Prejudice and Racism

JAMES M. JONES
Harvard University

ADDISON-WESLEY PUBLISHING COMPANY
Reading, Massachusetts · Menlo Park, California
London · Amsterdam · Don Mills, Ontario · Sydney

TOPICS IN SOCIAL PSYCHOLOGY
Charles A. Kiesler, University of Kansas, Series Editor

ISBN 0-201-03376-3
DEFGHIJKL-CO-798765

This Book is Dedicated to the Memory of
Stephen H. Bronz

a tragically lovely person, news of
whose death in an automobile accident
came to me today, January 21, 1971.
My debt to him for everything I have
written thus far is great. My sadness
at his death is greater.

Foreword

It is becoming increasingly difficult for anyone to be a generalist in social psychology. Not only is the number of published articles zooming, but new researchable areas of interest are multiplying as well. A researcher finds more fascinating topics these days than he used to, but he also finds himself behind in his reading of all but one or two of them. As a result, the quality of the broad introductory book in social psychology has suffered. No one can any longer be an expert in all of social psychology.

As an alternative, we offer the present series, *Topics in Social Psychology*, directed toward the student with no prior background in social psychology. Taken as a whole, the series adequately covers the field of social psychology, but it has the advantage that each short book was written by an expert in the area. The instructor can select some subset of the books to make up his course, the particular subset depending upon his biases and inclinations. In addition, the individual volumes can be useful in several ways: as supplementary reading in, perhaps, a sociology course; to introduce more advanced courses (for example, a graduate seminar in attitude change); or just for peeking at recent developments in social psychology.

This volume discusses perhaps the most pressing problem in our society today—prejudice and racism. In spite of so much already written on this topic, Professor Jones' book fills and important need. Previously, a concise but comprehensive treatment of prejudice and racism has not been readily available to most undergraduates. Dr. Jones neatly interrelates a broad spectrum of data from psychology, sociology, and history. Equally important, he shows his own angry and passionate feelings about these long-standing inequities. The combination makes this an exciting book to read.

Charles A. Kiesler

Preface

The touchstone of "scientific method" is objectivity. Social science, too, demands objectivity of its practitioners. However, we are all human beings with values. In matters of race relations particularly, it is not possible (nor in my opinion desirable) to divorce one's values from one's writing or research. I admit that the approaches taken in this book are influenced by my personal experiences and points of view. I have attempted to state things as clearly as I see them, and not to let traditional or commonly accepted viewpoints go unchallenged, if I feel a challenge is warranted.

At the same time, I do not want to give the impression of *simply* having an ax to grind. I have biases, and I am sure they will show. I hope that I have successfully labeled my biases so that personal views not tested by research and/or careful public analysis will not be mistaken for unsupported arguments. If you disagree with what I say, or reject it for lack of "objective" support, that is your prerogative. However, I ask you to contemplate the ideas carefully and try to relate these ideas to your own personal experience.

Racism in America is as old as the country itself, and older. I have attempted in the following pages to place the issues in their appropriate sociocultural historical context. Racism will not end with this book, but maybe, for some of you, awareness of the depths and complexities of racism in America will begin.

One of the clearest lessons I have learned in writing this book, is that it takes the interested concern of a lot of people to see it through. I would like to thank Chick Canfora, Susan Willard, and Margaret Morse, who did the bulk of the typing on the manuscript. Not only did they type swiftly and accurately while tolerating my excesses of disorganization and confusion, but their comments on various points in the manuscript have been provocative in my writing.

I would also like to thank Alvin Ramsey and Ronald Johnson for their assistance in researching background materials, compiling the bibliography, and reading and commenting on various portions of the manuscript. A great deal of gratitude is also expressed to Kelly Gersick for reading the entire manuscript and offering useful opinions and comments. I also found several discussions with him to be helpful in considering the way in which certain audiences would likely react to the book. Much appreciation is extended to Alvia Branch for her careful preparation of the index.

I owe a great deal to my colleagues Herbert Kelman, Thomas Pettigrew, and Zick Rubin for generously giving their time to reading various portions of the manuscript and providing comments and criticisms which were absolutely essential to the creation of a higher quality work. There are always several perspectives one can take on racial issues, and the comments of my colleagues have helped to make this book more representative.

Abundant gratitude is offered to Charles Kiesler who guided me through graduate school with thoughtfulness and sincere consideration. His confidence in me was always reassuring and ultimately was responsible for my writing this book. In addition, Professor Kiesler has been a most helpful critic of the entire manuscript. My own revisions in response to his criticisms have helped to make this a better book.

Finally and foremost, I am grateful to my entire family, my wife Olive, and my daughters Shelly and Itenash for their love and friendship during the writing of this manuscript. Shelly's gentle prodding, "How many more pages, Daddy?" helped keep me pointed ahead. Nashe always provided a cuddly, babbly, and energetic diversion when the writing was going slowly (and often when it was not, as well). Olive's ability to withstand a year and a half of "I can't, I've got to work on the book" is a tribute to Understanding. Not only did she support my writing, but her careful editorial hand over the entire manuscript, her comments and criticisms on reading and rereading draft after draft of various sections, and our numerous long discussions provided the most consistent input to the final manuscript. The ultimate criterion for the acceptability of a sentence or necessity of a particular point in many cases came to be Olive's judgment. I thank Olive, Shelly, and Nashe for their substantial contribution to my own contentment, without which this book could never have come about.

Boston, Massachusetts   J.M.J.
February 1972

Contents

CHAPTER ONE

Introduction — The Problem of the Color Line

The problem of the twentieth century is the problem of the color line.

W.E.B. DuBois

With nearly three-quarters of the century as evidence, the truth of this simple statement endures in stark defiance of all our efforts to contradict and destroy it. In 1903 the Wright brothers launched a feeble vehicle airborne for 59 seconds. Sixty-nine years later we watch men cavorting on the moon. In 1903 DuBois stated "the problem" of the twentieth century, and 69 years later we continue to affirm his diagnosis.

Recently a white Midwestern college student on a work trip to Cambridge came to my office to describe his study and obtain any assistance I could give him. His project was to investigate "why racial tension and conflict exist now in 1971." He felt perplexed that racial antagonism could persist so long when the fundamental ideals of the society were so egalitarian. I smiled and suddenly felt older than my years. The history of race relations was so ingrained in my mind that I felt as though I had been here from the beginning—since 1619. His idealism was refreshing but also wearisome. I thought of the task that his question set. I thought of my own attempts to answer this question.

When I tell graduate students I am writing a book on prejudice and racism, some say, "Ugh! Is there anything to it that hasn't already been said a thousand times?" With their cynicism they rebuff my young student's idealism. I have weighed these two perspectives and have decided to attempt to balance them by providing an historical perspective on the antecedents to contemporary racial conflict. Perhaps the young will get new information which enables them to see the problems in greater perspective. Perhaps those more experienced on the subject will find some of the ideas provocative enough to reawaken their interest and involvement.

I would like to believe that no one can dispassionately observe the thoughts and ideas expressed in the following pages. Many of the issues of prejudice and racism are still quite open. I will venture to frame these issues as I see them, hoping thereby to benefit the thinking of all who read this book.

WHAT IS PREJUDICE?

We know that the term "prejudice" is used by many people in many different ways. Some use the term to indicate petty, sometimes arbitrary, but generally quite personal dislikes (H.L. Mencken devoted six volumes to his *Prejudices*). In other cases the term can have *lethal* connotations, as when a Green Beret officer issues orders to "terminate with extreme prejudice" association with a particular individual. An even more subtle use of the term has recently come to light in the case of Jack Shaw, a former FBI agent. Having fallen into disfavor with the head of the Bureau, Agent Shaw was transferred to Butte, Montana. Rather than face exile, he tendered his resignation to the Bureau Director, who accepted it *with prejudice.* Because of this prejudicial acceptance the former agent has been unable to get a law-enforcement job anywhere in the country as of this writing.

In the American context, the term "prejudice" has usually been reserved for those attitudes and behaviors that have characterized particular kinds of relations between the white Protestant majority and the racial, ethnic, and religious minorities.* This emphasis is captured in the definition offered by Gordon Allport in his classic book on prejudice:

> Ethnic prejudice is an antipathy based upon a faulty and inflexible generalization. It may be felt or expressed. It may be directed toward a group as a whole, or toward an individual because he is a member of that group. (1954, p. 10)†

Allport concludes that "The net effect of prejudice, thus defined, is to place the object of prejudice at some disadvantage not merited by his own misconduct."

*We also speak of prejudice against Jews (anti-Semitism) and various other kinds of ethnic hostility. The present book is restricted to issues concerning black-white relations. For a general discussion of other kinds of majority-minority relations, see Robin Williams' *Strangers Next Door* (1964), Selznick and Steinberg's *The Tenacity of Prejudice* (1969), and Simpson and Yinger's *Racial and Cultural Minorities* (1965).
†References are listed at the end of the book.

There are two important elements in Allport's view of prejudice: (1) it is basically a negative attitude; (2) its existence puts the object of prejudice at an unjust disadvantage. Since an overwhelming amount of literature has focused on the white majority and black minority, and since these relations pose the most dramatic threat to the rather worn fabric of American society, in my own discussion of prejudice I will examine the negative racial attitudes whites have toward blacks, and the resultant social malaise.

The *psychological* position, which emphasizes feelings and attitudes, is in contrast to the *sociological* position, which emphasizes the primacy of "groupness." For example, Blumer (1958) argues that

> Race prejudice exists basically in a sense of group position rather than in a set of feelings which members of one racial group have toward the members of another racial group. (p. 3)

This statement makes explicit what the psychological view assumes. That is, to develop a negative attitude there must be some positive referent for comparison. Blumer suggests that this referent is the group to which the prejudiced individual belongs. However, the sociological view goes too far when it attempts to ignore the feelings which members of one racial group have toward members of another. Ultimately we must be concerned with the attitude one person has toward another and with what behavior that attitude implies for a specific situational interaction.

A thorough discussion of prejudice depends upon a socio-psychological concept—social comparison. Social comparison theory, first stated formally by Leon Festinger (1954), describes very simply the processes by which individuals come to place themselves accurately in their social milieu. If you want to know whether you are pretty or ugly, rich or poor, a fast or slow runner, smart or dumb, nice or mean, you must compare yourself with others. But you don't compare yourself to just *any* other person, only to people who are reasonably similar to yourself. For example, you would not estimate your own intelligence through comparison with that of a five-year-old child. Thus one formulates his perceptions and beliefs about himself on the basis of comparison with other members of his reference group.

Each individual, of course, belongs to many specific reference groups, but the sense of group position referred to by Blumer is a consequence of social comparison processes within a given group. The problem of prejudice follows from using the standards of one's own group when comparing the self to someone in another group. Moreover, this standard is unfairly used if one's own-group identification is always seen as the *positive pole* in the comparison process.

Prejudice is a negative attitude toward a person or group based upon a social comparison process in which the individual's own group is taken as the positive point of reference. The behavioral manifestation of prejudice is *discrimination*—those actions designed to maintain own-group characteristics and favored position *at the expense of* members of the comparison group. I agree with Raab and Lipset (1959) when they state that the behavioral manifestation of prejudice creates the social problem. Therefore, behavior is of more concern to us than the attitude view of prejudice.

WHAT IS RACISM?

In describing the "basic causes" of the wave of race riots that swept the United States in the summers of 1964 through 1967, the riot Commission made the following observation:

> Race prejudice has shaped our history decisively in the past; it now threatens to do so again. White racism is essentially responsible for the explosive mixture which has been accumulating in our cities since the end of World War II. (*U.S. Commission on Civil Disorders*, 1968, p. 203)

Note that *history's* problems were blamed on "race prejudice," while present racial tensions are blamed primarily on "white racism." Are racism and race prejudice interchangeable terms or is there discontinuity of history? Or has racism generally supplanted prejudice as a more inclusive term which encompasses, in addition to prejudice, ". . . hostility, discrimination, segregation, and other negative action expressed toward an ethnic group . . ." (Marx, 1971, p.101)?

Van den Berghe (1967) attempts a rather specific definition of racism when he defines it as ". . . any set of beliefs that organic, genetically transmitted differences (whether real or imagined) between human groups are intrinsically associated with the presence or the absence of certain socially relevant abilities or characteristics, hence that such differences are a legitimate basis of invidious distinctions between groups socially defined as races" (p.11). This suggests that racism is the natural process by which the physical and/or cultural characteristics of one group of people (e.g., black Americans) acquire negative social significance in a racially heterogeneous society.

Racism puts as much emphasis on the positive attributes of one's own race as on the considered negative attributes of the other. The following example from Abraham Lincoln is revealing.

> I am not, nor ever have been, in favor of bringing about in any way the social and political equality of the white and black races; I am not, nor ever have been, in favor of making voters or jurors of Negroes, nor qualifying them to hold office. . .I will say in addition to this that there is a physical difference between the white and black races which I believe will ever forbid the two

races living together on terms of social and political equality. And in as much as they cannot so live, while they do remain together, there must be the position of superior and inferior, and I as much as any other man am in favor of having the superior position assigned to the white race. (Abraham Lincoln, complete works, edited by Nicolay and Hay, the Century Company, 1894, pp. 369, 370, 457, 458)

Nor is black skin color the only criterion, as the following statement, made in 1909 by California *Progressive* Chester Powell, indicates:

[Racial discrimination] is blind and uncontrollable prejudice . . . yet social separateness seems to be imposed by the very law of nature. [An educated Japanese] would not be a welcomed suitor for the hand of any American's daughter [but] an Italian of the commonest standing and qualities would be a more welcomed suitor than the finest gentleman of Japan. So the line is biological, and we draw it at the biological point—at the propagation of the species. (Daniels, 1968, p. 49)

These statements represent what most writers call *individual racism.* Of the three types of racism—individual, institutional, and cultural—individual racism is closest to race prejudice and suggests a belief in the superiority of one's own race over another, and the behavioral enactments that maintain those superior and inferior positions.

Individual racism and race prejudice do not differ to a major degree. However, the white racism indictment of the Kerner Commission goes beyond the level of individual racism to the more general, more insidious, and more debilitating *institutional racism.* Carmichael and Hamilton (1967) describe institutional racism as

. . .[when] five hundred black babies die each year because of lack of proper food, shelter and medical facilities, and thousands more are destroyed and maimed physically, emotionally and intellectually because of conditions of poverty and discrimination in the black community. . .or when black people are locked in dilapidated slum tenements, subject to the daily prey of exploitative slumlords, merchants, loan sharks and discriminatory real estate agents. (p. 4)

This view represents one of two meanings of institutional racism, the conscious manipulation of institutions to achieve racist objectives. To this end, racist institutions are but extensions of individual racist thought. Thus, for example, "grandfather clauses" and "poll taxes" can be seen as the manipulation of the political process to achieve individual (or collective) racist ends.

Institutional racism also operates on another, subtler level. Colleges, graduate schools, and professional schools have for many years relied heavily on standardized test scores as criteria for admission. Black children and students routinely have inferior training in both test taking and the content of test materials. Therefore, in many cases the 600 SAT's or 700 GRE's requirement might as well be a "white only" sign on the gates of the educational institutions.*

We ask how *free* is free enterprise, how *equal* is equal opportunity employment, how *fair* are fair housing statutes? Is there a difference between *de jure* inequality and *de facto* inequality?

Institutional racism has two meanings, then: First, it is the institutional extension of individual racist beliefs; this consists primarily of using and manipulating duly constituted institutions so as to maintain a racist advantage over others. Second, it is the byproduct of certain institutional practices which operate to restrict on a racial basis the choices, rights, mobility, and access of groups of individuals. These unequal consequences need not be intended, but they are not the less real for being simply *de facto*.

Cultural racism, the third type, contains elements of both individual and institutional racism. Cultural racism can generally be defined as the individual and institutional expression of the superiority of one race's cultural heritage over that of another race. Racism is appropriate to the extent that racial and cultural factors are highly correlated and are a systematic basis for inferior treatment. When the Europeans first encountered the Africans they differed in fundamental cultural ways. African religion was polytheistic and utilized magic and superstition to a considerable extent. Western religion was monotheistic and emphasized rational thought. The invention of Johann Gutenberg made literacy an important value in Western society. African society had an oral tradition, but whites did not see that tradition as simply another way of communicating, teaching, and preserving the past—they saw it as a symptom of basic illiteracy.

It is cultural racism that has been most transparent to the eyes of American race-relation analysts. It is a matter of cultural racism when the achievements of a race of people are fully ignored in education. It is a matter of cultural racism when the expression of cultural differences is unrewarded or is interpreted negatively. It is not just black people who have been victimized by the cultural melting-pot myth, but all ethnic minorities. White Western-European religion, music, philosophy, law, politics, economics, morality, science, and medicine are all without question considered to be the best in the world.

Within the United States we are led to believe that black people contributed absolutely nothing to the American expression of these

---

*Of course, test scores can be "rich only" criteria also. Poor whites, however, have options which blacks never have, because racism restricts opportunity. Here, as in many other places in this book, the analysis of black problems can be applied to the poor or to other minorities. In the main, the analysis of racism can be applied on a case by case basis to other groups.

cultural forms. More significantly, any person, regardless of his cultural background, who cannot function well according to the dictates of white Western cultural norms does not have much opportunity for success in this society. Black Americans are now reacting to cultural racism by asserting their blackness, their African heritage, their cultural uniqueness.

To summarize briefly, racism has three faces: individual, institutional, and cultural. Individual racism is closely akin to race prejudice, but differs from the latter in (a) the importance of biological considerations and (b) the role of behavioral enactments. The concept of institutional racism has gained prominence since Carmichael and Hamilton (1967) and the United States Commission on Civil Disorders (1968) (hereafter known as the Kerner Report after the Illinois governor who chaired the commission) have sought to clarify and elaborate on it. I have introduced the term "cultural racism" to define the intersection of cultural and racial differences where superiority on *both* factors is assumed.

A CONCISE HISTORY OF EARLY RACE RELATIONS IN AMERICA

As I walk down the main street of a small town in northern Ohio I am aware of the curious stares of little children. I watch them tug at their mothers' skirts and point at me as if I had stepped from a TV fantasy. I see their mothers try to suppress this infantile curiosity in the interest of proper public behavior ("It's not nice to point!") while they themselves wait to stare daggers into my back.

Racial tension is probably higher now than at any time in American history. My idealistic undergraduate friend asks, Why now? Why now do black students willfully absent themselves from high schools, segregate themselves on predominantly white college campuses, and speak of revolution? Why haven't we righted the obvious wrongs of slavery? Why can't we make peace with our fellow man?

When we look around us we do not find answers, we find only symptoms of a diseased relationship. What do white rural farmers of southern Illinois know of 12-year-old black boys nodding on 137th Street in Harlem or dead of an overdose in a vacant tenement? What does the President of the United States know of a 15-year-old white girl hanging herself in an upper-middle-class northern Ohio community? Why is it that now a majority of white Americans would not even sign the original Bill of Rights? The country has become quite complex. Each of us is sheltered from the experiences of others by emotional rhetoric, selective reporting of the media, and growing urban sprawl. We cannot know for sure what others feel, why or if they hate, whether or not there exists a chance for humane interaction. Laws, plans, policies and programs come churning out of state houses and federal buildings at a rapid clip, but the problems do not get simpler—they become more complex.

It is difficult, indeed impossible, to make any sense out of the contemporary social, political, cultural scene without the benefit of history. History tells different stories to different people. Black Africans looked strange to the British in 1550, but the white menace evoked its own reaction in the black soon-to-be captives:

> The first object which saluted my eyes when I arrived on the coast was the sea, and a slave ship, which was then riding at anchor, and waiting for its cargo. These filled me with astonishment, which was connected with terror, when I was carried on board ... I was now persuaded that I had gotten into a world of bad spirits, and that they were going to kill me. Their complexions too differing so much from ours, their long hair, and the language they spoke (which was very different from any I had ever heard), united to confirm me in this belief.*

On this score did race relations begin: white Europeans shanghaiing black bodies for the long middle-passage.

Let us now briefly extract the salient aspects of the history of race relations. We are not so much interested in names and dates, or even events, but rather in the philosophical, ideological, attitudinal underpinnings of racial animosity in America.

Racist Attitudes–Racist Behavior–The Beginning

The first fact of history is that the British attitude was predisposed toward racism before any Englishman even beheld a black African. The very color black had long possessed strong negative meaning and emotional ties. You can well imagine how the British responded to *people* who were that color! Not only was black bad; its opposite, white, was *very good.*

We can call the reactions of white Englishmen to black Africans racist attitudes, but as with any attitudes, they are of little consequence unless conditions are present which link them to specific, correlated behaviors. The conditions of sixteenth-century England which started the long chain of events leading to the present were (a) the social, political, and economic consequences of the Renaissance and (b) the Protestant Reformation.

The Renaissance of the fifteenth and sixteenth centuries represented a formal break from religious domination of life and thought to an intense, individualistic world view. The measure of a man was his achievements on earth—the more numerous his capacities, the more impressive his personal worth. Leonardo da Vinci was perhaps the prototypical Renaissance man.

The upshot of this individualism was, in the social sphere, the dissolution of the feudal system and a heavy emphasis on individual

---

*From *The Interesting Narrative of the Life of Olaudah Equiano, or Gustavus Vassa the African. Written by Himself,* 1791.

liberty. However, the poor were not then (as they are not now) able to be free in a so-called free society, and widespread thievery, rape, and social chaos followed.

In the economic sphere, the accumulation of capital became an attractive way for an individual to beome worthy. Also, the adventurism of the Hawkinses, Drakes, and others led to a commercial revolution on the seas. It was not long before one of the principal commodities was black bodies.

Politically, the use of nation-states independent of religious control from Rome allowed for large-scale nationalistic competition for the world's wealth.

Freedom and individualism *without* social responsibility characterized sixteenth-century England and gave a strong push toward the enslavement of black Africans.

The Protestant Reformation began in 1517, when Martin Luther tacked his 95 theses on the doors of the Catholic Church in Wittenburg. More pertinent here, however, is John Calvin, whose doctrines (published in *The Institutes of the Christian Religion,* 1536) put man in direct contact with God on one of two levels—saved or damned. How did one know? He looked around at his fellows—those who led the good life were saved, the "Elect"; those who did not were damned.

The Calvinist influence prompted the Puritan Revolution in England in 1640. The strong Puritan tradition in the New World provided a handy formula for distinguishing between the "Elect" and the damned in a socioeconomic order of racist slavery.

In summary, the first significant point of the history of race relations is the predisposition toward racism in British thought, a racism that was realized through the application of social, political, economic, and religious principles of individuality *without* social responsibility.

Regional Variations in Black Oppression

The second significant historical factor concerns the regional patterns of enslavement and their ideological consequences. It is well known that slavery in the North (New England and New York, primarily) never attained the large-scale status of that "peculiar institution" in the South. No matter how strongly one emphasizes the economic and geographical reasons for these regional differences in the practice of slavery, the popular impression among Northerners (and Southern blacks) has been a mistaken belief that white racial attitudes have always been more tolerant in the North. It is this belief, perhaps, that led many blacks to move North, and my young college friend to ask, Why now?

That slavery existed in northern states is a fact. That the inhabitants of northern states felt a certain ambivalence toward slavery is indicated by the following Puritan law of 1641:

> There shall never be any bond-slavery, villenage or captivitie amongst us; *unlesse* it be lawfully captives taken in just warrs, and such strangers as willingly sell themselves, or are sold to us: and such shall have the libertyes and Christian usuages which the law of God established in Israell concerning such persons doth morally require, *provided this exempts none from servitude who shall be judged thereto by Authoritie.* (Jordan, 1969, p. 67; italics mine)

Thus was the spirit of political and legal double talk given early birth in America.

The recognized center of American finance is Wall Street in New York. But do you know the original function of Wall Street? It served as a market for the sale of Negro slaves! To be sure, one could also see advertised in the *New York Times* the sale of "Englishmen, Cheshire cheese, and a few Welshmen," but the predominant commodity at the Wall Street Market in 1711 was Negro slaves.

For a variety of primarily economic reasons, chattel slavery never flourished in northern states. Although some slavery did exist, blacks were principally entered as a commodity in the New England economic ledger. Although they lacked sufficient economic reasons for the wholesale exploitation of Negroes, the Englishmen of northern states nevertheless considered Negroes (even free ones) to be fundamentally different from themselves, and developed a set of legal, social, political, and educational policies through which—sometimes blatantly, sometimes subtly and insidiously—they perpetuated, reinforced, and widened racial differences. Jim Crow laws originated in the *North,* not in the South. Thus, the ambivalent attitude of Northerners toward Negroes has been over-shadowed somewhat by the obvious favorable comparison with Southern attitudes toward Negroes. However, as is so abundantly clear now, Northern blacks have never been fully admitted into the mainstream either.

The story of how King Cotton and Queen Tobacco ruled the South is well known and does not need to be recounted here. The interesting and important aspect of Southern slavery is how economic lust and dependence conspired to produce a sociopolitical racial orientation that differed so strikingly from that of the North.

The conspicuous display of inhumanity and moral bankruptcy that characterized Southern slavery has for many years obscured the spiraling attitudinal/behavioral consequences of racial relations. That is, since basic attitudes toward African blacks during this country's early history, and possibly up to the invention of the cotton gin, did not vary much between inhabitants of the North and South, we must look carefully at how the interaction of structure, attitudes, and behavior over time has produced such marked regional differences economically, politically, and socially.

The second point, then, is that the regional divergence in race relations has spawned an unwieldy two-ply pattern of attitudes, behaviors, and sociopolitical structures in this country. Thus any analysis of prejudice and racism must, in part, be a two-ply analysis. It is only in the past few years that the second ply (the Northern one) has been given due recognition.

The Great American Lie

Freedom. Equality. Justice. Praise the Lord and pass the ammunition. Praise America and lynch a nigger.

This country was born in revolution against tyranny and oppression while black people were at that very moment being tyrannically oppressed. We are taught in school that George Washington was the father of our country. For many blacks, he was probably the father of one of their slave ancestors. There is a place in Philadelphia called *Independence* Hall where one can go to see the crack in the *Liberty* Bell. Whose independence? Whose liberty? In Tennessee Williams' *Cat on a Hot Tin Roof,* Big Daddy could smell the mendacity of his children vying for his favor. The smell of American mendacity wafts across the land 200 years after independence.

Gunnar Myrdal (1944) spoke of the American Dilemma, that contradiction between the American Creed, "All men are created equal," and the facts of racist excess. Even now, conservative patriots are calling for a reaffirmation of what America has stood for. Liberty. Equality. Justice. When black Americans look at what America has stood for, they see many practices whose reaffirmation they would die to prevent.

We must be aware that some attempt was made to reconcile the spirit of the Revolution with the practices of the colonists. One can read about the conflicts and inconsistencies that surrounded the drafting of the Declaration of Independence (see Jordan, 1969, pp. 269-311). Many men, like Thomas Jefferson, had very definite antislavery sentiments; yet the compromise with the South (deletion of an antislavery phrase written by Jefferson) very clearly put the weight of the United States government on the side of the white majority in the matter of race. Thus was the United States government founded on contradiction and compromise. Widespread slavery practiced in the land of the free, and a legal constitution which proclaimed a slave to be three-fifths of a man.*

It is very important to note that the Declaration of Independence and the Constitution were major determinants of race relations in America. The initial racist attitudes of the English flourished upon the extensive contact with blacks provided by the slave trade and, ultimately, institutionalized slavery. Regional economic necessities resulted in divergent roles for Northern and Southern blacks; the former were trade commodities, the latter were cheap labor. The contradictions in the

---

*Since slaves were considered property, there was a need to determine for taxation and representation purposes how to count slaves. The Constitution concluded that slaves should be "divested of 2/5 the man."

ideological and practical foundations of America continue to exert their effect on the American conscience.

The remainder of American history presents us with the refinement and ramification of these political-social-economic-attitudinal dramas. We see North against South, black against white, patriots against bums, labor against management, wages against profits. Let's now take a brief, whirlwind trip through the nineteenth century of American history and watch some of the racial dramas unfold.

We begin, appropriately enough, with Gabriel Prosser's slave uprising in Richmond, Virginia, in 1801. Prosser's was not the first nor was it the last attempt to escape from bondage by force. In 1822 Denmark Vesey conspired to free several thousand slaves in Charleston, South Carolina. Nat Turner went on his famous "tear" in 1831, killing 60 whites. Ten years later, in 1841, slaves aboard the ship *Creole* overpowered their crew and escaped to the Bahamas, where they were granted asylum and freedom. Thus did blacks resist and strike out against their oppression.*

In 1807 (31 years after the United States declared that all men were created equal) the slave trade was abolished by Congress, though it continued as a black market operation for nearly 10 more years. By 1816, an American Colonization Society was organized to transport free Negroes back to Africa. Some free blacks, for example the black shipbuilder Paul Cuffe, returned to Africa of their own initiative. In 1817 Philadelphia Negroes organized to protest being exiled from their land of nativity. It is very important to know that black thought in America has *always* wavered between separatism and integration.

Slavery was not abolished in New York until 1827. In 1831, the same year as Nat Turner's rebellion, William Lloyd Garrison's *Liberator* first appeared. A year later the New England Anti-Slavery Society was organized, followed by the American Anti-Slavery Society in 1833. These events greatly exacerbated North-South antagonisms, which reached their peak with the Civil War.

But even as antislavery activity was escalating, in 1833 Prudence Crandall, a white woman, was arrested for conducting an academy for Negro girls (made so because all white children withdrew when the first black girl enrolled) in Canterbury, *Connecticut.* In 1835, integrated Noyes Academy in Canaan, *New Hampshire,* was closed by mob violence.

In the 1840's, while Harriet Tubman made her courageous forays to the South to free slaves, Sojourner Truth and Frederick Douglass spoke eloquently against slavery.

But in 1850 the United States Congress passed the Fugitive Slave Act, requiring free states to return fugitive slaves to their owners. This act was

---

*There were many slave uprisings. For a complete review see Herbert Aptheker's *History of Negro Slave Revolts* (1969).

passed as part of a compromise which closed the new Northwest Territory to slavery. However, this restriction on slavery was soon reversed by the Kansas-Nebraska Act of 1854, which left it up to each state to decide whether or not it would allow slavery. In the Dred Scott decision of 1857 the United States Supreme Court opened federal territory to slavery and denied citizenship to American Negroes with Judge Taney's infamous words: "Negroes have no rights that a white man is bound to respect."

In spite of official government complicity in the perpetuation of slavery, the Civil War erupted in 1861. The war was not precipitated by a desire to free slaves; rather, it was a last effort to preserve the Union. Thus, whereas preservation of the Union worked *against* American blacks in the Revolutionary era, it worked *for* them in the Civil War era, culminating in the Emancipation Proclamation. But we have already seen that Lincoln was not free of prejudice himself.

It is also important to note the frequent immigrant riots against Northern blacks from 1830 to the famous "draft riots" of 1863 when whites rioted against blacks because, ironically, blacks were taking jobs the whites had left to fight in the Civil War. Blacks, of course, were not allowed to fight. This country was founded and grew on the backs of black labor. Wave after wave of European immigrants have also grown and prospered by stepping to the top on black backs.

Reconstruction began with the rapid development of political, educational, and economic institutions and practices beneficial to newly freed *Southern* blacks. But for every forward step taken by blacks, reactionary moves by whites began to accumulate a base for the overthrow of Reconstruction.

In 1867 Howard University was opened, and the first national meeting of the Ku Klux Klan was held in Nashville. In 1870 Hiram Revel succeeded Jefferson Davis to the U.S. Senate, and Robert Wood was elected Mayor of Natchez, Mississippi. Both were black. Yet race riots in the South were common during Reconstruction. In 1875 the Mississippi governor *requested* federal troops to protect rights of Negro voters.

In that same year Congress enacted a Civil Rights Bill which gave Negroes the right to equal treatment at inns, in public conveyances, theatres, and other public amusement places. But alas, 1877 brought yet another compromise. Rutherford B. Hayes secured Southern support for his election to the Presidency by promising to withdraw federal troops from the South. Shortly thereafter, in 1879, large numbers of Negroes, unprotected from vigilante Klan raids, fled in a mass exodus to the North. In 1883 the Supreme Court greatly assisted Jim Crowism by declaring the Civil Rights Act of 1875 unconstitutional. And by 1907 Jim Crow stretched his clutching tentacles throughout the South in a death grip that only began to loosen half a century later.

At this point we break off our historical narrative. Chronologically we have reached our starting point—DuBois's statement of "the problem."

This brief sketch has outlined the historical foundation for twentieth-century race relations. Our analysis of the problems of prejudice and racism requires some knowledge of their origins and major determinants. It is from this background that we begin.

CHAPTER TWO

Growth of the Problem

Our nation is moving toward two societies, one black, one white—separate and unequal.

U.S. Commission on Civil Disorders, 1968

Deciding the case of *Plessy* v. *Ferguson* in 1896 the Supreme Court declared racial segregation—"separate but equal"—constitutional. In 1968 the United States Commission on Civil Disorders stated that the United States is *moving toward* racial separation *without* equality. Does this mean that the separation sanctioned by the Supreme Court has disappeared over the past seventy years but is now threatening to return? Does it mean that racial equality "no longer" exists? No, the Commission's statement is more ominous. It suggests that racial conflict has become so impacted that the long-present inequities are hardening into a racial antagonism more deep-seated and threatening than ever before. The line is drawn, and again we find our thoughts going back to DuBois.

Ours has been a remarkable century. In trying to follow the course of race relations we find ourselves in a maelstrom of world wars and undeclared "conflicts" compounded by fantastic economic growth, recognition of poverty and introduction of a national welfare system, in addition to tremendous upheavals in the relationships among the generations and the sexes. With accelerated social change has emerged the social scientist. Sometimes deftly, sometimes clumsily, this Charon has attempted to navigate our understanding through the complex network of American racial conflicts.

Lee Rainwater, a sociologist, sums up the responsibility of the social scientist in two points, (1) "Tell it like it is," and (2) "Try to understand why 'it' is that way, and to explore the implications of what and why for more constructive solutions to human problems" (Rainwater and Yancey, 1967, p. 162). With specific respect to race relations Rainwater sets forth four main goals, as follow.

1. To describe the disadvantaged position of Negroes,

2. To disprove the racist ideology which sustains the caste system,

3. To demonstrate that responsibility for the disadvantages Negroes suffer lies squarely upon the white caste which derives economic prestige and psychic benefits from the operation of the system, and

4. To suggest that in reality whites would be better rather than worse off if the whole jerry-built caste structure were to be dismantled.

In this chapter, we will review some of the facts of American race relations in the first half of the twentieth century. We will also analyze the trends in the social scientific investigation of race relations. Finally, we will try to evaluate the success of the social scientist in terms of Rainwater's statement of responsibilities and goals.

As the federal government has grown more powerful, it has engaged in more and more social engineering of the lives of the people it supposedly represents. In this effort the government appears to rely more and more (although still very little) on its chief informants, the social scientists. Inevitably, the social scientist has become an input in the pattern of social relationships he investigates and theorizes. In fact, since the mid-1940's the pattern of American race relations has become increasingly influenced by the research and theory of social scientists.

THE 1900's AND 1910's: EUGENICS AND JIM CROW

The first twenty years of this century were ushered in and out with race riots, lynchings, and burnings. Rioting was the Northern *modus operandi,* lynching and burning were the Southern. Anti-black riots occurred in New York City (1900); Springfield, Ohio (1904); Greenburg, Indiana (1906); and Springfield, Illinois (1908). One of the worst riots occurred in East St. Louis Illinois (1917); and in 1919, the summer of which has been described as "Red Summer," there were no less than 26 riots. The following account of the East St. Louis riot captures some of the flavor of this violent period in American race relations:

When the labor force of an aluminum plant went on strike, the company hired Negro workers. A labor union delegation called on the mayor and asked that further migration of Negroes to East St. Louis be stopped. As the men were leaving City Hall, they heard that a Negro had accidentally shot a white man during a holdup. In a few minutes rumor had replaced fact: the shooting was intentional—a white woman had been insulted—two white girls were shot. By this time, 3000 people had congregated and were crying for vengeance. Mobs roamed the streets, beating Negroes. Policemen did little more than take the injured to hospitals and disarm Negroes ... The press continued to emphasize the incidence of Negro crimes, white pickets and Negro workers at the aluminum company skirmished and, on July 1, some whites drove through the main Negro neighborhood firing into homes. Negro residents armed themselves. When a police car drove down the street Negroes riddled it with gunshot.

The next day a Negro was shot on the main street and a new riot was underway. The authority on the event records that the area became a "bloody half mile" for three or four hours; streetcars were stopped, and Negroes, without regard to age or sex, were pulled off and stoned, clubbed and kicked, and mob leaders calmly shot and killed Negroes who were lying in blood in the street. As the victims were placed in an ambulance, the crowds cheered and applauded.

Other rioters set fire to Negro homes, and by midnight the Negro section was in flames and Negroes were fleeing the city. There were 48 dead, hundreds injured, and more than 300 buildings destroyed. (Rudwick, 1966, pp. 23-53)

As brutal and bloody as race riots were, they took a back seat to lynchings and burnings. In 1918, 64 blacks were lynched; in 1919 the number rose to 83. Perhaps the most brutal act occurred in Valdosta, Georgia, in 1918. Mary Turner, a pregnant black woman, was hung to a tree, doused with gasoline, and burned. As she dangled from the rope, a man in the mob pulled out a pocket knife and slit open her abdomen. Out tumbled her child. "Two feeble cries it gave—and received for answer the heel of a stalwart man, as life was ground out of the tiny form," read one account (see Bennett, 1969, p. 294).

Even before white violence against blacks reached such an acute stage, blacks began to organize in their own behalf. In 1905 a group of black intellectuals met secretly at Niagara Falls, Canada. (They were not accommodated in hotels on the New York side.) DuBois and William Monroe Trotter organized what became known as the Niagara Movement. The following year, at its first national meeting, the Niagara Movement publicly demanded "full manhood rights—political, civil, and social." In 1909, a year after the Springfield, Illinois, riots, a group of white liberals headed by Mary White Ovington convened an integrated conference in New York City on the race problem. This conference established the National Association for the Advancement of Colored People. A year later, in 1910, the National Urban League was founded to deal with the social problems of urban black Americans.

The uneasy alliance between white liberals and black leaders was shaken when the Ovington group superseded the Niagara Movement and took only one black officer, DuBois, from among them. Monroe Trotter angrily withdrew and established his National Equal Rights League.

During this period, Jim Crow laws and customs governed much of public life, from transportation to restrooms and drinking fountains. By 1915 black ghettoes were being established in northern cities as blacks fled the violence and poverty of the South for the promise of jobs created by war in Europe. Conditions leading to racial conflict in the 1960's and 1970's existed in embryonic form fifty years earlier.

As race relations underwent violent change in the twentieth century, social thought polarized along the lines of the hoary nature-nurture, organism-environment controversy. At the turn of the century the Darwinian emphasis on "survival of the fittest," or natural selection, was the underpinning of American sociological theory. Influenced by Herbert Spencer in England, William Sumner of Yale presented the following American interpretation of Social Darwinism:

> Let it be understood that we cannot go outside of this alternative: liberty, inequality, survival of the fittest; or not-liberty, equality, survival of the unfittest. The former carries society forward and favors all its best members; the latter carries society downwards and favors all its worst members. (Quoted in Hofstadter, 1955, p. 51)

The implications of this position for race relations are abundantly clear. The development of the Eugenics movement affirms the racism inherent in American social Darwinist thought.

> The Eugenist believes that no other single factor in determining social conditions and practices approaches in importance that of racial structural integrity and sanity. (Kellicott, 1911, p. 44)

Social psychology developed as an antidote to this natural, biological emphasis. The social psychological view rejected the biological analogy, and saw the interdependence between the individual personality and the institutional structure of society. Echoing the ideas of colleagues Thorstein Veblen, Charles H. Cooley, and James Mark Baldwin, John Dewey wrote:

> We may desire abolition of war, industrial justice, greater equality of opportunity for all. But no amount of preaching good will or the golden rule or cultivation of sentiments of love and equity will accomplish the results. *There must be change in objective arrangements and institutions. We must work on the environment, not merely on the hearts of men.* (Dewey, 1922, pp. 21-22; italics mine)

Dewey's statement presages much of the later discussion among social scientists about the best way to deal with racial antagonism. More recently we have seen legal and legislative attacks on "objective arrangements and institutions" with some notable successes. But it is important to note that John Dewey charted this course early in the century. Although we now think of social action as a good and necessary thing, it has not always been so. Sometimes social action achieved reprehensible changes. For example, the applied eugenics activities of the National Conference on Race

Betterment passed a sterilization law in Indiana in 1907. The intersection of social thought and social action was established early in the century.*

The First Riot Report

The relation of whites and Negroes in the United States is our most grave and perplexing domestic problem. *[Sound familiar?]* Our race problem must be solved in harmony with the fundamental law of the nation and with its free institutions . . . The problem must not be regarded as sectional or political, and it should be studied and discussed seriously, frankly, and with an open mind.

These words could plausibly have been written at any time in this century, but in fact are found in a report on the causes of the Chicago riot of 1919 (Chicago Commission on Race Relations, 1922). The Chicago Commission stressed the environmental aspects of the racial problem by asserting the innate equality of blacks and whites. It attributed the observed differences to economic and social inequality. Although the Chicago Commission did not forthrightly indict white America (as the Kerner Report did 45 years later), it did point out the national scope of the problem and the need for thoughtful reform. The Chicago Commission specified that the 1919 riot was engendered by poor housing, inferior education, mistreatment by police, unemployment, job discrimination, and white prejudice.† Its recommendations also sound familiar: better police training for ethnic understanding and riot control; better jobs, housing, and education; equality before the law; integrated neighborhoods; and equal rights in public places. The simple documentation of the ills with the equally simple recommendation to "eliminate them" indicates how little the Chicago Commission knew about the complexities of American race relations.

Summary. The first two decades of this century were very important in the history of race relations. With the "separate but equal" decision of 1896 to uphold them, Southern whites established complete racial segregation *de jure*. With control of all political and economic institutions to support them, Northern whites used systematic racial discrimination to establish almost complete racial segregation *de facto*. When any tendency to disrupt the broad line of racial separation occurred, white violence against blacks was the response—riots in the North; lynchings, burnings, and other barbarisms in the South.

---

*In 1972, social action has been reified by proponents of Relevance in social science. Social action has not always been a desirable thing, and who knows how history will judge our current social activism.

†The Chicago Commission and Kerner Commission frame the concerns of this book. The Chicago Report blames, in part, white *prejudice,* while the Kerner Report blames white *racism* for racial violence in America. We will try in the remainder of this book to clarify the different assumptions and perspectives which these two terms represent.

The simultaneous emergence of social science and social action as potential contributions to the course of race relations must be noted. Early social theory—notably social Darwinism—lent itself easily to the perpetuation of racial inequalities. The social action to which that theory gave rise was avowedly racist.

THE 1920'S: ATTITUDES, ART, AND POVERTY

In many ways the 1920's represented the lull before the storm. Many of the industrial jobs created by World War I were still available to the blacks who had migrated to the North, even though they were forced to organize to protect their jobs (e.g., the Brotherhood of Sleeping Car Porters and Maids organized by A. Philip Randolph, and the Friends of Negro Freedom organized by other New York radicals). Black businesses increased as did the number of blacks in white-collar jobs. The Harlem Renaissance in literature (Claude McKay, James Weldon Johnson, Countee Cullen, and Langston Hughes), theatre (Paul Robeson and Bert Williams), dance (Florence Mills), and music (William Grant Still, W. C. Handy) introduced white Americans to black people (albeit often a stereotyped view, as in O'Neill's *Emperor Jones* and *All God's Chillun Got Wings* and Connelly's *The Green Pastures*).

But even as white Americans were being introduced to the "new Negro" (capitalization of the first letter of Negro was perhaps the first indication of newness), a West indian named Marcus Garvey was making plans for blacks to return to Africa. His Universal Negro Improvement Association (UNIA) chartered a steamship company called the Black Star Line to carry American blacks back to Africa. In addition, Garvey rejected the new Negro image in favor of the tribal African image of warriors and princesses. Although his separatist plans never materialized, he did have several thousand followers. The United States government reacted quite strongly to his influence, and after being convicted for using the mails to defraud, he was deported to England as an undesirable alien.*

In the 1920's New York society made the grand tour of Harlem, siphoning off pleasure in the evenings and leaving the natives to grovel in their poverty in the morning. For documentation of how white show business exploited, then dropped, black musicians and entertainers one can read W. C. Handy's autobiography. No aspect of life has been spared racial antipathies.

The Great Depression began early for Southern blacks. The boll

---

*Most accounts suggest that Garvey himself was innocent of the charges, but that other people in his organization had in fact used it to personal advantage. Also, many unwise business decisions helped promote the failure of the enterprise. See E. D. Cronon's *Black Moses* (1955) and Amy Jacques Garvey's *Garvey and garveyism* (1970).

weevil, soil erosion, and a general decline in agriculture hit Southern blacks hard. Those who had not left the South were mired in poverty. The crash of 1929 deepened Southern poverty and exploded the Northern economy—and, as in all hard times, blacks suffered worst.

The 1920's were also crucial for social psychology. As Floyd Allport (1920) began his empirical investigation of social phenomena, the concept of "attitudes" grew so important that social psychology came to be defined as "the scientific study of attitudes." But the emergence of an attitudinal/behavioral dichotomy assured that any analysis of race relations would be one-sided. (In line with this dichotomy social scientists have come to equate "prejudice" with "attitude," and behavioral manifestations of racial bias with "discrimination.")

The empirical positivism of social scientists' focus on attitudes was further advanced with the development of sophisticated statistical techniques by L. L. Thurstone (1927). The social scientist was thus fully armed and ready to attack the problem of race relations with a vengeance.

Systematic work on racial attitudes was begun by Emory S. Bogardus (1925; 1928). Interested in measuring the attitudes of one ethnic group toward another, Bogardus developed a "social distance" scale. Respondents were asked to circle one of seven social distance classifications to which they would be willing to admit a member of a given race. (Bogardus loosely defined "race" to include nationality and ethnic group.) The classifications were ordered by increasing degrees of social distance, from "To close kinship or marriage (1)" to "Would exclude from my country (7)."

The social distance scale was administered to a sample of 1725 native-born Americans representing 30 ethnic backgrounds. The results of this study are summarized in Table 2.1. Not unexpectedly, black, brown, and yellow peoples are least accepted by the predominately white Anglo-Saxon sample. In fact, the pattern is so striking that Bogardus posed a question familiar in the 1960's and 1970's: "Why the extensive social distance between Americans on one hand and Asiatics and Africans [the Third World?] on the other?" Bogardus' answer was simple:

> Where a person feels that his status or the status of anything that he values is furthered by race connections, then racial good will is engendered. But where a person's status or the status of anything that he values is endangered by the members of some race, then race prejudice flares up and burns long after the "invasion" has ceased. (Bogardus, 1928, p. 28)

Bogardus intended to portray racial attitudes clearly and accurately so that agents of social change would know what to do. Social scientific study of racial attitudes was seen as a prerequisite to social action. Furthermore, social action was seen as a means of changing attitudes and opinions. "The social distance test," Bogardus wrote, "would indicate

TABLE 2.1

Some Social Distance Ratings of Ethnic Groups by Black and White Americans

1. Reactions of 1725 Americans to 14 Different Races by Percentages

Regarding races listed below	1 To close kinship by marriage	2 To my club as personal chums	3 To my street as neighbors	4 To employment in my occupation	5 To citizenship in my country	6 As visitors only to my country	7 Would exclude from my country
English	93.7	96.7	97.3	95.4	95.9	1.7	0
Americans (native white)	90.1	92.4	92.6	92.4	90.5	1.2	0
Scotch-Irish	72.6	81.7	88.	89.4	92.	16.7	.4
Dutch	44.2	54.7	73.2	76.7	86.1	2.4	.3
Norwegians	41.	56.	65.1	72.	80.3	8.	.3
Spaniards	27.6	49.8	55.1	58.	81.6	8.4	2.
Armenians	8.5	14.8	27.8	46.2	58.1	17.7	5.0
Indians	8.1	27.7	33.4	54.3	83.	7.7	1.6
Jews (German)	7.8	2.1	25.5	39.8	53.5	25.3	13.8
Negroes	1.4	9.1	11.8	38.7	57.3	17.6	12.7
Turks	1.4	10.	11.7	19.	25.3	41.8	23.4
Chinese	1.1	11.8	15.9	27.0	27.3	45.2	22.4
Mulattoes	1.1	9.6	10.6	32.	47.4	22.7	16.8
Hindus	1.1	6.8	13.	21.4	23.7	47.1	19.1

2. Reactions of 202 Native American Negroes and Mulattoes to 9 Races by Percentages

	1	2	3	4	5	6	7
Negroes	96.	94.	94.	90.	92.	8.	0
Mulattoes	52.	66.	70.	70.	70.	10.	2.
French	32.	60.	80.	76.	72.	16.	2.
English	16.	42.	72.	72.	76.	14.	0
Americans (native white)	6.	34.	66.	72.	74.	0	8.
Japanese	6.	28.	30.	34.	40.	36.	10.
Germans	4.	22.	42.	44.	34.	30.	10.
Jews (Russian)	2.	12.	18.	24.	30.	34.	10.
Turks	0	6.	10.	16.	14.	38.	26.

Adapted from Bogardus (1928).

what changes in attitudes and opinions the native Americans would need to undergo in order to give the immigrants a square deal, what changes the immigrants must make, and where racial conflicts are likely to take place" (1928, p. 256). Bogardus' view of the proper work of a social scientist agrees closely with Rainwater's.

In the same period, Bruno Lasker (1929) was writing about race attitudes from a quite different perspective. As part of a national organization of social, education, and religious workers known as The Inquiry, Lasker contributed his study of *Race Attitudes in Children.* Lasker rejected the new uses of sample survey, preferring rather to rely on personal reports and testimony. He interpreted much of the observational/reportorial data and left the rest to stand as objective (or subjective) fact. He concluded that everything in a white child's environment (institutions such as family and school, photographs, public speeches, and so on) contributed to the child's negative attitudes toward blacks. Lasker's recommendations were simple: these environmental factors should be changed through education and religion, and by local, state, and federal government. Again we find current concerns are not new, but well-rooted in earlier decades of racial conflict and analysis.

Summary

The 1920's were characterized by three important trends. First, the largest black separatist movement to date was initiated by Marcus Garvey. This trend, with its emphasis on the positive elements of black—primarily African—culture was a precursor to modern developments in black politics and black culture.

Second, the rise of blacks in the arts to the point of becoming a class within the black population was highly significant. Then, as now, many of the leading black intellectuals and strategists were artists.

Third, social psychology developed primarily as an empirical social science. The development of rather sophisticated measurement pushed social psychology further toward a scientific self-image and the belief that social action could be accurately informed by the results of social scientific investigation. In the next decade experimental investigations of racial issues would proliferate, and a new dimension would be added to our understanding of "the problem."

THE 1930's: RACIAL STEREOTYPES AND FEDERAL BUREAUCRACY

The Great Depression struck savagely, fundamentally changing the nation's character. For the first time since Reconstruction, black Americans found the federal government sympathetic to their plight. President Roosevelt appointed black advisers in many areas (Robert C. Weaver in Interior, Laurence A. Oxley in Labor, Frank S. Horne in Housing, Mary McLeod

Bethune in Youth Administration, Ralph Bunche in State). Black Americans responded to New Deal aid and what seemed to be a sympathetic administration by switching from the Republican to the Democratic party.

In relieving the acute poverty of millions of Americans the New Deal was a big success. But federal programs such as the CCC and WPA left discrimination and racism essentially untouched, and made millions of black Americans grossly dependent on the federal government. For nearly 30 years welfare programs have had a cosmetic impact on American society. Moreover, the National Housing Act of 1935 placed public policy squarely behind racial segregation in public housing facilities, as administrators of that Act followed a principle of racial segregation. It was not until 1948 that this policy was altered. The Federal Housing Administration has also advocated racial segregation and its discriminatory mortgage policies have favored the development of all-white suburban communities. In the 1930's there was reason for almost anyone to be on welfare. But as the economy boomed behind a World War and two Asian "conflicts," there were fewer (if any) reasons for being on welfare—except that one was black.

A belief in the existence of equal opportunity led many whites to attribute the fact that a multitude of blacks were on welfare to innate laziness, ignorance, or apathy. Few focused clearly on the interactions of competition and conflict together with cultural or racial favoritism. What to do with the welfare system is now a problem of no minor significance, one which is not likely to disappear unless the conditions which perpetuate the lower-class status of black people are eliminated.

Racial antagonisms perhaps intensified during the 1930's because of the acute competition for the very few jobs and other necessities. In 1935 Harlem blacks rioted against white merchants and landlords. This was the first of the "modern" riots by blacks against white property instead of by whites against black people.

The Supreme Court showed signs of "modernity" in 1937 when it ruled that picketing of firms which refused to hire blacks was constitutional.* In black communities, "Don't Buy Where You Can't Work" programs were started, presaging the mass civil rights activities of the 1950's and early 1960's.

Interest in racial attitudes continued to dominate social science in the 1930's. Katz and Braly (1933) introduced the empirical investigation of stereotyping, although Walter Lippmann (1922) had introduced and analyzed the concept a decade earlier. In an elegantly simple procedure, Katz and Braly listed 84 diverse character traits (for example—intelligent,

---

*The Court had also shown earlier signs of taking a role in alleviating racial conflict when, in 1917, it struck down the grandfather clause and poll tax as efforts to disenfranchise black voters.

superstitious, happy-go-lucky, lazy, artistic, and industrious), and had 100 male American college students (from Princeton) select those traits they believed most characteristic of each of the following ten groups: Americans, Chinese, English, Germans, Irish, Italians, Japanese, Jews, Negroes, and Turks.

These Princeton men saw Jews as shrewd, mercenary, industrious, grasping, and intelligent. Americans were seen as industrious, intelligent, materialistic, ambitious, and progressive. Negroes emerged as superstitious, lazy, happy-go-lucky, ignorant, and musical. The authors concluded that the high degree of agreement in stereotyping indicated cultural forces which molded a "public attitude." Prejudiced attitudes, the authors argued, consist of both public and private attitudes. Private attitudes are based on individual feeling and experience, while public attitudes involve acceptance of cultural labels. Stereotypes, then, were seen as deplorable public attitudes, for "to the realist there are no racial or national groups which exist as entities and which determine the characteristics of the group members" (Katz and Braly, 1933, p. 289).

In 1935, Katz and Braly replicated their stereotyping study with Princeton undergraduates under two different sets of instructions. One instruction asked for the traits most commonly used to describe 10 ethnic groups; the second asked for subjects' personal descriptions of these groups. The results were similar to those of the 1933 study. The variation in instructions had virtually no effect, except that Negroes were placed one rank higher in private than in public preferences. The authors concluded that "racial prejudice is, thus, a generalized set of stereotypes of a high degree of consistency which includes emotional responses to race names, a belief in typical characteristics associated with race names, and an evaluation of such typical traits" (Katz and Braly, 1935, p. 191-192). By this definition, *black* college students in 1941 were also racially prejudiced. Bayton (1941) administered the Katz and Braly questionnaire to 100 black college students. Their racial stereotyping differed little from that of the white Princeton subjects of a few years earlier.

Since college attendance in the 1930's and 1940's usually went with middle- and upper-class status (for both blacks and whites), it is possible that the stereotypes were influenced more by class than by race. Dissociating these two variables is difficult at every level; hence, assertions about racial factors in attitudes must be evaluated cautiously. A later stereotyping study by Bayton, McAlister, and Hamer (1956) attempted to dissociate the race and class contributions to stereotypic attitudes. In that study, class was a more important determinant of stereotypes than was race.

The study of prejudice in the 1930's was primarily the study of attitudes. The belief that the study of attitudes was the first step in the study of prejudice was based largely on the view of attitude as "a disposition to act . . . a broad, generic (not simple and specific) determinant to behavior" (Allport, 1929). This attitudinal emphasis has had important consequences for the study and progress of race relations

First, the attitudinal approach places the burden of blame on the individual. Because of his culture and experiences he has prejudiced attitudes, and these attitudes describe his personality and his behavior. The most extreme result of this approach was *The Authoritarian Personality* (Adorno *et al.*, 1950). These authors concluded that basic personality distinguished prejudiced from supposed nonprejudiced individuals.

Second, and more important, in stressing attitudes social scientists employed value judgments in their operational definitions of prejudiced attitudes. There was a tendency to consider individuals who answered a question in a certain way not only as prejudiced, but as morally inferior human beings. The task of eliminating prejudice must be seen, in part, as a reorganization of the value systems of prejudiced individuals. The value position inherent in both theory and research in race relations must be recognized.

A curious assumption existed, implying the consistent relationship of attitudes to overt behavior; much of the attitudinal research in the 1930's did not question this assumption. A study by Richard LaPiere (1934) stands out as a warning beacon to all investigators of prejudiced attitudes who assume, as Allport did, that attitudes are broad, generic determinants of behavior.

Between 1930 and 1932 LaPiere traveled across the United States with a Chinese couple. (We know of the negative attitudes toward Chinese from the Katz and Braly and Bogardus studies.) LaPiere reported that

> [in] ten thousand miles of motor travel, twice across the United States, and up and down the Pacific Coast, we met definite rejection from those asked to serve us *just once*. We were received at 66 hotels, auto camps, and 'Tourist Homes,' . . . We were served in 184 restaurants and cafes . . . and treated with . . . more than ordinary considerations in 72 of them. (p. 232)

Six months after his visits LaPiere sent out a questionnaire asking "Will you accept members of the Chinese race as guests in your establishment?" He got replies from 81 restaurants and 47 hotels. The response was overwhelmingly negative—92 percent checked "No," and the remainder checked "Uncertain, depend upon circumstances." A control group of establishments LaPiere had not visited responded similarly.*

Thus as early as 1934 LaPiere sounded a cautionary note for the attitudinal true believers and their paper and pencil tests. "It would seem far more worth while to make a shrewd guess regarding that which is

---

*It might be argued that the same results would not have been obtained had LaPiere traveled with a black couple. That is possible, but more recently Kutner, Wilkins, and Yarrow (1952) made a similar study with blacks and got similar results.

essential than to accurately measure that which is likely to prove quite irrelevant," LaPiere advised (p. 237).

Another highly significant contribution to the analysis of race relations was Otto Klineberg's article on the nature of race and intelligence (1935). In this volume, Klineberg sought to demonstrate the lack of decisive evidence on the innate intellectual inferiority of black Americans. He argued against the hereditary intellectual inferiority view that pervaded social science at the time. His piece was one of the earliest attempts to reverse the racist inclination that many social scientists had.

Summary

For a brief time in the 1930's blacks and whites faced a common predicament—bread lines were not segregated. Large-scale federal intervention turned the nation around and prepared for the rapid economic growth that ensued. However, the legacy for black Americans was devastating. Blacks were locked into a bureaucratic welfare system which left them economically impotent. With few exceptions, last hired (if at all) and first fired was the rule for blacks. Welfare stepped in to maintain the moribund patient for many years.

While racial attitudes may have buttressed the discriminatory practices responsible for the highly unfavorable position of blacks, the proliferation of bureaucratically run welfare institutions created a transparent vise which tightened year by year on the poorly housed, fed, clothed, and educated black masses. The transparency of individual and institutional racism as *basic* causes of racial inequality was contributed to by the dominant focus of research on racial *attitudes*.

THE 1940'S: GROWING CIVIL RIGHTS ACTION AND ATTITUDE CHANGE THROUGH CONTACT

As we have seen, the federal government began to make a commitment to ease the plight of the poor, and of blacks, during the 1930's. As the Great Depression lifted with the coming of war, much of the federal bureaucratic maze remained. The numerous jobs that bureaucracy spawned as well as the labor shortage of wartime gave blacks more economic power. Pressures to eliminate discrimination and segregation in federal agencies forced the United States government, for the first time, to face its own involvement in racial strife and inequity.

The growth of black militancy showed in 1941 as A. Philip Randolph threatened a march on Washington to dramatize demands for fair treatment in defense industries, the armed forces, and government apprenticeship programs. Rather than face the march of a threatened

100,000 black Americans, President Roosevelt issued Executive Order 8802 banning discrimination in war industries and apprenticeship programs.* Randolph called off his march.

The civil rights movement burgeoned. The Congress of Racial Equality (CORE) was organized in 1943 and staged its first sit-in in Chicago. The black press became so vocal that the government considered prosecuting black publishers for impeding the war effort.

With the economy booming as in World War I, many blacks migrated North and West to get jobs or simply to escape the oppressive South. However, despite Executive Order 8802, there was still large-scale discrimination in war industries. Moreover, many whites still recovering from the shock of the Great Depression felt their jobs and neighborhoods threatened by black migration. These tensions exploded into another series of race riots in 1943. The worst was in Detroit, where 25 blacks and 9 whites were killed.

Because of black determination, reaction against Nazi racism, the rise of the Third World, and growing recognition of American hypocrisy, segregation came under frontal attack. In 1945, the year the war ended, a group of black NAACP lawyers decided to implement the teachings of their mentor at Howard University, Charles Houston. Led by Thurgood Marshall, they formulated plans for a direct legal attack on segregation. A year later President Truman appointed a Committee on Civil Rights, which concluded in its report, *To Secure These Rights,* that racial injustices must be abolished. In 1948 President Truman ordered the armed services integrated; a year after that, Jackie Robinson became the first black baseball player in the major leagues.†

Responsibility Number One: Tell it like it is

Rainwater suggested that the social scientist's first responsibility was to tell it like it is. Swedish sociologist Gunnar Myrdal did just that.

> The Negro in America has not yet been given the elemental civil and political rights of formal democracy, including a fair opportunity to earn his living, upon which a general accord was

---

*It was learned later that Randolph could not really come up with anywhere near the number of people reported. Nevertheless, this early use of confrontation tactics worked.

†Prior to Truman's order, black soldiers were segregated in every branch of the armed services. Some all-black companies were formed which did some fighting. Most black soldiers, however, were given little but cooking and cleaning responsibilities. Racial discrimination in the military has persisted since the early Revolutionary War days. Even though Truman ordered racial integration in 1948, there still exist various forms of racial inequity in the military.

already won when the American Creed [rights to Liberty, Justice and Equality] was first taking form. And this anachronism constitutes the contemporary 'problem' both to Negroes and to whites. (Myrdal, 1944, p. 24)

Thus in 1944 Myrdal formulated "the problem" posed by DuBois 40 years earlier. In *An American Dilemma*, a massive work of remarkable depth, quality, and insight, Myrdal and his large and impressive staff documented the character and consequences of racial relations in America. The theme of the book is the contradiction between the American creed of equality and opportunity for all, and the general exclusion of black people from its benefits.

Although black writers had written several important books on the plight of the urban black—e.g., DuBois' *The Philadelphia Negro*, James Weldon Johnson's *Black Manhattan*, and Claude McKay's *Harlem*—St. Clair Drake's and Horace Cayton's *Black Metropolis* (1945) was the most influential sociological study of urban black Americans. In this lengthy but highly readable study of Chicago's South Side, the authors eloquently documented the insights and experiences of Richard Wright's searing novel, *Native Son*. In addition to *An American Dilemma* and *Black Metropolis*, John Dollard's *Caste and Class In a Southern Town* (1937) and E. Franklin Frazier's *The Negro Family in the United States* (1944) broadly reviewed the sociology of race relations. Psychologists and sociologists alike have fed on these sources of information ever since.

The interest in attitudes remained, however, and studies continued to affirm the stereotyping data of Katz and Braly (1933, 1935) and the social distance data of Bogardus (1928). The questionnaire approach to attitudes produced copious quantitative data on social distance and stereotyping, but it was unable to capture the intensity of racial attitudes.

Some Voices of White America

More illuminating was a collection of interviews with white Americans published in 1946 by the Social Science Institute at Fisk University. In these interviews, conducted between 1940 and 1946, the respondents gave their impressions of and basic orientations toward black Americans. Here are some samples:

Female, age 45, assistant to city official in Philadelphia:

They have to overcome their racial condition. They are inclined to be lazy . . . It is our duty to help them . . . The solution lies in their own hands . . . I have a friendly feeling toward them.

Female, age 50, civic and club worker in Philadelphia:

I got along with them first-rate, because I knew how to handle them. They are like children. The only time they get up-ish is when they have too much white blood. These superstitions are one of the worst things they have ... That's in the blood ... Those in the city, now, are a sassy bunch. I think they should be separated in the schools. Their minds are really not the same ... The Japanese are not as repulsive as the Chinese ... I am far more tolerant than my mother.

Male, age 60, physician in Charleston, South Carolina:

Racial antagonism is universal ... Take the Russian-Japanese War. The American sympathies lay with Japan, but when it came to accepting individual Japanese ambassadors in Washington, the individual sympathy was for the Russian. That's race prejudice. Certainly the white race is further along the path of evolution ... We don't want them to determine political issues because he is not capable ... He is better off under our system of politics, but he doesn't get justice in the courts because people are prejudiced.

Male, age 50, businessman in Durham, North Carolina:

They are like children; the state of their mental development is low ... In spite of all that, I like the darkie. You may think I am prejudiced, and I am, but they are likeable ... Wits weren't developed in the tropics ... I have a feeling of aversion toward a rat or snake. They are harmless, but I don't like them. I feel the same toward a nigger.

Male, age 45, newspaper editor in Durham, North Carolina:

We have no friction, especially on the Negro side, except when outsiders come in and begin to try social equality ... There is no disposition on the part of any white people, except the low element, to mistreat the Negro or take unfair advantage of him ... A Negro is different from other people in that he is an unfortunate branch of the human family who hasn't had the opportunity, who hasn't been able to make out of himself all that he is capable of ... Unfortunately, many think of them as a race because they have more of a lower element that we have to keep under subjection because of their animal nature ... In a way, we know them less intimately. I believe that I have a better, higher regard because I grant them a certain amount of intelligence. The next generation will go further in this regard. That possibility doesn't alarm me. They will all die out before we get that far.

Male, age 38, newspaperman in Newport News, Virginia:

Our colored people are hard-working, self-respecting, and do not attempt to mix anywhere with the whites. There are some who try to butt in with their rights ... The best evidence of the fair treatment they get are the public school facilities. They have very excellent nigger schools ... The Negro is a black and kinky-haired person from whose body comes a not entirely pleasant odor. He is always regarded as an inferior person and race, mentally and morally, destined by birth and circumstances to serve the white people . . . I don't understand the northerners. How would they like a nigger to marry their daughter?

Female, age 40, housewife in Little Rock, Arkansas:

As long as you deal with them as your workers, everything is all right. They have no resentment . . . Our cook, here, would just do anything for us . . . We have several Harvard graduates here. I can't see where they are any different from the others; they act very humble, and realize that they are still Negroes . . . Negroes have their own characteristics. First their utter lack of responsibility. They have an inborn sense of rhythm and music. As a race, they are not honest . . . They are not a very stable race; they are here today and there tomorrow. But they are happy, carefree people and get more out of life than any other race. Their morality is low.

Female, age 20, stenographer in Newark, New Jersey:

They aren't different, except for their color . . . most of the colored people I know are servants or laborers. I never knew any who did skilled work . . . If I were a monarch and had power to do what I wanted to do with the Negroes, I don't know just what I would do. It would not be a good idea to send them back to Africa. It's necessary for them to mingle with the whites; to learn each other's ways.

This sampling of racial attitudes reveals all of the stereotypes Katz and Braly found and more. Blacks are unfortunate branches of the human family, childlike, lazy, inferior intellectually and morally, but are hard-working and good *except when they butt in with their rights!* "All men are created equal . . . [and are] endowed by their Creator with certain inalienable Rights, that among these are Life, Liberty and the pursuit of Happiness." The American Creed, the *white* American Creed, did not apply to blacks in 1776, nor did it in 1946. The American Dilemma marches on.

Although the attitudinal studies continued, the lessons of LaPiere (1934) and other investigators led several researchers to seek more general explanations. One of the first such attempts was made by John Dollard, Leonard Doob, and their Yale associates, in *Frustration and Aggression* (1939). These writers argued that prejudice is a form of aggression and that aggression results from frustration. Race prejudice, they suggested, is displaced aggression resulting from the frustrations of unemployment and insecure economic conditions. Thus, their argument ran, the lynching of blacks was not the result of frustration or anger with blacks as blacks, but rather a consequence of generally low and unstable cotton prices.

This approach is known as the *scapegoat* theory of prejudice. It suggests that blacks are the innocent victims of displaced white aggression.

This theory seems quite compelling when one observes a pigeon in a conditioning box viciously attacking a dummy pigeon whenever his customary reward is withheld. However, such reasoning applies better to emotional acts of violence than to the years of considered legal, political, social, and economical disadvantage suffered by blacks. It also narrowly focuses on the South, ignoring the physical and psychological oppression to which Northern blacks were and are subjected.

A second approach emphasized basic personality differences between prejudiced and less-prejudiced people. The best known of these studies was *The Authoritarian Personality*, by Adorno and others (1950). This volume reported on three different kinds of questionnaire techniques designed to measure anti-Semitism, ethnocentrism, and antidemocratic feeling or fascism. These authors felt that prejudice varied so greatly from situation to situation that a broader concept such as ethnocentrism would be more relevant.

Adorno and his associates developed the third of their question-naires—the F-scale— to measure anti-Semitism and ethnocentrism without mentioning specifically the groups toward which antagonisms were expressed. The F-scale was considered to be more general and more broadly predictive. The mental sets or attitudes represented in the F-scale were considered representative of the kind of prejudiced personality observed in interracial situations. The totalitarian or prejudiced personality was delineated as follows:

Conventionalism: Rigid adherence to conventional middle-class values.

Authoritarian submission: Submissive, uncritical attitude toward idealized moral authorities of the ingroup.

Authoritarian aggression: Tendency to be on the lookout for and to condemn, reject, and punish people who violate conventional values.

Anti-intraception: Opposition to the subjective, the imaginative, the tenderminded.

Superstition and stereotypy: The belief in mystical determinants of the individual's fate; the disposition to think in rigid categories.

Power and "toughness": Preoccupation with the dominance-submission, strong-weak, leader-follower dimension; identification with power figures; overemphasis upon the convention-alized attributes of the ego; exaggerated assertion of strength and toughness.

Destructiveness and cynicism: Generalized hostility, vilification of the human.

Projectivity: The disposition to believe that wild and dangerous things go on in the world; the projection outwards of unconscious, emotional impulses.

Sex: Exaggerated concern with sexual "goings-on." (Adorno, *et al.,* 1950, p. 228)*

This personality approach tended to slice the world into two types of people—prejudiced and nonprejudiced. Prejudiced people scored high on the F-scale, while nonprejudiced people scored low. Rate yourself on these items. Do you score high? Do you consider yourself prejudiced?

This view, like the scapegoat view, tended to obscure very important regional variations in race relations. Both theories spoke directly to Southerners, and indicted specific types of individuals. They diverted attention from the North, and from whites who did not fit the characteristic of their theories. Pettigrew (1958) later showed that the notion of an authoritarian personality was not a sufficient explanation of prejudiced *behavior* by demonstrating that F-scale scores were *not* higher among a random sample of Southerners than among a similar sample of Northerners.

This generalized personality approach was given some support by Hartley (1946), who presented a Bogardus social distance scale but added three fictional nationalities (Wallonian, Pirenian, Danerian). Hartley found that students who showed relatively prejudiced attitudes toward traditional outgroups showed prejudiced attitudes toward the fictional groups. ("I don't know anything about them; therefore, I would exclude them from my country," was one comment.) On the other hand, those relatively tolerant toward traditional out-groups were tolerant of the fictional groups. ("I don't know anything about them, therefore I have no prejudices against them," one such subject noted.)

While the personality approach put prejudice squarely in the heads and hearts of individuals, Oliver Cox (1948) made a far more sweeping indictment. Cox concluded that "race prejudice is a social attitude provocated [*sic*] among the public by an exploiting class for the purpose of stigmatizing some group as inferior so that the exploitation of either group itself or its resources, or both may be justified . . . Race prejudice is a socio-attitudinal facilitation of a particular type of labor exploitation . . ." (p. 939). The importance of economic exploitation of course had been recognized from slavery on. But in the 1940's the emphasis on attitudes and on personality and intergroup hostility was so great that the economic interpretation was largely overlooked.

The new emphasis among social scientists on the prejudiced personality suggested strongly that changing people's attitudes was not the

---

*One is struck by the close correspondence between these personality traits and present day images of the personality of middle-Americans. It seems that now, for the first time, there exists a real American stereotype.

way to deal with racial antagonism. Moral appeals and rational argument simply would not work with an authoritarian personality. Other means for dealing with the problems of race had to be discovered—and this brought social scientists back to Dewey's (1922) emphasis on changing the environment.

Two viewpoints, then, had developed. On the one hand, the personality theorists implied that prejudicial attitudes cannot be changed through information and therefore more impersonal institutional means, such as legislation, were necessary. On the other hand, the attitudinal approach suggested that changing of folkways, or attitudes based on tradition, experience, and social expedience, was a necessary step toward benign intergroup relations.

Combined, the two approaches argued strongly for social change through legislation. The rigid personality would not be influenced by moral appeals or rational argument, while the prejudiced, ill-informed attitudes could be altered only by personal contact. As Bettelheim and Janowitz (1950) stated: "The law and the courts stand within our legal system as an immediate focal point for changing some of the basic norms of interpersonal contact outside the primary groups, including those of inter-ethnic relations" (p. 177).

In the late 1940's most social scientists believed that racial integration was the only possible way to ease racial tensions. They felt that only integration could eliminate the gross educational, social, psychological, and economic disparities between the races.

A few years earlier, Lippitt and Radke (1946) had condemned the literature on prejudice for "a narrow emphasis on the surface aspects of the problem" (p. 167). In the late 1940's and early 1950's social scientists began to emphasize the dynamic elements of prejudice and to outline ways of reducing it.* Again and again, social scientists asked whether laws can change customs—whether enforced personal contact can reduce interracial hostility. A well-known "social experiment" on this subject was conducted by Morton Deutsch and Mary Collins (1951) in the new federally sponsored public housing. The authors selected interracial housing projects (1) where blacks and whites were assigned living units without regard to race, and (2) where blacks and whites were assigned to separate sections of the same project. The fully integrated projects were in New York City, and the internally segregated projects in Newark. Projects selected from the two cities were matched according to racial ratio. The Newark project, called Bakerville, with two blacks to every white, was matched with Sacktown in New York, which was 70 percent black. A second matched pair consisted of Frankville in Newark, half blacks and half whites, and Koaltown in New York, which was 40 percent black and 60 percent white.

---

*See, for example, Rose (1947), Williams (1947), and Bettelheim and Janowitz (1950).

Data were obtained through intensive and long (from one and one-fourth-
to two-hour) interviews conducted with housewives in their own apart-
ments.

TABLE 2.2

*Interracial Contact Patterns and Attitudes of White Housewives
Toward Negroes in Two Housing Projects ***

		Integrated projects		Internally segregated projects	
		Koaltown	Sacktown	Bakerville	Frankville
1.	Closest casual contact				
	As neighbors in the building	60%	53%	0%	0%
	Outside on benches	46	64	7	21
	Shopping in stores on streets around project	12	13	81	60
2.	Intimate contact visiting, helping, clubs, etc.				
	None	61	28	99	96
	Once or more	39	72	1	4
3.	Type of relations				
	Friendly	60	69	6	4
	Accommodative	24	14	5	1
	Mixed	7	11	2	3
	None	5	0	87	88
	Bad	4	6	0	4
4.	Feelings expressed				
	Like, desire, friendship	42	60	9	5
	Mixed, reserved	30	12	12	27
	Avoidant, dislike	28	28	79	68

*Adapted from Deutsch and Collins (1951), Tables 2, 3, 9, and 12.

If interracial contact ameliorates racial attitudes, the racial attitudes of housewives in the integrated projects of Koaltown and Sacktown would be more favorable than those of housewives in segregated Bakerville and Frankville. (See Table 2.2.) Since very few of the whites in either the segregated or integrated or internally segregated projects would have picked a project with black families on the basis of their initial attitudes, we can assume that the differences found by Deutsch and Collins were due to the interracial contacts.

White housewives' attitudes toward blacks became more positive in the integrated projects and changed little if at all in the segregated project. Deutsch and Collins concluded: "From the point of view of reducing prejudice and of creating harmonious, democratic intergroup relations, the net gain resulting from the integrated projects is considerable; from the same point of view, the gain created by the segregated bi-racial projects is slight."

Also concerned with the effects of social contact on attitudes, Festinger and Kelley (1951) conducted a field experiment designed to produce desirable attitude changes. In the town studied, hostility had developed toward a public housing project; the townspeople feared it would become a slum. Project residents felt inferior even though their actual status differential from nonproject residents was quite small. Project residents were also hostile toward each other, and anticipated hostility from each other. The task was to reduce the hostility within and without the project. Festinger and Kelley reasoned that lessening hostility through interpersonal contact required

1. *motivational control* of attitudes by changing what people want;

2. *perceptual control* of attitudes by changing the person's experience with relevant objects, events, attributes and relationships; and

3. *social control* of attitudes by changing the social attitudes and group norms with which the person comes in contact.

To lessen hostility, the authors initiated nursery school programs, teenage clubs, and adult softball and crafts. The intent was to involve all the members of the community in changing motivational, perceptual, and social systems. The authors found that hostile attitudes lessened *only among people who participated in and had favorable attitudes toward the program.* Unfortunately, for the project as a whole the program made matters worse. The authors concluded: "If a group of persons are held together by common interest in community activities, and carry on communication about attitudes and opinions on which they differ, the conditions for attitude-change are present" (p. 76).

The Deutsch and Collins and the Festinger and Kelley studies suggest that "social engineering" (i.e., putting people in positions they would not choose themselves, for purposes of social change) may have general usefulness in the area of reducing racial conflict. The Festinger and Kelley study, though, warns that the positive effects of contact may be limited to certain kinds of people and situations. Gordon Allport (1954) later organized the research on interracial contact and extracted from the results hypotheses about the optimum contact conditions. We will look at the contact hypothesis in greater detail in Chapter 4.

Summary

Many important events of the 1940's coalesced to create optimum conditions for changes in race relations. The mood of militance was early established by A. Philip Randolph's threatened march on Washington in 1941. Two Executive Orders were issued which put the government on record as taking some responsibility for the elimination of racial inequities. The spirit of the NAACP lawyers produced a flurry of attacks on the legal structure of segregation and discrimination. The weakened legal structure was more susceptible to the large-scale attacks to come in the 1950's.

General theory of race prejudice, particularly the personality theories, converged with the demonstrated effectiveness of interracial contact in diminishing racial hostility. This state of affairs in social science was particularly supportive of legislative attempts to abolish segregation of the races.

Thus, conditions bred a mood for civil rights activity, and the nature of social-scientific research and theory were ripe for the initiation of massive attacks on "the problem."

CHAPTER THREE

Attacks on the Problem

We conclude that in the field of public education, the doctrine of 'separate but equal' has no place. *

United States Supreme Court, 1954

THE 1950's: CIVIL RIGHTS AND MODERN AUTHORITY

Thus began the modern phase of the black American's struggle for freedom and equality. Not to be overlooked in attacking the problem is the important role of the social scientist. When it struck down the separate-but-equal doctrine of *Plessy* v. *Ferguson,* the Supreme Court noted that segregation had a "detrimental effect on colored children"; more recently, investigators have emphasized the detrimental effect on white children as well. But in 1954, the Court appealed to *modern authority,* i.e., social scientific research, for the basis of its decision that the separate-but-equal doctrine was detrimental to colored children.

The immediate importance of *Brown* v. *Board of Education* was largely symbolic, as the "all deliberate speed" desegregation timetable of a 1955 decision invited ingenious legal procrastination at which the Southern lawyer politician is peerless. The full impact of the decision has only begun to be realized in the last few years as the Court's decision has been enforced by more recent judicial decisions and more vigorous Justice Department activity.

---

*From the text of the unanimous opinions, Supreme Court in *Brown* v. *Board of Education,* May 17, 1954, reprinted in full in Clark (1963, p. 159). This decision came about because an eight-year-old Topeka, Kansas child was obliged to walk across a railroad track and take a bus to a black school twenty-one blocks away because her community school was all-white. The social meaning of bussing changes, depending on whether it is serving or splitting segregated schools.

Two months after the Supreme Court decision, a White Citizens' Council was formed in Indianola, Mississippi. Citizens' Councils sprang up all over the South and swore to fight integration by every lawful means. Considering the operation of Southern law at this time, they were assured a wide variety of such "lawful means." For example, shortly after the Supreme Court decision, a Mississippi circuit judge (educated at Yale) wrote a book entitled *Black Monday* in which he intoned:

> When a law transgresses the moral and ethical sanctions and standards of the mores, invariably strife, bloodshed and revolution follow in the wake of its attempted enforcement.

> The loveliest and purest of God's creatures, the nearest thing to an angelic being that tread this terrestial ball is a well-bred cultured southern white woman or her blue-eyed, golden-haired little girl . . . . We say to the Supreme Court and to the northern world, you shall not make us drink from this cup . . . . We have, through our forefathers, died before for our sacred principles. We can, if necessary, die again (Brady, 1955, pp. 45;88-89).

Can laws change customs? Deutsch and Collins said yes; Festinger and Kelley's study said maybe; Tom Brady said NO!

Meanwhile, evidence was accumulated to document the negative consequences of being black in white America. E. Franklin Frazier (1949) reported the psychological anguish black Americans experienced in their oppressed role as underclass for a privileged white caste. Kardiner and Ovesey (1951) corroborated many of Frazier's observations.

Studies of Racial Identification

Although there were many studies cited in the Supreme Court decision, the most famous of these was a study on racial identification in black children by Kenneth and Mamie Clark (1947). One hundred thirty-four black children aged 3-7 from racially segregated nursery and public schools in Arkansas, and 119 black children of the same age range from integrated schools in Springfield, Massachusetts, were shown four dolls—identical in every detail but skin and hair color. Two were brown with black hair, while two were white with blond hair. With respect to their own skin color, the black subjects were classified as light or nearly white, medium (from very light brown to fairly dark brown), and very dark. The experimenter asked each child to give him one doll that

1. you like best;	5. is a white child;
2. is a nice doll;	6. is a colored child;
3. looks bad;	7. is a Negro child;
4. is a nice color;	8. looks like you.

Racial identification. The study showed that the black children had a very keen sense of racial awareness. When asked to give the white doll, 94 percent chose the white doll; when asked to give the colored doll, 93 percent chose the colored doll; when asked to give the Negro doll, 72 percent chose the colored doll.

The authors cautioned, however, that "awareness of racial differences does not necessarily determine a *socially accurate* racial self-identification." For example, only 66 percent of the children chose the colored doll as looking like them. It was expected that *accurate* self-identification would have produced 100 percent choice of colored doll. But if we look at the choices of the doll that looked like them as a function of the subjects' skin color, the presumed inaccuracy of self-identification is questionable. Of the *light* children (nearly white), 80 percent chose the white doll and only 20 percent chose the colored doll. But among the dark children 81 percent chose the colored doll, while only 19 percent chose the white doll. The medium-colored black children chose the colored doll at a rate of 73 percent and the white doll at 26 percent. Thus the apparently low average of 66 percent choosing the colored doll is heavily influenced by the *accurate* choices of light-skinned children, of whom only 20 percent chose the colored doll. These data, then, do not provide clear evidence for erroneous self-identification by black children.

North-South differences. If segregation negatively affects racial identification and preference, one would expect the Southern black children to differ strongly from the Northern black children. But the Clarks found that "the children in the northern mixed school situation do not differ from children in Southern segregated schools in either their knowledge of racial differences or their racial identification" (p. 174-175). However, Northern black children preferred the white dolls more than the Southern black children did.

Racial preferences. The Clarks found that the majority of black children preferred the white dolls. Sixty-seven percent preferred the white doll *to play with;* 59 percent said the white dolls *were nice dolls;* and 60 percent said the white dolls had the *nice color.* On the other hand, 59 percent of the subjects said the *colored dolls looked bad.*

In general these data are interpreted as an indication of the negative racial self-concept acquired very early by black children. But since the white dolls in the study had not only white faces but also blonde hair, the preferences of the children could well represent an aesthetic judgment of hair color, or the child's representation of societal norms.*

*For example, Sara Kiesler (1971) showed that black and white children preferred a *purple* stick figure to others drawn with regular black and blue writing colors. There have been numerous attempted replications and clarifications of this classic study in recent years. We will review several of them in Chapter 4.

Since the results of this study were used frequently in argument against racial segregation in schools, the lack of difference between segregated Southern and integrated Northern black children's racial attitudes should have been noted. This finding suggests that it is not only simple racial segregation but the role requirements and social structural supports that are fundamental to the issues being investigated. Once again the North escaped indictment while the South came under attack.

In 1952 Mary Ellen Goodman wrote a sensitive and passionate book, *Race Awareness in Young Children,* in which she portrayed much of the racial dynamics suggested by the Clarks' study. Through interviews and play situations in an interracial nursery school in New England, she found that forms of ugly and insidious race awareness were widespread by the age of four. Miss Goodman observed that "four-year-olds, particularly white ones, show unmistakable signs of the onset of racial bigotry . . . [and that] Negro children not yet five can sense that they are marked, and grow uneasy" (p. 218).

The children, of course, responded profoundly to the racial attitudes of adults. But to say simply that children copied or learned the attitudes of the dominant socializing agent (the family) would be very misleading. Miss Goodman accurately pointed out that each child *"generates his own attitudes* out of the personal, social, and cultural materials that happen to be his." Children respond to the objects they perceive. Miss Goodman summarizes the meaning children derive from the facts of skin color differences with the simple fraction

$$\frac{white}{brown}.$$

Once again we encounter the "color line"—a horizontal line separating black from white, *with white always on top.*

In the 1970's Law and Order is a popular phrase with different meanings for different people. The lawlessness which issued from the Supreme Court decision of 1954 is impressive in its own right. In 1955, Emmet Till, a fourteen-year-old black boy from Chicago was kidnapped, lynched, and his body was mutilated in Money, Mississippi. The Rev. Dr. Martin Luther King, Jr. took leadership of a bus boycott in Montgomery, Alabama, and in 1956 his home was bombed. That same year a black woman, Autherine Lucy, was admitted to the all-white University of Alabama but suspended only four days later following a riot at the school. A white mob prevented the enrollment of black students at a high school in Mansfield, Texas. The Tennessee National Guard was called up to quell mobs demonstrating against school integration; National Guardsmen dispersed a similar mob in Sturgis, Kentucky. The Birmingham, Alabama home of the Rev. F. L. Shuttlesworth, an aide to Dr. King, was destroyed by a dynamite bomb. The following year Shuttlesworth was mobbed trying to enroll his daughters in a white Birmingham school.

In 1957 a Nashville, Tennessee elementary school with enrollment of one black and thirty-eight white children, was destroyed by a dynamite blast. In the same year Governor Orville Faubus of Arkansas led defiance of a Federal Court integration order, and nine black children had to be escorted into Little Rock's Central High School by the 101st Airborne Division. And in 1959 Mac Parker was lynched in Poplarville, Mississippi.

The six years following *Brown* v. *Board of Education* saw the perfection of such nonviolent tactics as the boycott, the establishment of such militant groups as Martin Luther King's Southern Christian Leadership Conference (S.C.L.C.), and the slow, painful integration of small numbers of Southern white schools.

Social scientists, meanwhile, concentrated on two areas: (1) sociologists were concerned with social stratification and proliferation of social roles; (2) some social psychologists remained chiefly interested in attitudinal change in race relations and in the prejudiced or authoritarian personality.

Social Roles in Mass Society

The social-role approach was summarized in a brief paper by Lohman and Reitzes (1952), who rejected the stress on attitudes in race relations. Instead they suggested that behavior is determined mainly by the social-role requirements in a given situation. As society has become larger and more differentiated, the authors argued, more and more roles have developed. This has led to greater impersonalization. Thus conflict between individuals has been replaced by conflict between social roles enacted by individuals. These roles are determined primarily by social structures. The authors conclude: "Most situations of racial contact are defined by the collectively defined interests of the individuals concerned and do not merely manifest their private feelings toward other races" (p. 241). In these terms desegregation in the South can be seen as creating conflict between public officials in their roles as defenders of the Southern way, and the federal government, considered by many Southerners to represent chiefly Northern interests which would challenge and disrupt the Southern way. The conflict, then, was not between the angry whites, led by men like Faubus, and the handful of black children and their supporting parents who attempted to integrate the schools. Rather, it was between the social ideals of white supremacy and segregation in the South, and the attack on those ideals by the federal government. Recall that Tom Brady did not issue his challenge to the black people of the South, but to "the Supreme Court and the Northern world." Throughout the 1950's and early 1960's, that hatred of many Southerners for the white liberal who went south to "cause trouble" was at least as great as Southern animosity toward Southern black organizers. The social-role approach is also applicable to the North, as became clear in the mid-1960's.

Interracial Contact

A second major thrust in the attitudinal approach developed from the contact theory of reducing intergroup conflict. In the 1930's social psychologists had mainly tried to describe attitudes; by the 1950's the focus was on how to change attitudes.

In his classic monograph on prejudice, Allport (1954) summarized the characteristics of interracial contact situations, concluding that prejudice will be diminished when the two groups: (1) possess equal status in the situation, (2) seek common goals, (3) are cooperatively dependent upon each other, and (4) interact with the positive support of authorities, laws, and custom. The South became a major testing-ground for contact theory as school desegregation followed, in all deliberate speed, the 1954 Supreme Court decision.

Numerous investigations of the effects of desegregation on black and white children were conducted during the 1950's. As Allport suggested, interracial contact needs a supportive social milieu in order to effectively diminish racial hostility. It is not very likely that the coercive, emotional atmosphere of the South was supportive of desegregation attempts. For example, E. Q. Campbell (1958) studied the attitudes of 746 white high-school students toward blacks six months before and six months after their school was desegregated. He found a large number of both positive and negative changes. Positive changes seemed associated with greater classroom contact and friendship, and negative changes seemed to be influenced more by prevailing parental attitudes. A similiar study by Whitmore (1957) found a diminution in prejudiced attitudes though it was unrelated to classroom contact.

The conditions listed by Allport for positive attitude change as a result of contact are quite stringent compared to the social scientific evidence upon which *Brown* v. *Board of Education* was presumably based. Hence, even if segregation is abolished because of its strong negative impact on black children (recall the study by the Clarks), it does not follow that mere racial desegregation will diminish racial hostility.* The idea that interracial contact can improve race relations is predicated on two assumptions: (1) Interracial hostilities exist partly because of misperceptions of other people's beliefs, attitudes, opinions and goals. According to this assumption, interracial contact should diminish these perceived discrepancies and thus foster positive attitudes by removing this basis for interracial hostility. (2) Through interracial contact, differences

---

*As Pettigrew (1971) has recently pointed out, "mere desegregation" should not be confused with "true integration." The optimum conditions for interracial contact do not apply to conditions of mere desegregation. True integration would exist within a supportive social milieu with cooperative racial dependency. Contact theory, then, has not always been adequately tested by school desegregation.

between races will be shown not to be causes for derision or animosity, but rather a basis for interesting and varied relationships. Both of these assumptions are valid. There has been a tendency to emphasize the first, however. We will review the literature on the effects of interracial contact in more detail in Chapter Four.

In examining the effects of interracial contact (that is, racial integration) it is important to consider both the extent to which racial groups share beliefs and purposes, and the extent to which their different ethnic backgrounds are major distinguishing characteristics. The only way groups can come together in common purpose is to unite around those beliefs and goals they share and to mutually respect those differences (inherited and cultural) which they enjoy.

Summary

The 1950's formed the backdrop for the enormous complexities of race relations in the 1960's. The 1954 Supreme Court decision intensified conflict in the South, while diverting attention from the teeming ghettos and urban crisis. It also established the social scientist as a major force in race relations.* The Southern responses to the Supreme Court decision anticipated the rise of black demands for equal rights, and increasing resistance on the part of whites. There was also sounded the warning note that mere desegregation would not have totally positive effects.

THE 1960's: CONFRONTATION AND THE RELEVANT SOCIAL SCIENTIST

In the 1960's the problem of race relations was so intertwined with other problems of a huge and complex society that one hardly knows where first to turn.

The Student Nonviolent Coordinating Committee (SNCC) was organized in 1960 and took leadership of the sit-in movement in the South. The following year, 13 members of the Congress of Racial Equality (CORE) took a freedom ride—traveling in an integrated bus from Washington southward. At Montgomery, Alabama, crowds of whites pulled the Freedom Riders from the bus and beat them, then overturned the bus and burned it. Attorney-General Robert F. Kennedy was obliged to send 600 United States Marshals to Montgomery to restore law and order.†

---

*Some of my social-science colleagues are pessimistic about their role as major "forces" in race relations. Whether they are "effective" forces may be debatable, but there is no question that expert testimony and fact-finding commissions have played increasingly prominent roles in *public* governmental justifications of its policies.

†Note that only a short time ago, Law and Order had a very different meaning than the current political shorthand for white conservatism. Then it was blacks who sought the law for protection from white violence.

While civil rights workers pushed hard for integration in the South, Elijah Muhammed led the Black Muslims on a different path. The Black Muslims followed a philosophy preached earlier by Marcus Garvey. Through Malcolm X, their most popular minister, they proclaimed the beauty of black people and culture and the horrors of white oppression. Their emphasis on black pride and self-help counseled racial separation as a desirable and necessary means of collective black advancement.

Because the Muslim philosophy offered clear indictments of white people, they were branded "militant" and generally discredited in the popular press (blacks as well as white).* They were even linked to the Ku Klux Klan. The Black Muslim philosophy is important because (1) it produced a new brand of black hero, Malcolm X (although he was not widely acclaimed by the black community until after his break with the Muslims and subsequent assassination); and (2) it presented in understandable terms the seminal ideas of a black cultural revolution.

The Southern civil rights workers' tactics of confrontation, and the Muslims' ideology of black pride fused by the end of the decade. Accompanying this fusion has been a shift from a moral thrust mainly for rights to a thrust for power through economic, political, cultural, and quasimilitary means.

The decade of the 1960's witnessed the continuing escalation of the intensity and velocity of black efforts to improve their position in this society. From advocating integration under John Lewis, SNCC moved by stages to the enunciation of Black Power by Stokely Carmichael in 1965. As early as 1962, Robert Williams had organized armed defense of blacks against marauding Klansmen in North Carolina. In 1964 the Deacons for Defense and Justice in Louisiana used rifles and rode around protecting the black community from rampaging whites. In Oakland, California, Huey P. Newton and Bobby Seale organized a similar kind of protective vigilante group in 1966 under the name of the Black Panther Party. This quasimilitary self-protection, together with increasingly violent rhetoric, created an ideological conflict for various politically moderate supporters of civil rights activities.

The mid-1960's explosions ripped open the powderkeg of the black Northern ghetto—New York, Philadelphia, Rochester in 1964; Los Angeles and Chicago in 1965; Chicago, Cleveland, Lansing, Omaha, and others in 1966; Cincinnati, Buffalo, Detroit, and Newark in 1967; and dozens throughout the country after the assassination of Martin Luther King in 1968. Most Northern whites accustomed to thinking of race relations as a

---

*In light of recent events it is interesting that the Muslims were seen as so militant and prone to violence. A recent report linked favorable attitudes toward the Muslims to participation in the Watts riots of 1965 (Cohen, 1970). By current revolutionary standards the Muslim philosophy is not militant at all.

Southern problem, were rudely jolted by these demonstrations of trouble in their own backyards. With few exceptions (notably the Harlem riots of 1935 and 1943) previous racial riots had consisted of interracial fighting or the destruction of black communities by white mobs.

As the black struggle widened, black-white relations became more strained, not only through direct confrontation in the South or through violence in the urban ghettos, but also in the ranks of civil rights organizations.

In the 1960's a growing sense of dissatisfaction with the prominent, for many *too* prominent, role of whites in the civil rights movement culminated in the black power position of "whites to the rear or out." The popular advice to white sympathizers was "go get your white community straightened out." Although it was seen as new policy at the time, the issues it embodied were not.

Historically the major role in the abolitionist movement was credited to William Lloyd Garrison who, in 1831, put out the first issue of *The Liberator.* David Walker, a black man, issued his *Four Appeals* in 1829, calling for blacks to rise up and overthrow their white oppressors. Later, Frederick Douglass, the black abolitionist, was not even on speaking terms with Garrison, the white abolitionist.

The NAACP grew out of the all-black Niagara Movement of 1905. However, its inception as a duly constituted organization in 1909 was under the auspices of a white woman, Mary White Ovington. Recall it was the prominent role of whites in the organization that alienated Monroe Trotter and led to the formation of a counter, all-black group.

Under Stokely Carmichael, SNCC not only enunciated Black Power, but also advised white members that their role would have to be distinctly secondary. After the Kerner Commission Report, citing white racism as the root cause of the riots, charges of racism flew like wildfire, stinging many white so-called liberals.

But just as the leadership tensions were not new, the issues of racial integration or separation themselves were not new. The racial problem in this country has not been confined to slavery, segregation and "red-neck" bigotry. It has infiltrated the ranks of every region, philosophy, movement and policy. It seems to many that the events of the 1960's are basically different from past events, and that issues have been reconstituted on a new level. In an important sense, this newness of the problem is illusory. We have taken a basically historical perspective in an attempt to demonstrate those elements of "the problem" which seem to recur generation after generation.

In the 1960's the rhetoric changed to racism, and charges flew in new directions. It is most important to realize that these new perspectives did not reflect newly created problems but recently *discovered* ones.

From the cauldron of race relations in the 1960's, three critical developments are salient:

1. The development of confrontation tactics in the early phase of the civil rights movement. Confrontations continued in the late '60's, switching from nonviolence to violence.

2. A sense of black solidarity. While by no means totally agreeing on tactics or even goals, black leaders moved steadily toward demanding black power, rather than merely equal rights. This ideology is expressed most forcefully by the Black Panther Party ("Power to the People"), but it is evident also in attempts by a variety of black community organizations to exercise control over research, allocation of funds, schools, and so on.

3. The rampant proliferation of role conflicts. The importance of this kind of conflict is amply demonstrated in a statement from an organizer of a white ethnic working class symposium in Washington in 1970:

> America is *not* a melting pot. It is a sizzling cauldron for the ethnic American who feels that he has been politically courted and legally extorted by both government and private enterprise.
>
> The ethnic American is sick of being stereotyped as racist and dullard by phony white liberals, pseudo black militants, and patronizing bureaucrats ... checked by the political rhetoric of the illusionary funding for black-oriented social programs, he turns his anger to race—*when he himself is a victim of class prejudice. (New York Times,* June 17, 1970, p. 41; italics mine)

Sex, race, class, age, education, region, life styles, and labor affiliation—in all these areas role conflicts are evident. But it is far from evident how the massive bureaucracy of government can adopt the nimbleness such complexities demand of it.

One way in which the government has tried to inform its political policies is through large-scale social-science commission investigations of employment, education, and domestic violence—racial problems of major consequence.

Correspondingly, the role of the social scientist in government policy-making has burgeoned. Social scientists sit on national councils, give testimony before national commissions, and lend authority to a variety of political programs. The work of social scientists is exemplified by the report and we will look at three of the most important ones.

The Moynihan Report

In March, 1965, Assistant Secretary of Labor Daniel Patrick Moynihan issued a report from the Office of Policy Planning and Research entitled *The Negro Family: The Case for National Action.** The purpose of the

---

*For a full analysis of the contents and history of the Report, see Rainwater and Yancey, *The Moynihan Report and the Politics of Controversy* (1967).

report was expressed in these statements:

> ... It has to be said that there is a considerable body of evidence to support the conclusion that Negro social structure, in particular the Negro family, battered and harassed by discrimination, injustice, and uprooting, is in the deepest trouble. While many young Negroes are moving ahead to unprecedented levels of achievement, many more are falling further and further behind. ...
>
> At the heart of the deterioration of the fabric of Negro society is the deterioration of the Negro family.
>
> It is the fundamental source of the weakness of the Negro community at the present time . . . .
>
> A national effort toward the problems of Negro Amercians must be directed towards the question of family structure . . . . Such a national effort could be stated thus:
>
> The policy of the United States is to bring the Negro American to full and equal sharing in the responsibilities and rewards of citizenship. To this end, the programs of the federal government bearing on this objective shall be designed to have the effect directly or indirectly of enhancing the stability and resources of the Negro American family. (Moynihan, 1965, p. 4-48)

With respect to the black family, Moynihan makes these points:

1. *The family structure of lower-class blacks is highly unstable, and in many urban centers is approaching complete breakdown.* The breakdown of the black family is to be contrasted, according to Moynihan, with the stability of the white family. The statistics from the census of 1960, presumably supporting this assertion, showed that 22.9 percent of urban nonwhite American women, compared to 7.0 percent of urban white women, had absent husbands or were divorced.

2. *Nearly one-quarter of urban black marriages are dissolved.* Moynihan buttresses this assertion with the statistic that 26 percent of black, compared to 10 percent of white, ever married are divorced, separated, or have husbands absent.

3. *Nearly one-quarter of black births are now illegitimate.* The Report points out that reported illegitimacy rates have been increasing for all races since the census of 1940, but by 1963 the increase had produced a rate of only 3.1 percent among whites, but 23.6 percent among blacks.

4. *Almost one-quarter of black families are headed by females.* This figure is contrasted with approximately one-sixteenth of white families.

5. *The breakdown of the black family has led to a startling increase in welfare dependency.* The Report points out that a majority of black children receive public assistance under the Aid to Families with

Dependent Children Program at some point in their childhood. In 1965, the families of 14 percent of black children were receiving welfare, compared to the families of only 2 percent of white children.

The suggested causes of the breakdown of the black family were: 1) slavery's systematic destruction of family bonds, recognizing only maternal control for the young; 2) the failure of Reconstruction, closely followed by Jim Crow laws and customs which robbed the black man of his just place at the head of the family; 3) urbanization, which trapped blacks in urban ghettos while whites fled to suburbs; 4) the violent and continuing impact of unemployment and poverty; 5) the wage system, which makes no provision for the size of a person's family (penalizing blacks, who have, on the average, larger families); and 6) the dramatic population growth producing larger black than white families.

The Report goes on to suggest that the consequence of this breakdown in black family structure is a "tangle of pathology" which has arisen because

> The Negro community has been forced into a matriarchal structure which, because it is so out of line with the rest of the American society, seriously retards the progress of the group as a whole, and imposes a crushing burden on the Negro male, and in consequence, a great many Negro women as well. . . .

> Ours is a society which presumes male leadership in private and public affairs. The arrangements of society facilitate such leadership and reward. A subculture, such as that of the Negro American, in which this is not the pattern, is placed at a distinct disadvantage. (p. 29)

Analysis of the Moynihan Report is difficult because its insights and conclusions are based on unsophisticated social scientific research methods; furthermore, its subject matter and conclusions are so controversial that the numerous highly emotional reactions to it preclude any simple objective analysis. In spite of these obstacles, the Report needs to be discussed because involved in its assessment are many of the most fundamental issues of race relations today. Our analysis of the Report will focus on three things: 1) family stability; 2) methodological weaknesses; and 3) the idea of a "culture of poverty."

By continually referring to the breakdown of the black family, the Moynihan Report seems to imply that the white American family is a stable, enviably competent producer of well-adjusted, achievement-oriented youth. Yet in the early 1970's, a major problem of *white* America is described as the "generation gap," a euphemism for social problems such as alienation, drug use and abuse, violence, and crisis in confidence.* A

---

*More recent writers (e.g., Pitts, 1969) refer to these changing times in terms of a growing counter culture with different value systems. Other writers (e.g., Lipset, 1971) reject this view as naively ahistorical.

report of the 1970's on the white family might begin familiarly: "It has to be said that there is a considerable body of evidence to support the conclusion that white social structure, in particular the white family, battered and harassed by male chauvinism, misplaced values, hypocrisy, and traditionalism, is in the deepest trouble." Yet the Moynihan Report implied that if black family structure more closely resembled white family structure, black Americans would be better off.

The Report singles out the matrifocality of many black families as the chief pathological symptom of the dissolving black social structure. Yet one cannot help but wonder if male domination might not be symptomatic of other maladies which can afflict a family.* The problem of family structure is more complex than the simple "matrifocal" argument suggests. The solution offered by the Moynihan Report is rather like the captain of a sinking ocean liner "rescuing" passengers of a disabled ferryboat.

The fact of the instability of lower class black families cannot and need not be disputed. What arouses the emotional involvement of concerned parties is the attribution of cause and effect. Moynihan's Report suggests that the instability of lower class black families is the *cause* of black problems. Congruent with this analysis, the Report advises the federal government to adopt policies designed to enhance the stability of the black family.

If one looks at the instability of the black family as an *effect* of racist discrimination, bias, and oppression, one might advise the federal government to deal directly with this malady—to eliminate racism in all forms from this society. The Report leaves one with the feeling that it blames the victim by focusing on the "tangle of pathology."

The focus and interpretation aspects of the Report's analysis of family stability aside, the methodology itself was deficient on several key points. For example, the fact that nearly one-quarter of black births are recorded as illegitimate is of highly questionable significance. On this point Ryan (1967) summarizes the inadequacy of Moynihan's analysis:

> We can conclude only that Negro and white girls probably engage in premarital intercourse in about the same proportions, *but* that the white girl more often takes Enovid or uses a diaphragm; . . . if she gets pregnant, she more often obtains an abortion; if she has the baby, first she is more often able to conceal it (for example, shotgun marriage) and second, she has an infinitely greater opportunity to give it up for adoption. (p. 460)

Ryan's observations significantly qualify the suggestion that illegitimacy means a breakdown in moral values with corresponding negative impact on family structure among blacks.

---

*Moreover, there is much evidence to suggest that many traditional African societies were matrilineal and some were matrifocal. Among blacks, the woman has always had a prominent role in family life, not just as a childbearer, but as a worker as well. Women's liberation and attacks on sexism approach this same issue from the other side.

The data consistently failed to show significant differences between black and white Americans (on the basis of race alone). The Report generalizes from lower-class black Americans to all black Americans, compares lower-class blacks to whites regardless of class, and, in addition, make questionably causal inferences. For example, it presents a table showing that when the father is present black children have higher IQ's than when the father is absent. But it would be expected that the presence of a father would go along with higher socioeconomic status, and data confirm the high correlation between socieconomic status, IQ, and achievement.

The fact that Moynihan made sweeping conclusions based on shoddy analysis suggests one possible interpretation of his intentions. Perhaps he sought to convince the federal government to adopt a unified and binding commitment to right the wrongs suffered by black Americans. He might also have thought that the best way to appeal to the paternalistic and racially biased thinking of the government was through a report fostering the notion of gross black pathology and misfortune, stressing the need for federal guidance and intervention. Put another way, the Report could be seen as the attempt of a white liberal politician using the language and methods of social scientific analysis to shake a white moderate politician into commitment to national action.

Since Moynihan made no *specific* proposals or recommendations for action, the major impact of his analysis was to create controversy concerning his diagnosis of the problems of black America. Many social scientists have rejected his analysis as uniquely applicable to black Americans. Nevertheless, the publicity and authority of an official report by a lawyer-politician acting as a social scientist can have an enormous impact on how Americans think about race relations.

Until the mid-1960's almost all the federal government's involvement in civil rights was in response to pressures from blacks or to national crises. The Moynihan Report proposed that the federal government take the lead in identifying and dealing with the problems on a national scale. It was this goal, apparently, that guided the writing of the Report. However, such an approach can have both positive and negative consequences. Wise and effective federal policies are plainly good, just as unwise and ineffective ones are plainly bad. It is sometimes difficult to predict which are which when programs are begun.

Perhaps the most important aspect of the Moynihan Report was its claim that the poor, in general, represent a substratum within the lower-class substratum of the larger society. It further suggests that people who fall within that economic substratum exhibit a unique set of traits which, taken collectively, identify a "culture of poverty." The culture of poverty is seen as defective and unhealthy. The problem for black Americans, according to the Report, is an overrepresentation in this category.

The general acceptance of this point of view has led many social scientists to argue that black culture is *no more than* lower-class culture. Because the problem for the national government is poverty, this focus on the poorest people in the black community has led to the general impression that most black people are products of broken homes, grow up hating themselves, and early learn the ways of crime and immorality. The black child, according to this stereotype, loses motivation to work and just waits until he grows up to get on welfare. This composite picture from several sources (not only Moynihan but also Kenneth Clark's *Dark Ghetto,* Claude Brown's *Manchild in the Promised Land,* and several others) portrays the negative characteristics of poor black Americans.

The "defective culture" view of black Americans has dominated social science literature. However, recognizing that adaptations to an impoverished socioeconomic condition undoubtedly affect the behavioral and psychological responses of black Americans, it is by no means sufficient to capture all of the ramifications of the black experience in America.

Research aimed directly at the question of black versus lower-class subcultural characteristics produces equivocal results. For example, investigating a national sample for differences in value orientation, Rokeach and Parker's (1970) findings suggested that "value differences *do* distinguish the rich from the poor, but not Negroes from Whites" (p. 97). Johnson and Sanday (1971) interviewed lower-class people in Pittsburgh and concluded, "The data indicate that for the sample studied, there are two subcultures—one black and one white" (p. 128).

The importance of these issues is that proper programs designed to promote constructive social change must be based on proper understanding of subcultural influences. It is not enough for a politician or administrator to take a set of census statistics and, on the basis of fairly simple-minded analyses, propose national action that can affect the lives of millions of people. The community responses of control, participation, and celebration of positive aspects of their experience are in part a reaction to the frequently ill-informed, paternalistic effort of federal organizations.

The Coleman Report

Section 402 of the Civil Rights Act of 1964 requested the United States Commissioner of Education to conduct a survey investigating the lack of availability of equal opportunities for individuals by reason of race, color, religion, or national origin in public educational institutions at all levels in the United States. This survey was conducted in late 1965 under the leadership of the sociologist James S. Coleman of Johns Hopkins University. The Coleman Report was published by the government in 1966 under the title *Equality of Educational Opportunity.* The purpose of the survey was to determine answers to four questions:

1. To what extent are public schools racially and ethnically segregated?

2. Do schools offer equal educational opportunities in terms of criteria such as quality of buildings and teacher-student ratio?

3. As measured by standarized achievement tests, how much do students learn?

4. How are students' achievement and the kinds of schools they attend related?

The sketchy social-scientific support for *Brown* v. *Board of Education* was concerned mainly with the psychological effects of segregated schools. But why and how does segregated schooling produce the gross inequalities that are observed? The Coleman Report gives some of the answers.

Public school segregation. Segregation is a fact of life in public schools, regardless of the region of the country. Of all racial groups white children are obviously the most segregated, for in 1966 almost 80 percent of white elementary and high school students attended schools that were from 90- to 100-percent white. Like prejudice, segregation works both ways. At the same time, 65 percent of all black elementary school students attend schools that are between 90- and 100-percent black.

Segregation of teachers shows the same pattern, though not quite so strongly. The average black elementary school student attends a school in which 65 percent of the teachers are black; the average white elementary school student attends a school in which 97 percent of the teachers are white. Again, the pattern of segregation among teachers is most pronounced in the South. Nearly 20 years after the 1954 Supreme Court decision the ruling still has had little impact on the actual racial composition of public schools in the United States. Segregated schools are tantamount to a difference in training of teachers, quality of facilities, and the nature and character of the student body. Let us consider how these differ as a function of the racial composition of the school.

The schools and their characteristics. Coleman's data showed considerable variation by race and region; still, some generalizations are possible. For example, facilities which seem related to academic achievement are underrepresented in predominantly black schools. Such schools have fewer science and language laboratories, fewer library books per pupil, and fewer textbooks. Although these differences prevail in general across the country, specific regions show even greater variation. In the metropolitan Far West, 95 percent of black and 80 percent of white high-school students attend schools with language laboratories, compared with only 48 and 72 percent respectively in the metropolitan South. Predominantly black schools are more frequently in buildings over forty years old, and less frequently in ones under twenty years old. Furthermore, black students—particularly in the South—are less likely to attend schools that are regionally accredited, that conduct extensive intelligence testing, or that have well-developed extracurricular programs.

As for instruction, the teachers of black children tend to be slightly less capable, according to such criteria as scores on verbal tests, whether or not they majored in an academic subject, whether or not their parents attended college, and the highest degree they earned. The differences, however, are very small; and on several criteria the teachers of black children measure higher than the teachers of white children. On the basis of the questions asked by Coleman's team it seems unlikely that differences in teacher quality and training were responsible for differences in quality of education observed between black and white children.

Coleman's team also found that the classmates of white children more frequently have encyclopedias in their homes, have mothers who are high-school graduates, are from small families, are enrolled in college-preparatory programs, and take more courses in English, foreign languages, and science. These data suggest that white children, more than black children, have classmates who come from environments which foster achievement in school settings.

So far we have briefly summarized some of the observations made in the Coleman Report which suggest that black children receive inferior educations as compared to whites. Now let us look at the results of Coleman's findings about student achievement.

Achievement in the public schools. Assuming that a main function of schools is to teach children skills which will be useful for competing in society as presently constituted, and further assuming that standard achievement tests measure the schools' success in imparting these skills, the Report tries to correlate differential achievement with the racial composition of schools. The Report acknowledges that the standard achievement tests upon which these summary data are based are by no means culture-free, but are specifically culture-bound. Like the Moynihan Report and every other report on American racial relations, the Coleman Report takes the characteristics of the dominant and dominating white majority as the yardstick by which to measure the black minority.

Not surprisingly, Coleman found that black Americans score consistently lower on achievement tests than whites, and that these deficiencies *increase* as the black child moves through elementary and secondary school. Evidently, whatever the factors producing a difference between black and white children when they enter the first grade, the educational process in public schools increases that disparity. This generalization has a regional qualifier. The differences between black and white first graders are greatest in the South, and the disparities in the South increase even more rapidly than elsewhere as children progress through school. It should be noted also that Southern children scored generally lower than Northern children without regard to race.

Relation of achievement to school characteristics. According to the Coleman Report, the quality of facilities, teachers, and student-body affects black children more than white children. Coleman found one of the most important criteria to be the educational background and aspirations of other students. Black students were shown to be more sensitive to this variable. This finding led Coleman to state:

> If a white pupil from a home that is strongly and effectively supportive of education is put in a school where most pupils do not come from such homes, his achievement will be little different than if he were in a school composed of others like himself. But, if a minority pupil from a home without such educational strength is put with schoolmates with strong educational backgrounds, his achievement is likely to increase. (Coleman, p. 22)

The Report went on to observe that the main difference in school environments of black and white children involves the composition of their student bodies, and that this composition strongly affects the achievement of black and other minority people. It followed that bussing black children to predominantly white schools would raise their achievement, and that bussing white children to predominantly black schools would not substantially affect their achievement. Thus, despite its use of considerably more skillful experimental design, data collection, and data analysis, the Coleman Report, like the Moynihan Report, ignited a conflagration of opinion and controversy.

The main thrust of the Coleman Report was to show that a majority of public schools are racially and ethnically segregated, and that resultant educational opportunities are grossly unequal. To support its conclusion that public-school integration is the best way to insure equality of educational opportunity, the Coleman Report tried to show that black children in integrated schools achieve more than black children in segregated schools. The major evidence for this conclusion, however, came from the careful analysis of the Coleman data by the U.S. Commission on Civil Rights in 1967.

Relation of integration to achievement. Testing black children in integrated schools indicated minute positive effects of integration. Support for the Report's contention that black students do better in integrated schools was underscored by observing that in every case except one, black students who had been in classes comprised of more than one-half white students had higher average test scores.

We should note, however, that in only two cases did the average score of black children who had attended one-half-white classes exceed the average score for those black children who had had *no* white classmates. This suggests that whatever positive effect integration has on black students' achievement occurs only if the classes are more than one-half white.

At a time when the proportion of black children in public schools has exceeded 50 percent in some cities (in Washington D. C., it is now over 90 percent) it seems highly unlikely that racial integration of public schools can ever mix large numbers of blacks into classes with a majority of white children. Furthermore, it is highly unlikely that masses of urban black students can, or should, be bussed to suburban schools to attain the degree of integration recommended by Coleman.*

Both the Coleman Report in 1966 and a report by the United States Commission on Civil Rights (*Racial Isolation in the Public Schools*) in 1967 strongly urged the Federal government to bring about school integration. The arguments behind these recommendations are straightforward:

1.   A student's achievement in school is significantly determined by the social class of his fellow students.

2.   A student's achievement in school is also significantly determined by his own social class.

3.   The social class of black children in predominantly black schools is considerably lower than the social class of children in predominantly white schools.

4.   Black children in predominantly white schools achieve more than black children in racially mixed or in predominantly black schools.

5.   White children in all-white schools achieve no more than white children in predominantly white schools.

In contrast to *Brown* v. *Board of Education,* which had been hailed with a single voice by the black community, these recommendations of integration provoked ambivalent and sometimes antagonistic responses. Black leaders were beginning to cut the shackles of a "We've-got-to-be-like-THEM" philosophy and were formulating the goals for an educational system relevant to black children in a predominantly white society.

In addition to the issues of community control of schools and a relevant education for black children, educators and researchers were concerned with raising the achievement of black children confined to ghettoes and unsatisfactory school situations. Title I of the *Elementary*

---

*Pettigrew (1969) has offered the concept of a Metropolitan Educational Park as a possible solution to racial unbalance in urban-suburban public schools. This plan would create school districts on the borders of suburban and central city communities. The districts would be pie-shaped, radiating toward the suburbs from a central point in urban centers. This is by far the most reasonable proposal for integration in public schools thus far advanced. However, it seems rather unlikely that people in suburban communities will see any advantage to sharing a school district with inner-city black residents.

and Secondary Education Act of 1965 provided massive funds to improve the educational opportunities within segregated schools. Generally labeled "compensatory education of the culturally deprived," these programs were based partly on the liberal notion that schools should rectify the damage wreaked by socioeconomic inequities. They were also seen as an alternative to desegregation of the public schools. The failure of these programs to produce marked changes in achievement has fed racist arguments concerning racial differences in intelligence and has also pressured the federal government to push harder for integration. But, alas, by the time the federal umpires got around to straightening out the ground rules, they found that key members of the black team no longer wanted to play!

Between 1965 and 1967 two governmental reports on race relations were released to the public. The Moynihan Report laid major blame for racial inequities on special discrimination against the black male, which led to the deterioration of the black family. The Coleman Report stressed the inequities in education which went along with segregated schools. The former made no specific recommendations, but called for a national commitment to the repair of the black family. The latter proposed integrated schooling as an important means of diminishing racial tensions and inequities. Both called for massive federal programs.

But in 1968 another governmental report looked at a different aspect of the problem—violence. The National Advisory Commission on Civil Disorders (the Kerner Commission) concluded from its investigation of the wave of riots occurring in the summer of 1967 that: "White racism is essentially responsible for the explosive mixture which has been accumulating in our cities since the end of World War II" (p. 203).

The Kerner Report

And so this chapter ends as it began, with the Kerner Report. In 1964 the fuse burned down in the North. A white New York City policeman fired a shot, and a black boy lay dead in the street. When the firing stopped, when the burning stopped, when the looting stopped four years later, race relations were more tense and critical than at any other time in this century.

In the midst of this period, President Lyndon Johnson established the Kerner Commission. In welcoming the Commission in the summer of 1967, Johnson said that the American people "are baffled and dismayed by the wholesale looting and violence that has occurred. . . ." A curious statement. For 350 years the equation white/black has described American race relations. But in 1967 President Johnson wanted to know what happened—and why—and what could be done to prevent it from happening again and again! As had the commissions before it (Chicago,

1922; New York, 1935, 1943; Civil Rights, 1946), the Kerner Commission once more documented the causes of the most recent blatant manifestation of "the problem."

Population redistribution. The first cause the Kerner Report noted was the gross shift in the black population of the United States. In 1910, 91 percent of black Americans lived in the South, and 27 percent lived in cities. By 1963, only 55 percent of black Americans lived in the South, while 69 percent lived in cities. The problem, the Report observed, "has shifted from a Southern rural locus to primarily a Northern urban locus." Between 1900 and 1920, the annual average out-migration of Southern blacks was about 45,000. During the 1920's, after the peak lynching years of 1918-19, out-migration increased to 75,000 per year. Slowing down during the Great Depression, out-migration soared from 1940 on as the hope of jobs and greater equality in the North and in the West attracted millions of Southern blacks.

In addition to a changing geographical distribution, black population has risen in both absolute and relative numbers. This increase has been due to a decreasing death rate and a rising fertility rate. In 1900 the annual death rate per 1000 non-white Americans was 25, and for white Americans only 17. However, by 1965 the death rates per 1000 were 9.6 and 9.4 respectively.* The similarity of death rates is even more striking in view of the nearly two-to-one black lead in mortality within the first year (40.4 versus 21.5 deaths per 1000 live births).

Fertility rates, on the other hand, remain considerably higher for black than for white American women, as they have since 1900. In 1965, there were 133.0 births per 1000 black women 15 to 44 years of age, but only 91.4 births per 1000 for white women of the same age range. As a consequence, the average age of black Americans is 21.2, while the average age of white Americans is 29.1.

We can also note that large numbers of young black Americans are segregated into small communities in urban areas. A study by Taeuber and Taeuber (1965) computed a segregation index based on the percentage of blacks who would have to move from their block to desegregate the area. The average segregation index in metropolitan areas was 86.2; in only eight cities was it less than 70, while fifty cities scored above 90. But we have noted that segregation in itself does not necessarily harm those who are segregated. We saw, for example, that the most segregated school children were whites. Certainly most whites, and especially well-to-do ones, live in segregated neighborhoods—according to class even more than to race. The issue again breaks down to basic economic considerations.

---

*These figures are probably quite conservative when comparing blacks with whites. The trends observed, however, should not be substantially affected.

Black Americans have lower incomes, poorer jobs, and higher unemployment. Furthermore, a higher percentage of black women are in the labor force. These inequalities are greatest in central cities. They are attributed by the Kerner Report and by increasing numbers of Americans, black and white, to white racism. Chapter Five deals with this issue and with the distinctions between racism and race prejudice.

Summary

In the last two chapters, we have reviewed the unfolding of racial relations during the present century. From 1954, when the social scientist was recognized by the United States Supreme Court as "modern authority," his role in influencing—indeed in formulating—governmental policy has grown. Society has become more complex, and the government's growing involvement in the control of society has given it a greater role in the resolution of race relations. To the extent that government policy is influenced by socioscientific research, we must pay close attention to that research as we attempt to analyze race prejudice and racism in the next chapters.

We have taken an historical perspective on race relations because the issues which currently garner major attention are complexly interrelated. The development of these complex interrelations has occurred over the 350 years from the beginning of the slave trade in the colonies to the present. In attempting to unravel the thread of race relations we need to recognize the constituent strands.

One strand is the attitudes and personalities of the parties involved—white and black. Emphasis on this aspect of the problem, as we have seen, has been largely the domain of the psychologist. The dominant analysis to which this focus gives rise is race prejudice. It is this approach which will be featured in the following chapter.

A second strand is the behaviors that occur between blacks and whites, and the nature of the institutions and groups which shape and influence these interactions. Emphasis on this aspect of the problem has been more central to the work of sociologists and social psychologists. Although the *term* prejudice has dominated the field for many years, the type of analysis which this approach yields is more conducive to the study of racism. Chapter Five will focus on racism.

CHAPTER FOUR

Perspectives on Prejudice

THE ALUMNAE

"I'm not prejudiced against all policemen in general, I just dislike each and every one of you individually."

Fig. 4.1. Prejudice—a negative attitude generalized to all members of a group. *Beating the rap!* (Reproduced by permission of the Register and Tribune Syndicate, Inc. © 1970.)

FRAMES OF REFERENCE

Prejudice Defined

The above cartoon suggests some ingredients of a literary definition of prejudice. *Webster's New Twentieth Century Dictionary* (1965) offers six such definitions:

1. a judgment or opinion formed before the facts are known, preconceived idea, favorable or more usually unfavorable.

2. a judgment or opinion held in disregard of facts that contradict it, unreasonable bias as a *prejudice* against Northerners.

3. the holding of such judgments or opinions.

4. suspicion, intolerance, or hatred of other races, creeds, regions, occupations, etc.

5. injury or harm resulting as from some judgment or action of another or others.

6. foresight. (p. 1420)

The term prejudice is derived from the Latin *praejudicium,* from *prae* meaning before, and *judicium* meaning judgment. We can summarize the main points of this formal definition with the following statement that prejudice is

> the prior negative judgment of the members of a race or religion or the occupants of any other significant social role, held in disregard of facts that contradict it.

This definition fits well the etymological history of the term, as well as some of the popular research uses. However, Professor Thomas Pettigrew would extend the definition to emphasize the emotional and cognitive aspects by defining prejudice as

> an affective, categorical mode of mental functioning involving rigid prejudgment and misjudgment of human groups.*

No simple definition can capture all the meanings which individuals give to the word prejudice. Within the two definitions offered above, different people will select different words or ideas to use as *their* meaning of prejudice. In the remainder of this chapter, we will use these definitions to guide our analysis and discussion; but we will not allow them to exert too great an influence on our selection of topics and ideas.

To determine whether or not a given judgment qualifies as prejudicial, we must obtain answers to three essential questions:

1. *Is it a prior judgment?* That is, was the judgment made before all the facts were known?

2. *Are there facts which contradict it?* Answers to this question are complex because they involve the determination of what is a fact.

3. *Are these facts known to the judge at the time of his judgment?*

Assuming it is possible to determine the facts in the case, we must ascertain whether the facts were known at the time of judgment, or if not, whether the judge had made a "reasonable" attempt to secure those facts.

I mention these considerations to suggest that according to the formal criteria specified by the literary definition of prejudice, it is not an easy matter to make accurate, *objective* determinations of prejudiced judg-

---

*Personal communication, June 28, 1971.

ments. Nevertheless, we can agree that there are attitudes and attitude-statements, behaviors and behavioral consequences which are highly relevant to an analysis of interracial conflict and strife in America.

Attitudes and Behaviors

A very large portion of the research on prejudice has been concerned with attitudes. In fact attitudes have been so central to research on prejudice that we could substitute "attitude" for "judgment" in our earlier definition and have an accurate reflection of popular usage. We saw in Chapter 2 that attitudes were lifted to a position of preeminence in social psychology through a combination of circumstances, including 1) the popularity of the theory which stressed the predispositional character of attitudes, 2) the budding scientific aspirations of social psychology which found attitudes a particularly handy concept for scientific interests and methodologies, and 3) a desire to address important social problems within the context of a scientific commitment. Many social scientists have taken shots at the lofty status of attitudes over the years, and now the importance of behavior in social-psychological conceptions is beginning to catch up.

We must recognize that the starting point for any analysis of relevant social experience *begins with behavior.* Any concept of attitude is inferred from some behavioral index whether it be overt motor behavior (Joe hit Bill), overt symbolic behavior (Joe scowled at Bill), overt verbal behavior (Joe said, "I hate Bill"), or symbolic verbal behavior (in a questionnaire, Joe included Bill's name in a list of people he disliked). The common inference from each of these behavioral observations is that Joe has a negative attitude toward Bill. Social scientists have been concerned with attitudes because attitudes are assumed to closely correspond with *overt motor behaviors* that are problematic for society. Therefore we are interested in the negative attitudes that whites in Lamar, South Carolina, have toward blacks to the degree that they can be shown to *cause* white residents to overturn school buses with black children aboard.

However, we are also interested in the attitudes of whites toward blacks as *consequences* of the actions taken against the black children. If a young child witnesses his mother engaging in violent behaviors with small black children as objects of her wrath, what must the child make of it? It is a significant event in his life, and the child might come to ask himself, "Why?". His answer in most cases will *not* be that his mother is a racist bigot (the answer that many others of greater distance give), but that those kids (or black people in general) must be awful and deserving of this kind of treatment.* One might soon expect this negative attitude to generate

---

*Melvin Lerner (1969) has shown that belief in a Just World will lead people to derogate the *victim* of unprovoked aggression. The greater the aggression, the more subjects derogate the victim.

behavior of its own; perhaps a child product of such barbarism would be heard to say something like "I don't want to go to school with no niggers." Or much worse, he might think killing a nigger or a nigger-lover was an entirely appropriate thing for him to do.

In our analysis of race relations, therefore, we are interested in both attitudes and behavior. We are interested in attitudes for two reasons:

1.   Attitude studies provide a description of the phenomenal world of the respondents. Large-scale attitude and opinion surveys reveal with some accuracy what people think about themselves and others.

2.   We can combine certain attitudinal indices to predict certain kinds of behaviors. (It must be understood, however, that rarely are we really able to *predict* behavior; more commonly we *postdict.* The Kerner Report is an example where the data collection did not commence until after the significant behavior had occurred. The Report then postdicted the attitudes and events which contributed to the riotous outbreaks of the mid-1960's.)

We are similarly interested in behavior for two reasons:

1.   Cataloguing the host of behaviors which describe racial relations provides a description of the real problems which confront us. Overturning school buses, bombing houses, assassination, and so on are behaviors which describe some of the areas of principal conflict.

2.   Behaviors are the fundamental units from which attitude structures are inferred by people as well as by social scientists.

For example, choose two people whom you see regularly. Do they like you? (attitude). How do you know? The *evidence* for the attitude you attribute to these people likely will be a list of behaviors, overt or verbal.

Consider now the social scientist investigating prejudice. One team of investigators was interested in measuring racial attitudes of a group of male undergraduates. To determine whether white students held positive or negative attitudes toward blacks, they asked for volunteers to show a group of African students around the campus. On the basis of the rate of volunteering, the researchers inferred whether the students had positive or negative attitudes toward black Africans (cf. Marlowe, Frager, and Nuttal, 1965).

In both of these examples, attitudes are inferred (or you might say constructed) from basic behavioral data. We will, in the following pages, be interested in the reciprocal relations of attitudes and behaviors. Certainly in many situations the way we feel or think motivates our behavior. But in the developmental view the way we feel or think now is determined in part by the way we have thought and *acted* in the past. The historical perspective taken in the first three chapters is an attempt to chronicle the development of attitudes and behaviors.

A Paradigm for the Analysis of Prejudice

While it is possible to have a prejudice against things, our analysis is concerned only with prejudices toward people or human groups. We therefore define our inquiry in the realm of interpersonal relations where person A has some relation (r) with person B. We will refer to this relation as an interpersonal paradigm and will represent it as ArB. For any kind of analysis we can focus our attention on one of several different points in the paradigm. For example, we can ask questions about the type or number of relations joining A and B; we can consider the characteristics of B as object and A as actor, or look at any of several such combinations.

The research on racial stereotypes can be understood in this paradigm as holding the object B (Negroes) and the actor A (whites) constant, while varying the attitudinal relations which join them. It should be noted, however, that as we hold A and B constant with respect to race, there is the possibility of differences in other dimensions such as sex, occupation, socioeconomic status (SES), age, education, and so on. The numerous ways in which it is possible to characterize any potential A or B in our analysis introduces the concept of social roles. Role conflict in this paradigm would be indicated by consistent negative relationships between A's and B's with certain role characteristics.

For the purposes of the following analyses we will consider those relations which are positive or negative (approaches-avoids) attitudes or actions (dislikes-harms). Our analysis proceeds along two points: (1) *Description*—specifically what *are* the ArB relationships important in race relations? (2) *Explanation*—what are the *causes* of the observed relationships? For the most part, research in race relations has been directed toward answering question (1) above by describing in very great detail the attitudes and behaviors which characterize racial relations in America.

TABLE 4.1

A Paradigm for the Analysis of Prejudice

A (Actor)	r (Relation)	B (Object)	
		Other (Bo)	Self (Bs)
Race	Action	Race	
Occupation	Attitude	Occupation	Same as A
Religion		Religion	
Sex		Sex	
Age		Age	
Region		Region	
Political affiliation		Political affiliation	
Education		Education	
SES		SES	
.		.	
.		.	
.		.	

In addition to the basic ArB relation, we have bifurcated the B object to include either another person or group *(Bo),* or the actor himself *(Bs).* We include the actor's relation to himself because there is an almost continual comparison of oneself with others in situations involving social judgment.

Cultural differences are often of the form "*we* do it this way but *they* do it that way." As Blumer (1958) has defined the problem of prejudice as a sense of group position, there is an implied own-other group *(Bo-Bs)* comparison. Attitudes of the actor toward himself are as relevant to us as his attitudes toward the other person. The assumption of similarity between self and other is an important determinant of racial hostility. Moreover, theoretical notions of relative deprivation or social evaluation (Pettigrew, 1967), and social comparison theory (Festinger, 1954) have provided both descriptive and explanatory frameworks for the analysis of interracial conflict.

Just as the social analyst attempts to explain particular ArB configurations, people in their everyday lives are also compelled to do so. As Americans most of us are taught early that we must have "good" reasons for doing the things we do, and the "goodness" of a reason has been determined primarily by prevailing social norms. In almost all research and theoretical writing on prejudice, the discussion has been influenced by individual explanations for particular ArB relations. In the case of a particular ArB paradigm we seek to determine whether A's relation to B is (1) a consequence of characteristics of B; (2) a consequence of characteristics of A; or (3) a consequence of some situational determinants. Consider the following example: Joe, a white male (A), sells his house and moves away within three weeks of the time Ahmad, a black male (B), buys the house next door. Is Joe's relationship to Ahmad a function of characteristics of Joe? (He is prejudiced against blacks.) Of Ahmad? (He is an undesirable neighbor, generally.) Or is it simply situational? (Joe was transferred to a new job in another part of the country.) Prejudice is usually claimed when the answer to this question violates one, two or all of the following social norms:

1. *Rationality*—beliefs, perceptions and expectations based on reasonable attempts to (a) secure accurate information, (b) correct misinformation, (c) use logical deductions, and (d) make cautious inferences.

2. *Justice*—in all areas of public concern individuals are treated equally except insofar as unequal treatment is based on abilities or achievements functionally relevant to the requirements of the situation.

3. *Human-heartedness*—the relationship is based upon (a) love and brotherhood, (b) tolerance and human sympathy, (c) a general positive affection for one's fellow human being.

These social norm criteria, listed by Harding and others (1969), all apply to characteristics of the actor (A). Because of the high level of interpersonal violence, the complicated socioeconomic structure which strongly influences group conflict, and the numerous examples of injustice permeating this society, it is difficult to apply these criteria objectively to the specific situations of race prejudice.

I have attempted in this section to set some guidelines for the following analysis of prejudice. We have constructed a paradigm as a point of reference to which we can repeatedly refer as we proceed through diverse bodies of data and theory. Hopefully, this paradigm can serve as an organizing (not explanatory) tool for our inquiry into prejudice.

Historically, research in race relations preceded theory. It was not until contradictory or conflicting empirical results were obtained that a strong move toward theory was initiated. Theoretical ventures were undertaken for the purpose of explaining disparate empirical findings. Let us follow this lead in the next two sections by first reviewing prejudice research and then examining theory. This will enable us to understand the empirical findings behind various theories. We will then be in a better position to evaluate the theories as they are discussed.

RESEARCH ON RACE PREJUDICE

Much theory and research on race prejudice is predicated on the assumption that wholesome, normal persons are rational thinkers and actors. Our *homo sapiens* status in the animal kingdom sets us apart, because our knowledge is derived through rational, objective thought and analysis. And most importantly, our actions *follow from* this rationally derived knowledge. Individuals who consistently short-circuit these rational thought processes are said to prejudge, and are frequently assigned inferior positions in the *homo sapiens* hierarchy. Those who prejudge people on the basis of race are said to be afflicted with race prejudice. For many theorists, race prejudice is a symptom of a basic adaptive inferiority (e.g., the personality theories of race prejudice).

We should note, however, that a person can never know and will never like everything and everybody. No judgments are based on *all* the facts. The question is this: how much information does one need before his judgment can surpass "prejudgment" status? Are there legitimate bases for disliking another person or human group? We all make generalizations in arriving at decisions and planning courses of action. The social criteria for certification of rational judgments have strong situational determinants and certainly vary from person to person. We could take another approach and consider, instead, the criteria for *irrational* judgment (i.e., prejudgment).

One criterion might be the availability and use of facts. We might ask these questions: (1) What are the "facts"? What is the available information that is valid and relevant to the decision or judgment to be made? (2) What percentage of the available information is actually used in the judgment? and (3) Are the inferences drawn rationally congruent with available facts? That is, given that we know what the relevant and valid facts are, and know what facts were used in the judgment, does the judgment fit the canons of rationality? These are complicated and difficult criteria on which it would be nearly impossible to find agreement among social scientists, among logicians, or among most men of presumed rational persuasion.

The difficulty of making these determinations should not, however, be taken as license to give up trying. In fact the more important the issue to the judge, or the more significant the consequences for another, the more effort one should expend in gathering and analyzing the facts.

A second criterion concerns how unyielding a person's judgment is to evidence which contradicts it. Here we might ask: (1) Is there valid evidence which contradicts the judgment? (2) Has the respondent been exposed to this contrary evidence? and (3) Has the respondent gone out of his way to avoid or misinterpret contrary evidence? Harding and others (1969) claimed that the person must make every reasonable attempt to seek out and consider such information. But what constitutes a reasonable attempt? If contrary evidence has eluded the respondent in question, we must then consider whether or not the tag of prejudice is appropriate, and a further question: (4) Given that the contrary evidence is valid, and given also that the respondent has been exposed to it, do these conditions constitute a rational mandate for revision of the prior judgment?

With these very stringent criteria for determination of a prejudiced judgment, it is not difficult to see that little of the data accumulated in prejudice research would stand up to such rigorous demands. Data collected through simple questionnaires or interviews do not present a careful analysis of all these criteria. One cannot conclude without serious reservation that the data reflect the existence of race prejudice. Most of the research has measured attitudes which were *presumably* arrived at through a prejudicial prejudgment. These data do not have direct bearing on prejudice strictly defined.

If we expand our perspective beyond the formal definitions of prejudice, we begin to move away from the idea of judgment and look more towards hostile behavior and intergroup conflict. At that level of analysis the research data are more to the point. Dropping the term prejudice for a moment, we can document fairly accurately some of the parameters of intergroup hostilities and conflicts. From these observations we can attempt to infer the individual psychological processes that underlie the manifestations of racial hostility.

I. Attitudes

We have suggested that attitudes are important for several reasons. One of the prime reasons we adhere to the social scientific methodology known as -

attitude measurement is that we learn something about what people think, feel, expect, or desire in their perceived social world. We might quibble with the interpretations, conclusions, and theoretical gerrymandering which social scientists impose on questionnaire responses, but the raw data are there for our scrutiny. When a respondent fills out an attitude questionnaire or rates a group on some character traits, he is telling us *something.* He has *behaved* in a particular way. But exactly *what* he is telling us may not be so clear.

Recall that in 1933 some Princeton men tried to tell us something. Among other things they told us that the group of people represented by the word Negro could be characterized as superstitious, lazy, and ignorant. Furthermore, they told us, Jews were shrewd and mercenary. Americans, on the other hand, were industrious and intelligent. Katz and Braly told us that these characterizations did not reflect the Princeton men's own (private) judgment of Negroes, Jews, or Americans, but their understanding of the cultural patterns which are publicly and single-mindedly affirmed in our society. Katz and Braly considered the replacement of individual scrutiny with a public label to be the process of stereotyping. The importance of stereotyping in prejudice theory and research has persisted through the years from the early discussions of Walter Lippmann to the recent replication of the original Katz and Braly study by Karlins, Coffman, and Walters (1969).

Stereotypy: Study of Public Racial Attitudes

The analysis of stereotypy fits our ArB model at the most general level. Although A is defined as the population from which respondents come, B is left wholly unqualified. Therefore, when respondents assign traits to "Negroes," they are establishing a relation to B based objectively on the simple category of race, while the range of other possible categories (class, education, sex, and so on) which are also relevant to B-Negro is not controlled.

When a person is asked to assign character traits to a race or nationality, he cannot assign them to the group as a whole but must select some presumably representative sample from which summary statements might be generalized to the entire group. Bayton, McAlister and Hamer (1956) believed that racial stereotypes were heavily influenced by class considerations, so that the sample of Negroes from which the traits of lazy, ignorant, etc. were generalized was that of lower-class Negroes. Conversely, the traits ascribed to whites were based on a sample of upper-class whites. The authors tested their assumptions by administering the Katz and Braly stereotype procedure to black and white college students. Subjects were asked to select those traits which described upper- (or lower-) class white Americans, or upper- (or lower-) class Negroes. The results were interesting (Table 4.2).

TABLE 4.2

Percentage Assignment of Traits by Race and Class

Objects (*B*)

		BLACK		WHITE	
		Upper class	Lower class	Upper class	Lower class
Rater (*A*)	BLACK	Intelligent 61%	Loud 55%	Intelligent 48%	Physically dirty 36%
		Ambitious 35	Superstitious 44	Ambitious 28	Ignorant 34
		Progressive 25	Very religious 35	Progressive 27	Rude 33
		Neat 24	Lazy 28	Sophisticated 26	Lazy 19
		Ostentatious 23	Ignorant 26	Tradition-loving 21	Loud 18
	WHITE	Intelligent 66	Superstitious 53	Intelligent 59	Happy-go-lucky 20
		Ambitious 39	Lazy 51	Ambitious 49	Materialistic 20
		Ostentatious 34	Physically dirty 29	Materialistic 45	Ignorant 19
		Industrious 34	Unreliable 28	Pleasure-loving 33	Lazy 19
		Courteous 30	Musical 27	Industrious 25	Loud 19

Adapted from Bayton, McAlister, and Hamer (1956).

The similarity in stereotypes for class overshadows the dissimilarities for race. Recall the earlier warning about the entangled race-class issue. The issue to consider here is this: Why do respondents (black and white) use a lower-class black reference group when ascribing traits to Negroes, and an upper- (or middle-) class reference group in ascribing traits to whites? The answer is not a mystery. In 1947, 65 percent of black Americans could be considered lower-class with an income of less than $3000 a year. The corresponding figure for whites was 23 percent. Without analyzing the correspondence between the traits assigned and the characteristics of people designated lower-class, the problem frames itself. It is not that Princeton men overgeneralized negative-trait characteristics to Negroes, but that the apparent reference group they used (lower-class Negroes) comprised such a large portion of the Negro category.

The vagueness in the stereotypy literature on who (characteristics of *A*) is judging whom (characteristics of *B*) is amply demonstrated in the 1969 literature review by Harding and others. In summarizing the stereotypy literature these authors point out that "Sometimes the low status of a group in a particular society is so firmly established that even the traits used by group members to characterize themselves are predominately unfavorable" (p. 8). Harding's group cites a study by Bayton (1941) as support for this assertion; Bayton administered the Katz and Braly adjectives to Negro college students and obtained a listing quite similar to that obtained in 1933 by Katz and Braly themselves. However, this judgment of "Negroes" was a judgment of lower-class Negroes, as the Bayton, McAlister and Hamer (1956) study suggests. Evidence for this comes from the observation that black students assigned to *themselves* different and more positive traits. Thus when Harding and his co-authors claim that group members characterize themselves in unfavorable ways, we realize that it is not the relationship

A (Negro)   r (negative) B_S (Negro)

suggested by these authors, but

A (Negro, middle class)   r (negative) B_O (Negro, lower class)

that is being described.*

It should be clear from this example that *methodologically* the Katz and Braly technique *forced* subjects to stereotype groups by asking for undifferentiated group judgments. However, the fact of stereotyping cannot be considered a mere artifact of research techniques, as the interviews of Chapter 2 so clearly demonstrate.

---

*Solomon Asch has reported on a 1946 study ("The doctrine of suggestion, prestige, and imitation on social psychology," *Psych. Rev.* (1948), 55). His findings showed how importantly the *perceptions* of an object influence judgments or attitudes about it. Asch found that subjects' attitudes toward an excerpt from the Declaration of Independence were negative if sponsorship was attributed to Lenin, but positive if attributed to Thomas Jefferson.

We are interested in stereotypes as attitudinal descriptions of perceived social reality. These data may have a special cumulative interest; we would expect stereotypes to change as the realities of social experience change. The 1969 investigation by Karlins, Coffman, and Walters provides a look at trends in stereotyping in a population of Princeton males at three time points: (1) the study by Katz and Braly in 1933; (2) a study by Gilbert in 1951; and (3) their own in 1967. From the Katz and Braly list of 84 trait names, the authors had Princeton men select the ten which they would most frequently use to characterize ten religious, ethnic, or racial groups. Next, the subjects selected the five which were most characteristic of each group and, in addition, rated each of the 84 traits for favorability on a scale from -2 to $+2$. These favorability ratings were not made in the Katz and Braly or the Gilbert studies. The authors then computed a favorability index for each group in each of the three studies by multiplying the frequency of each trait by the mean favorability rating obtained in the 1967 study. Table 4.3 summarizes the results of this study for American, Jew, and Negro.

TABLE 4.3

Social Stereotypes in Three Generations of Princeton Men

1933		1951		1967	
AMERICAN					
Industrious	48	materialistic	37	materialistic	67
Intelligent	47	intelligent	32	ambitious	42
Materialistic	33	industrious	30	pleasure loving	28
Ambitious	33	pleasure loving	27	industrious	23
Progressive	27	ambitious	21	intelligent	20
Favorableness	(.99)		(.86)		(.49)
JEW					
Shrewd	79	shrewd	47	ambitious	48
Mercenary	49	intelligent	37	materialistic	46
Industrious	48	industrious	29	intelligent	33
Grasping	34	ambitious	28	industrious	33
Intelligent	29	mercenary	28	shrewd	30
Favorableness	(.24)		(.45)		(.66)
NEGRO					
Superstitious	84	superstitious	41	musical	47
Lazy	75	musical	33	happy-go-lucky	27
Happy-go-lucky	38	lazy	31	pleasure loving	26
Ignorant	38	ignorant	24	lazy	26
Musical	26	pleasure loving	19	ostentatious	25
Favorableness	(−.70)		(−.37)		(.07)

Adapted from Karlins, Coffman, and Walters (1969), Tables 1 and 4.

The first thing to note is the dramatic shift in favorability ratings for the three groups. The marked decline in favorability for the term American is due largely to the overwhelming characteristic of *materialistic* which had a mean favorability rating of −.45. The large increase for Jew was due principally to the elimination of the negative term mercenary (mean = −.88) and the decline in the application of shrewd (mean = .18). The strong upturn for the term Negro, which nevertheless held a favorability rating of only .07 in 1967, was due largely to the elimination of the trait *ignorant* which had a mean rating of −1.37. Comparing the favorableness ratings of the 1933 Katz and Braly study with the 1967 Karlins, Coffman, and Walters study, we see a general decline in favorableness for Americans, English, Germans, Irish, and Italians, with a corresponding increase in favorableness for Chinese, Japanese, Jews, Negroes and Turks.

As Princeton men go, so goes the country? Probably not. But there is reflected in these stereotyping data a trend toward greater tolerance, or rejection of intolerant attitudes, as indicated by the unwillingness of subjects to make the stereotyping judgments. Comments of the sort obtained in the 1951 study by Gilbert ("I think it ludicrous to attempt to classify various ethnic groups") were also characteristic of the study done by Karlins, Coffman and Walters.

However, to say that the trend toward tolerance and favorableness presages the demise of stereotyping is inaccurate. An index of stereotype *uniformity* (the extent of agreement among subjects on the assignment of traits to different ethnic groups), reveals a general decline in uniformity between the 1933 and 1951 studies, but a resurgence of high uniformity in the 1967 study. While the popular stereotypes seem to be fading in terms of trait content, the *tendency to stereotype* has not. The fact that favorableness of Negro just barely passed zero is also significant. Times are changing, but the gap is still very wide.

The study of stereotyping behavior was one of the first experimental inroads made by social psychologists in the study of prejudice. The emphasis on attitudes characterized by the stereotyping studies has persisted over the years, and it makes review of these studies an appropriate beginning to the review of the research literature on prejudice. But what have we learned about prejudice from a consideration of studies of stereotyping behavior?

As we have defined it, prejudice is a prejudgment held in disregard of contradictory evidence. This meaning of prejudice applies to an individual person. A *social* stereotype amounts to a summation of *personal* stereotypes. What we have learned principally from these stereotyping studies is the degree of consensus about trait characteristics in different populations of subjects. This is interesting to know about but does not tell us a great deal about prejudice.

More to the point of prejudice is the apparent reluctance to make gross ethnic judgments of the sort required in stereotyping studies. This reluctance suggests that prejudgment or illiberal inferences about group characteristics is fading, even though social stereotypes remain. These studies, then, imply that at least among Princeton men, judgmental activities associated with prejudiced attitudes have declined over the past 35 years.

Demography of Racial Attitudes

In the ArB paradigm there are three units of analysis: (1) characteristics of person A—for example, race, socioeconomic status (SES), religion, age, sex, region of the country, education; (2) behaviors or attitudes linking persons A and B; (3) characteristics of person B. Each of these units is susceptible to a wide range of variability, independent of each of the other units. Person A in our analysis can be represented by any one of a number of demographic configurations (e.g., young, white, female, urban, Northern, eighth-grade education), as can person B. In addition, B can be a group. Question: Do different demographic characterizations of A and B affect the kinds of behaviors (attitudes) which link them together? Of course we know the answer is yes, so let us look at the distribution of attitudinal relations linking A's and B's of varying characteristics.

Racial attitudes—white on black. Let us begin with the simple constraint that A is white (and non-Jewish) and B is black. Let us consider attitudes linking the two as represented by answers to the following five questions:*

1. Generally speaking, Negroes are lazy and don't like to work hard. *(Agree)*

2. Do you think that white children and Negro children should go to the same schools, or to separate, but equal schools? *(Separate)*

3. Do you think there should be laws against marriages between Negroes and whites? *(Yes)*

4. Before Negroes are given equal rights, they have to show that they deserve them. *(Agree)*

5. As you see it, are Negroes today demanding more than they have a right to? *(Yes)*

---

*These are the five questions asked of a national probability sample of 1913 white respondents just before the national election in 1964. Selznick and Steinberg (1969) used responses to these questions to indicate racial bias. They seem rather simple-minded by today's standards of sophisticated racial bigotry. They do reflect the kinds of questions race researchers ask, however. The inability to ask questions as subtle as the dynamics of race relations is part of the problem with questionnaire studies of prejudice.

Selznick and Steinberg computed an antiblack index by assigning a score of +1 to the responses in parentheses for each of the five questions. The average number of items on which an antiblack response was made was 2.6. The authors chose a mean score of three or more items to indicate an individual with strongly antiblack attitudes. Table 4.4 summarizes some demographic associations with antiblack sentiment.

TABLE 4.4

Some Demographic Characteristics of Antiblack Attitudes Among Whites

		North	South	Total
A.	EDUCATION			
	Grade School	58%	86%	68%
	High School	41	77	49
	Some College	25	50	32
	College Graduate	16	43	23
B.	SEX			
	Males	40	76	50
	Females	41	69	48
C.	AGE			
	Less than 35	29	63	39
	35-54	37	71	46
	55 or over	55	81	63
D.	INCOME*			
	Less than $5,000			58
	$5,000 to 9,999			44
	$10,000 to 14,999			41
	$15,000 or more			46
E.	RURAL-URBAN			
	Urban	41	64	46
	Rural	40	81	55
	TOTAL	40	72	49

Adapted from Selznick and Steinberg (1969), Tables 55, 56; p. 176, 178.

*Not given by region.

The associations can be summarized as follows:

1. Antiblack attitudes are more prevalent in the South than in the North (72 percent versus 40 percent).

2. There is a strong negative association between antiblack attitudes and education (from 68 percent for grade-school educated to 23 percent for college graduates).

3. The apparent relationships of antiblack attitudes with age and income are due primarily to the association of these two variables with education. When the effects of education are extracted, the relationships with age and income disappear.

There is considerably greater antiblack sentiment in the South than in the North, but there are some subtle variations in the patterning of attitudes that are worth noting. First, in relation to education level, there is a decrement in antiblack attitudes which accompanies each new level of educational advancement. For example, in the North, 17-percent fewer high-school than grade-school graduates are antiblack (58 percent and 41 percent, respectively). A similar though weaker relationship is observed in the South, where 9-percent fewer high-school than grade-school graduates are antiblack (86 percent and 77 percent, respectively). Regional variations in the association of antiblack attitudes to educational advancement are shown in Fig. 4.2.

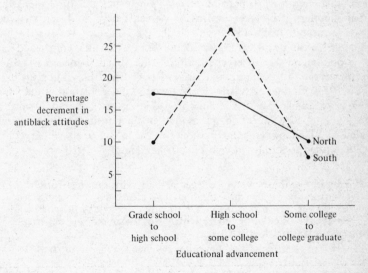

Fig. 4.2. Decrement in antiblack attitudes as a function of educational advancement and region.

In the North the major reduction in antiblack attitudes accompanies the educational advancement from grade-school to high-school graduates. Once the college level is reached, graduation only slightly reduces antiblack attitudes (9 percent).

The South shows a quite different pattern. The reduction in antiblack attitudes accompanying a high school diploma is small (9 percent). However, when a white Southerner goes to college, the reduction in antiblack attitudes is sizeable (27 percent). Once in college, graduating does not strongly influence his racial attitudes (7 percent).

There are two plausible interpretations of the large decrement in antiblack attitudes among Southerners who have had some college education. The first is that antiblack attitudes in the South are based on traditional, unchecked stereotypes and cultural ideologies. The informational input of college education might break into this closed ideological system and produce dramatic changes. The second is that the major socializing agents of the Southern community (family, peers, *schools*, public officials) maintain a nearly total hegemony over the attitudinal development of the white Southern child; going away to college breaks that domination and allows new ideas and perspectives to take form. Thus going away to college may either produce new informational inputs, and/or diminish the influence of antiblack socializing agents.*

We can note that with regard to sex and rural-urban living, there are no differences in the Northern sample, but in the Southern sample, males more than females (76 percent versus 69 percent) and rural more than urban dwellers (81 percent versus 64 percent) have antiblack attitudes. White Southern males have through the years made consistently loud reference to the beauty and grace of the Southern white woman and have correspondingly formulated the notion of the "black menace" as a threat to this paragon of goodness and virtue. Recall Tom Brady's homage in his book, *Black Monday*. Apparently the threat of desegregation of the public schools of Lamar, South Carolina, in 1970 was not community control, bussing, or quality education, but as one onlooker at the bus-burning scene stated it: "Things keep going like they is and in five years all our women will be nigger prostitutes" (*New York Times*, March 8, 1970). †

---

*Of course Southern white colleges are not virtuous institutions which actively promote racial understanding. The effect may be simply learning how to answer race questions *nicely*. In any case, it may be worthwhile to investigate the mediating influence of Southern college experience on reduction in antiblack attitudes.

†Black-white sex conflicts have always been very important in race relations. It is a growing theme in current black-on-black discussions (see early issues of *Essence* magazine, Spring, 1970) and was very prominent in the psychological development of Eldridge Cleaver (see his *Soul on Ice*). But it is most difficult to know how to treat sex in a discussion of prejudice and racism without becoming embroiled in psychoanalytic musings which, though perhaps plausible and provocative, are beyond the scope of our more limited inquiry. Continuing pressure from women's liberation groups, and the sexism analogy to racism will keep the relatedness of the problems before us. Perhaps their interaction will be cogently formulated soon.

The rural South represents the lowest income, least education and oldest population of any of the regions of the study. The high degree of antiblack attitudes (81 percent) likely represents the cumulative effects of these variables.

The relations between white and black Americans as measured by the composite responses to the five questions on page 73, point to sources of racial tension in this country. They summarize the distribution of racial animosities—white against black—across several demographic characteristics. We can make similar kinds of associations when we reverse the race of A and B.

Racial attitudes—black on white. Gary Marx (1969) computed an antiwhite index from black responses to five questions. The antiwhite response is given in parentheses.

1. Type of neighborhood preferred, if all equally well kept up. *(All black)*

2. Some people have told us that there are white store owners who take advantage of Negro customers. How many white store owners would you say are like this? *(All or nearly all)*

3. Most whites who take part in civil rights demonstrations aren't really interested in the problems of Negroes. *(Agree)*

4. I am suspicious of whites who try to help Negroes. *(Yes)*

5. It bothers me to see immigrants succeeding more than Americans who were born here. *(Yes)*

The first item was considered an index of *social distance,* and the antiwhite response was weighted +2. The second and third questions were *belief* items, and the antiwhite responses received +1 scores. The fourth and fifth questions were *feeling* items and similarly were given +1 for antiwhite responses. The author used composite scores of 4, 5, or 6 as an index of strong antiwhite sentiment.*

Table 4.5 summarizes some demographic correlates of antiwhite sentiment among blacks. With the exception of the age variable, these relationships are about the same as those seen in the antiblack attitudes of whites.

---

*From a general black perspective, the so-called antiwhite responses are not antiwhite, but quite natural and realistic. For example, on the social distance item, a preference by blacks to live among blacks is taken as hostility toward whites, a possible but by no means necessary implication. One need only review the pattern of the rise of immigrants from poverty to solid first-class American citizenship while black Americans continue to occupy the bottom rung of this society to see the legitimate grievance in the "antiwhite" response to item 5. The plethora of pawnshop charlatans and subtle-heavy-handed clerks in urban black communities affirms yet another reality. We will take up these and related issues in Chapter 5, The Realities of Racism.

Antiwhite attitudes are greatest among blacks (1) in the South; (2) from lower socioeconomic classes; (3) with less formal education; (4) who participate least in American society. Age notwithstanding, blacks and whites with the greatest antipathies toward each other are alike on several demographic dimensions. It seems ironically cruel that those persons most alike are in the greatest conflict. Perhaps it is a natural consequence of a fiercely competitive society that those individuals most alike are in greatest competition. The importance of conflict and competition in racial relations is considerable, but our analysis of *prejudice* does not easily encompass them. We will devote more time to the nature of competition and conflict in Chapter Five.

The Marx data were collected late in 1964. A lot has happened in this country since then, and we might expect changes in the profile of black attitudes these data create. Moreover, the questions comprising the antiwhite index seem now to be too simple for the issues at hand.

A recent book by Peter Goldman, *Report from Black America* (1970), presents more current data on a wide range of attitudes held by black Americans. In Table 4.6, I have presented a sample of black attitudes toward whites, violence, black politics, the United States and some of its institutions, and, finally, toward racial integration.

TABLE 4.5

Some Demographic Characteristics of Antiwhite Attitudes Among Blacks

1. Region	N.Y. 19%	Chicago 22%	Atlanta 24%	Birmingham 25%
2. Social Class	Lower 28	Middle 22	Upper 16	
3. Age	Under 30 27	30-44 25	45-59 23	60+ 17
4. Sex	Male 21	Female 25		
5. Education	8th 27	Some college 14		
6. Social Participation (Symbolic)*	Low 33	Moderate 24	High 18	
7. Social Participation (Actual)†	26	22	22	

Adapted from Marx (1969), Tables 108, 110, 112-116; pp. 186-191.

*Symbolic social participation is indicated by number of newspapers and magazines read.

†Actual participation is indicated by organizations belonged to, voting, and socialization with friends.

TABLE 4.6

Some Attitudes of Black Americans

	NORTH		SOUTH	
	Younger* (N=121)	Older (N=365)	Younger (N=123)	Older (N=368)
1. Violence necessary	36	20	29	13
2. Riots justified	47	30	25	27
3. Whites want to keep Negroes down	51	38	47	40
4. Following groups helpful				
a. The federal government under Nixon	14	17	24	38
b. The federal antipoverty program	50	69	66	75
c. White college students	41	54	27	37
5. Negroes band against whites	45	26	31	22
6. Like African styles	65	30	38	23
7. Favor Black Power	68	42	49	30
8. Country worth fighting for†	60	83	70	83
9. Work with whites	78	90	83	76
10. Go to school with whites	73	85	82	72
11. Like children bussed to white schools	32	40	54	51
12. Prefer racial integration‡	59	83	80	81

From P. Goldman, *Report from Black America* (1970) Appendix C.

Younger is less than thirty; *older* is over thirty.

†Comparable figures for white respondents are 85 and 89 for younger and older, respectively.

‡The question was posed as racial integration versus community control of schools and so on.

As you can see from Table 4.6, black attitudes are not uniform. I have broken the data down by region and age, for these seem to exert the greatest influence on attitude development. The data for income level are omitted because they are inversely related to age in their association with attitudes. That is, younger blacks have attitudes more similar to middle-income blacks ($6450 and over), while older blacks are more similar to lower-income blacks (less than $3068). I shall not try to summarize this table, but I will simply point out the greater hostility toward whites, the greater attraction to blacks, and the growing rejection of the United States and its institutions which characterized *young* black people. This trend is much greater among young Northern than young Southern blacks. There is still a large majority, even of young Northern black people, who want to work with whites (78 percent) and go to school with whites (73 percent). However, the majority preferring racial integration to community control is quite small (59 percent) among this regional-age group.

Of course there are many different possible versions of "community control" and "racial integration," and we do not know which ones are envisioned by the respondents. We can recognize, however, that simplistic proposals for ensuing racial tensions will not likely meet with success. We might also recognize that now perhaps more than ever before, the attitudes of black people must be considered before any proposal for dealing with racial problems even has a chance of working.

Racial attitudes—race versus beliefs. To be black in America is to constantly question the motives of whites with whom you have contact. Is the clerk just mean, or does he dislike blacks, or dislike me because I am black? Was the apartment really taken or was an excuse given to keep from renting to a black person? In attempting to assess the motivation or intention underlying a negative action initiated by someone white, a black person always has several possible inferences: 1) white person has negative personality; 2) white person has negative attitude toward black people; 3) white person has a negative attitude about me personally; and 4) white person and I have different beliefs. An interesting theoretical and empirical controversy arises from such queries. Stated in its general form, the question is: Considering an attitudinal relation (r) between two people (*A* and *B*), which characteristic is more important in determining *A*'s relation to him: *B*'s RACE or *B*'s BELIEFS?

One side of the argument stems from early work on the Authoritarian Personality. This view stressed personality differences in cognitive processes as a central problem of race prejudice. Milton Rokeach (1960) and his students and colleagues were interested in demonstrating that to characterize a person as *dogmatic* was more inclusive than to characterize him as authoritarian; and that to be highly opinionated was more inclusive than to be highly ethnocentric. The dogmatic-opinionated versus authoritarian-ethnocentric comparison provided differing accounts of hostile racial attitudes. The former distinction emphasizes the importance of the beliefs and opinions one holds, the latter stresses one's group affiliation and ethnic identification. Rokeach argued that white racial attitudes were based more on the assumed dissimilarity of beliefs than on the objective racial characteristics of blacks.

Rokeach, Smith, and Evans (1960) conducted an empirical investigation of race and belief determinants of antiblack attitudes. White undergraduates at a Northern and a Southern college were given descriptions of a pair of target persons. Subjects judged on a 9-point scale how likely they were to become friendly with each of the persons. The target persons were presented in pairs in one of three ways:

1. Race varied—Belief constant (Type R)
   a) A white person who believes in God.
   b) A Negro who believes in God.

2. Belief varied—Race constant (Type B)
   a) A white person who believes in God.
   b) A white person who is an atheist.

3. Race and Belief varied (Type RB)
   a) A white person who believes in God.
   b) A Negro who is an atheist.

A comparison of the first pair indicates the importance of race; the second pair indicates the importance of belief, and the final pair indicates which of the two dominates in a head-on confrontation.

Target persons varied on race (white or Negro) and on beliefs (eight in all, four general ones, and four race-relevant ones). In addition to religion, general beliefs concerned socialized medicine, communism, and labor unions. Race-relevant beliefs included speed of desegregation, integrated Greek societies, racial equality, and integrated housing. Subjects were asked to indicate their own feelings about each of the eight belief statements. Thus it was possible to determine for each subject whether a given target person's belief was in agreement or disagreement with his own. In terms of similarity to the raters, the four possible targets would rank as follows: (1) white-agree; (2) white-disagree; (3) Negro-agree; (4) Negro-disagree. The important question is contained in the comparison of items (2) and (3). Preference for the former supports the race interpretation, preference for the latter supports the belief interpretation.

Subjects preferred white to Negro persons when belief was held constant and preferred people who agreed to those who disagreed on the eight belief items when race was held constant. This is what everyone would expect. But which of these two choices was dominant when they were pitted against each other in the Type RB pairing? If choices were made primarily on the basis of race, they should be most highly correlated with R choices. If, on the other hand, RB choices are made primarily on the basis of belief, they should be highly correlated with B choices. The authors' expectations were confirmed. The range of correlations between RB and B choices was .74 to .91, while the range of correlations with R choices was only −.07 to .28. This relationship held regardless of region of the country. This result suggests that belief is a more important determinant of racial attitude than race.

This result, if confirmed, would have provided a very optimistic turn for discussions of racial strife in America. It suggests that education and enlightenment about belief similarities between conflicting racial groups would have a strong analgesic effect on those hostile relations. However, the belief-prejudice interpretation seemed strikingly inadequate to explain the racial conflict that has surfaced in so many creative forms over the years. Dissenting voices were quick to cry out.

Harry Triandis (1961) noted that the belief-congruence interpretation of prejudice was perhaps correct for the attitudinal relation "friendship," but the close social distance of friendship was inadequate because prejudice more typically involved larger social distance (e.g., live in neighborhood, go to school with, etc.). Triandis argued that if one considers a wider range of social distances more accurately reflecting the areas in which prejudice operates in the real world, race would be a more important determinant than belief.

To test this hypothesis, Triandis administered a social distance questionnaire consisting of a 100-point scale from willingness to marry a person (0 social distance) to willingness to lynch a person (97 social distance). This scale was used to rate each of sixteen stimulus persons who were constructed by factorially combining four characteristics:

Race—Negro or white
Religion—same or different
Occupation—coal miner or bank manager
Philosophy—same or different

Not at all surprisingly, the stimulus person receiving the smallest social distance rating for the white University of Illinois undergraduates was someone who was white, same philosophy, same religion, and a bank manager. The largest social distance was assigned to a Negro of different religion and philosophy who was a coal miner.

Triandis was attempting to demonstrate that race was more important than belief in determining a wide range of social-distance choices. The characteristic corresponding to Rokeach's belief variable was *philosophy*. Whereas Rokeach had assigned to the hypothetical stimulus persons (e.g., atheist) specific beliefs which bore some relationship to beliefs actually held by the subjects, Triandis told the subjects that some unspecified beliefs of the target person were similar to or different from their own (e.g., same or different religion). The results confirmed Triandis' criticism of the Rokeach position. Race accounted for social-distance ratings in a ratio of about 4-1 to belief.

Rokeach responded to Triandis (Rokeach, 1961) by pointing out the noncomparability of the treatment of belief. He argued that Triandis' manipulation was vague (simply same or different philosophy) and that the simple proposition, ". . . the more salient a belief, the more will belief congruence override racial or ethnic congruence as a determinant of social distance," could successfully incorporate both sets of data. But where is prejudice in all this?

The original Rokeach, Smith, and Evans (1960) report concerned the question of one or two kinds of prejudice. The debate seemed to surface about which was the stronger determinant of *social distance*. Is social distance to be considered synonymous with prejudice? Our answer must be no. We have seen at the beginning of this chapter that theoretically it is very difficult to demonstrate clearly the operation of prejudice. Considerably more information than is possible to obtain in one experimental setting is required for this determination. The empirical controversy of Rokeach and Triandis should more accurately be considered in terms of interpersonal social attitudes. The research question then becomes this: Which characteristics of an individual have the greatest impact on another person's evaluative judgment of him? Of course interpersonal attraction is not unrelated to prejudice. Others things equal, the more similar two people are the more likely they will be attracted to each other (see Berscheid and Walster, 1969, for a thorough review of this literature). However, one difference—race—may negate a whole range of similar attributes. The demographic data in racial attitudes suggest this may be so. Thus the question of race prejudice goes beyond simple interpersonal attraction theory. To have a proper perspective on race prejudice it is necessary to understand the unique psychological-historical-cultural dynamics of the race question. With this in mind we can say that at the level of discussion reported in the literature, this controversy did not concern prejudice.

But let's follow the question to its conclusion. Byrne and Wong (1962) reported a study which essentially confirmed the thesis of Rokeach. These authors found that highly prejudiced white students at the University of Texas assumed greater attitude dissimilarity between themselves and a black stranger than between themselves and a white stranger. This important result suggests a correlation between race and belief which is quite difficult to eliminate in the uncooperative (scientifically speaking) real world. In the same article, Byrne and Wong found that attitude similarity resulted in positive ratings, attitude dissimilarity in negative ratings *regardless* of the prejudice of the subjects or the race of the stranger. A summary of these findings suggests the following analysis:

Belief is the more important general criterion for interpersonal attraction (within a limited range of social distance). However, a willingness to make inferences about belief dissimilarity *solely* on the basis of race seems to characterize the prejudiced person. Apparently the answer lies somewhere in the prejudiced personality.

As research reports continued to appear, the above analysis became more plausible. Stein, Hardyck, and Smith (1965) found that white ninth graders responded to "stimulus teenagers" in terms of belief when extensive information about the target's beliefs was supplied. When such information was withheld, responses were more heavily influenced by race. It seems, therefore, that students' judgments were based on the assumption of belief dissimilarity, as in the Byrne and Wong study, since negative judgments were made for blacks under conditions of minimal knowledge of beliefs.

The implications of these studies are clear for our analysis of social contact as a means of reducing intergroup hostilities. If through contact one removes the need to guess about the beliefs of blacks (and vice versa), presumably erroneous negative judgments will be diminished. Through interracial contact, greater belief similarity would be revealed, and racial hostilities based on *assumed* belief dissimilarities would be diminished. Other evidence from the Byrne and Wong (1962) and Byrne and McGraw (1964) studies suggests that the prejudiced person will not be positively influenced by contact unless nearly complete belief similarity can be achieved. This is a state which does not exist and cannot be created through any contact situation. We will return to some of these considerations later in this chapter when we review the research on the effects of social contact on racial attitudes.

Two final studies rounded out the controversy. The first, by Triandis and Davis (1965), used large-scale factor-analytic techniques to demonstrate that both race and belief were influential in subject judgments; race more so for more intimate kinds of behaviors, belief more so for less intimate behaviors. This finding supports the earlier results of Stein *et al.* (1965) who, although finding the greatest effect for belief, found a significant race effect for intimate social behaviors (like bringing home for dinner, may date sister, etc.).

The second study by Rokeach and Mezei (1966) was conducted in a more realistic interactional situation. Subjects were given a chance to interact with others who were white or black, and who expressed attitudes which either agreed or disagreed with the experimental subjects. Each subject agreed with two of four people (one white and one black agreed; one white and one black disagreed). The results indicated that similarity of belief was considerably more influential in subject choices than race. The authors reaffirm Rokeach's earlier contention that ". . . the locus of racial and ethnic discrimination is to be sought in society, not in the individual's psyche. If society's restraints were removed and man was still observed to discriminate, it would be in accord ... with his basic psychological predisposition ... to organize the world of human beings in terms of the principle of belief congruence" (Rokeach *et al.,* 1960, p. 184).

Belief and race are the yin and yang of racial conflict. In a country where belief plays such an important role (belief in God, belief in country, belief in the American creed, belief in free speech and so on), there is almost instant exoneration if one's piques and antagonisms are based on personal beliefs, especially if they can be rationalized around religion or patriotism—that is, religion and patriotism as narrowly defined by the keepers of America's images. Although they accept Conscientious Objector statuses for hundreds of American youth, many draft board members threatened to resign when the Supreme Court overruled Muhammed Ali's draft evasion conviction. They apparently could not accept Ali's *Muslim beliefs* and ministerial practices. It is probably true that belief dominates race in the determination of most forms of discrimination. It is equally true, however, that a large portion of what passes as belief-based hostility is but a cover for primary feelings of racial or ethnic hatred.

We must realize that the interrelationships of race and belief in the determination of people's racial attitudes cannot be overemphasized. The demand characteristics of experimental conditions are particularly salient when the issues dealt with are so important. With caution imposed by the above provisos, we can summarize the empirical propositions suggested by the research in this section as follows:

1. Belief congruence is the most frequent determinant of interpersonal attraction.

2. When *A* knows only *B*'s race, he assumes belief dissimilarity.

2a. There is a tendency for prejudiced persons to assume belief dissimilarity of blacks more frequently than do persons judged as non-prejudiced.

3. Race is a more frequent determinant of *A*'s relation to *B* when that relation is an intimate one.

Having asserted that belief-congruence is an important factor in inter-group relations, let us now look at how blacks' and whites' views of themselves and each other correspond, *or fail to.*

Racial attitudes—some comparisons. Thus far we have looked at interpersonal attitudes. That is, we have considered those attitudes which establish relations between two people or between a person and a group. Another way to compare two groups is to compare their attitudes toward a third object or event and look for similarities and dissimilarities between them. One attempt to make such comparisons was that of Campbell and Schuman (1969) in a report prepared for the Kerner Commission. The general demographic characteristics of black and white attitudes correspond quite well with the data reported by Marx (1969) and Selznick and Steinberg (1969). Of interest in the Campbell and Schuman study is the direct comparison of black and white attitudes about the same events or judgments. Table 4.7 summarizes several of these comparisons. It does not take detailed analysis of these figures to see that there is a sizeable disparity between the attitudes of blacks and whites. White respondents characterized the riots of 1967 as actions planned in advance for the

TABLE 4.7

A Comparison of Black-White Attitudes on Some Important Issues

Issue	Percent Agreement	
	Black *N*=2814	White *N*=2945
Negroes miss out on jobs and promotions because of discrimination	70%	56%
Negroes miss out on good housing because white owners won't rent or sell to them	76	68
Purpose of riots:		
Protest	58	43
Looting	9	28
Cause of riots:		
Discrimination and unemployment	70	38
Black Power and looters	16	57
Planning of riots:		
In advance	18	49
Not at all	34	11
Prevention of riots:		
Better employment and end discrimination	40	12
More police control	8	46
Effect of riots:		
Helpful	33	13
Harmful	23	64

Adapted from Campbell and Schuman (1969), Tables IIk, m; IIIb, e; Va, b, c, d, e, pp. 23; 30; 47-49.

purpose of looting or general rabble-rousing. The riots were seen as harmful to the cause of black people, and their prevention best achieved by increased police control. This view is contrasted with the black view which sees the riots as spontaneous protests against discrimination. For blacks, the riots were not seen as terribly helpful, but they were seen as more helpful than harmful. In marked contrast to the white view, the best way to prevent riots is to make available better employment possibilities and realities.

In addition to having quite dissimilar views about the riots, blacks and whites have quantitatively different views of the extent to which racial inequities are caused by discrimination. Among blacks inferior jobs and housing are blamed on discrimination by 70 and 76 percent of the sample, whereas for whites these figures are only 56 and 68 percent. Moreover, the figures for whites are perhaps inflated; consider the responses to another question in the survey, which asked: "On the average, Negroes in (Central City) have worse jobs, education, and housing than white people. Do you think this is due mainly to Negroes having been discriminated against, or mainly due to something about Negroes themselves?" Only *19 percent* of the white respondents attributed the inequities described in the question to discrimination. A total of 56 percent attributed them to something about Negroes themselves.

A recent study by Wilson (1970) compared black and white attitudes toward several civil rights activities. His research was an empirical followup of an assertion made by Gunnar Myrdal (1944) suggesting that blacks and whites both preferred economic opportunities and legal and political rights as the most desirable goals for civil rights actions. Both groups, on the other hand, were expected to eschew such goals as intermarriage and school integration. The hypothesized real agreement but perceived disagreement between blacks and whites on the relative favorability of civil rights goals was termed "rank order of discrimination." Wilson contended that if such relative agreement could be obtained, policy makers could take advantage of this happenstance agreement and create a climate of maximum social influence.

Students at the University of Alabama, and black students at Fisk University were given a list of 14 civil rights goals and asked to rank them twice, first in the order of their own preference, second in the order they estimated the other race would prefer. During the same experimental session, subjects filled out another questionnaire from which estimates of their degree of prejudice were obtained (e.g., "Negroes have their rights but it is better to keep them in their own districts and schools and to prevent too much contact with whites."). The white students were divided into high- and low-prejudiced groups on the basis of their scores on this questionnaire.

The civil rights goals emphasizing *rights and opportunities* concerned (1) rights to vote and hold public office, (2) equal employment opportunities, (3) equitable administration of welfare funds, and (4) equal legal rights. Those goals implying *social integration* included (1) school integration, (2) open housing laws, and (3) social mixing including intermarriage. As the rank order hypothesis predicts, rights and opportunities are given higher priority than social integration for *both* blacks and whites. The average ranks for the rights and opportunities items were 3.7, 4.0, and 7.0 for blacks, unprejudiced whites, and prejudiced whites respectively. The respective ranks for integration items were 8.5, 11.7, and 13.

Table 4.8 lists the rank correlations of interest. The pattern of correlations can be summarized as follows:

1. Black students predict the rankings made by prejudiced white students quite well, but the rankings of unprejudiced whites quite poorly. This finding suggests that when predicting *white* rankings, black students assume they are prejudiced.

2. White students both high and low on the prejudice scale are able to predict fairly accurately the rankings made by blacks, but unprejudiced whites do it better.

TABLE 4.8

Comparative Correlations of Civil Rights Priorities for Black and White Students

	Rank correlations	
	Prejudiced whites	Unprejudiced whites
Blacks predict rankings of . . .	.80	.17
Black rankings predicted by . . .	.62	.82
Black self-ranking with self-rankings of . . .	.00	.51
	----.61*----	

Adapted from Wilson (1970), Table 2; p. 121.

*Correlation between prejudiced and unprejudiced white rankings.

In addition to the correlations, there are important differences in specific goals. White students ranked law enforcement relatively high (6) and equal legal rights relatively low (9 for prejudiced) on civil rights priorities. Black students, on the other hand, ranked law enforcement quite low (13), but equal legal rights quite high (2). Moreover, these discrepancies were accurately perceived by both black and white students. White students expected blacks to rank law enforcement fourteenth and black students expected whites to rank it first. These results lead the author to conclude that ". . . this profound degree of both perceived and actual disagreement does not harken well for the future course of race relations" (p. 121).

However, not all studies show such sizeable discrepancies in racial attitudes. Studying the value orientations of a national sample of white and black people from all socioeconomic statuses, Rokeach and Parker (1970) found substantial similarities among black and white values.

Summary

The research reviewed thus far has been concerned with various aspects of racial attitudes. The empirical investigations cited have not been tied directly to theory on prejudice (with the possible exception of the race vs. belief controversy). Rather, these studies are important primarily as descriptions of racially relevant social attitudes (college phenomenologies). They hold some important observations.

The Karlins, Coffman and Walters (1969) study demonstrates an important trend in social attitudes away from the negative racial stereotyping which characterized the early Bogardus and the Katz and Braly investigations. In addition to a shift away from negative stereotyping, Princeton men informally report increasing reluctance to make widespread generalizations. It is not immediately clear whether the apparent increase in tolerance is due to genuine change toward greater goodwill, or simply reflects greater sophistication about this kind of research and the implications that are drawn from stereotyped judgments. The persistence of the formation of stereotypes, indicated by the high uniformity of trait assignment to groups, suggests that the ethnic judgments continue to have strong normative influences in the country at large. The results seem to fit the old admonition, "If you can't say something nice about somebody, don't say anything at all."

We must keep in mind that the studies reviewed here have to do with attitudes, not necessarily behavior. The demographic attitude data of Marx (1969) and Selznick and Steinberg (1969) seem to show that interracial hostilities are greater in the South than in the North. However, Goldman's (1970) results suggest that black hostility toward whites is greatest among the young, Northern blacks. Violence and racial conflict still occur in both the South and the North, but the tension accompanying racial contact in many Northern institutional and residential settings cannot be ignored.

The research cited on race and belief as determinants of racial attitudes leads to the conclusion that in most areas of interpersonal relations belief is a more important consideration than race. On the face of it, this finding would seem to diminish the importance of racism and racial antagonism as bases for major forms of social conflict. Quite the opposite often results. In the absence of other information, there is a tendency to attribute different beliefs to people of different races. In fact, even when other information is known, there is a tendency to either deny the contrary information, to distort its meaning, or to adduce additional information which bolsters one's initial attitude. The various psychological gymnastics of which prejudiced or bigoted persons are capable are central to the understanding of prejudice.

We have pointed out the many different ways in which race and belief combine in the determination of attitudes and behavior. An additional caveat comes from the studies of comparative racial attitudes. Blacks and whites do, in fact, differ in many of their beliefs. These differences are imagined in some cases ("all the black men want to do is sleep with our white women"), and quite real in others (whites want more police to stop riots; blacks want more jobs). In either case, the realities of racism must not be obscured by the research findings which place greater emphasis on belief than on race.

The Development of Racial Attitudes in Children

One of the most important and often-discussed findings in the area of racial attitudes concerns doll preference as an index of racial attitude. The classic study which we have discussed previously was conducted by Kenneth and Mamie Clark in 1939. There are two methodological assumptions underlying the doll-selection studies: (1) Racial preference and identification revealed by doll choice technique is associated with actual preference and identification in real life; and (2) the *color* differences of dolls are represented as *racial* differences by children. The preference questions can produce three kinds of results:

1. Children identify with and/or prefer dolls of race-congruent color (own-race identification and/or ethnocentrism).

2. Children identify with and/or prefer dolls independent of color (no racial identification and/or preference).

3. Children identify with and/or prefer dolls of race-incongruent color (other-race identification and/or preference).

Let us begin our brief review of the doll-preference studies with a summary of the results of the classic Clark and Clark (1947) study.

1.   Fifty percent or more of the black children preferred the white doll at every age level.

2.   This doll preference reached a peak at the age of five years where the white doll was chosen 75 percent of the time.

3.   Race awareness increased with age from a minimum of 61-percent correct race choice for three-year-old children to 93-percent for seven-year-old children.

4.   Light-skinned children preferred the white doll more than darker-skinned children did (70 percent versus 59 percent).

5.   Children from Northern integrated schools (in Springfield, Massachusetts) showed greater preference for the white dolls than did children in Southern segregated schools (in Little Rock, Arkansas).

6.   Northern and Southern children were comparable in their ability to identify the dark-skinned doll as a "Negro doll."

7.   Light-skinned Negro children more frequently identified the white doll as "looking like them" (80 percent versus 26 percent and 19 percent for medium- and dark-skinned children, respectively).

The interpretations of these results have been the subject for considerable discussion over the years. It is suggested that since black children chose (preferred?) white dolls, they preferred white skin. It is further suggested that since black children identified themselves with the white doll, they desired themselves to be white.

It is not difficult to understand why the black children seemed to prefer the white dolls. Until recently, colored dolls have been relatively rare. Moreover, beauty has been monopolized by standards of light skin, rosy cheeks, and long straight hair. Any child who (a) is trying to reconstruct the phenomenology of the society or (b) has internalized society's standards would choose (or prefer) the white doll.

The fact that 33 percent of the black children identified the white doll as looking like themselves is not so easily understood in cultural terms. Here, methodological factors are most relevant. Only two types of dolls, dark and white, were used, but black children varied over a range of colors from light-skinned (almost white) to very dark. Considering only the brown or darker-skinned children, only 19 percent erroneously identified the white doll as looking like them.

A more recent study by Greenwald and Oppenheim (1968) attempted to clarify these color factors by using three dolls, a dark-brown, a white, and a mulatto (or light-brown) doll. These authors replicated the Clark and Clark procedure using black and white nursery-school children four and five years old. In this study all of the dolls had brown hair, instead of the usual blonde hair for white dolls.

The results for identification were quite interesting. Combining the children's choices of dark brown and mulatto dolls in response to the question which one looks like you, 78 percent of the light-skinned, 69 percent of the medium-skinned, and 93 percent of the dark-skinned children selected either the dark or the mulatto doll. For dark-skinned children, the percentage misidentifying themselves with the white doll is reduced from 19 percent (in the Clarks' study) to a mere 7 percent. It is, however, interesting still to note that the medium-skinned children chose the white doll at a rate of 31 percent and the light-skinned at only 22 percent. The greater misidentification of *medium-* than light-skinned children suggests the possibility of psychological dynamics in these doll-choice studies.

Results for the white children are of considerable interest; 47 percent selected the white doll in response to the identification question, while 44 percent selected either the dark or the mulatto doll. The white children might reasonably have selected the mulatto doll (25 percent did this), so we are left with a figure of 19 percent of the white children selecting the dark-brown doll as "looking like" themselves. This figure is the same as the percentage of black children identifying with the white doll in the original Clark and Clark study.

One of the concepts used to describe the apparent preference of blacks for white skin has been "identification with the aggressor (or oppressor)." The present results for white children might be similarly interpreted as "identification with the *oppressed.*" This concept is not offered facetiously, as there is much cultural evidence to support it. For example, Elizabeth Taylor, for many years the paragon of white beauty, recently attended the wedding of her son whose bride wore an Afro hair style. Not only hair styles, but also life styles, music styles, speech styles, and other facets of black culture are being adopted by young, white America. But this carries us a long way from choosing dolls.

What, then, do doll studies tell us about racial attitudes? What does it mean for a child to select a doll of a particular color in an experimental situation? The preference results obtained by the Clarks has been replicated many times since their results were published (cf. Radke, Trager and Davis, 1949; Radke, Sutherland and Rosenberg, 1950; Trager and Yarrow, 1952; Landreth and Johnson, 1953; Asher and Allen, 1969; and, more recently, Porter, 1971). It seems that if doll choice actually does reflect racial attitudes, there should be a dramatic shift in preferences from 1939 to the present; yet the results of Asher and Allen (1969) are nearly identical to those of the Clarks.

The typical doll-choice finding has been integrated to suggest that for black and white alike, "black is *not* beautiful." Hraba and Grant (1970) presented the most dramatic recent experimental demonstration of "black is beautiful." Still using the doll choice technique, these investigators showed that black children preferred *black dolls* in roughly the same proportion as black children had preferred *white dolls* in the Clarks' study.

This result is closer to our expectations in 1972, but we must ask why in Lincoln, Nebraska—and not in Boston, Massachusetts (Porter, 1971), or Newark, New Jersey (Asher and Allen, 1969), or in New York City (Greenwald and Oppenheim, 1968)?

One explanation for the general failure of doll-preference techniques to produce expected changes might be the poor relationship between doll-color choice and racial attitudes. If a child could make the same kinds of selections from realistic human choices with implications for behavioral relationships, the results might be more congruent with our expectations. A more realistic study of racial choice has recently been conducted by Sara Kiesler (1971).

Kiesler had 165 kindergarten children select photographs of other children under one of three conditions: (1) where the children were simply asked to choose one or the other photograph as the experimental task; (2) where children selected the photograph of the child they would prefer to *play* with in the anticipated next phase of the experiment; or (3) where children selected the photo of the child they would prefer to *work* with in the anticipated next phase of the experiment. To add realism to the expectation that the other photographs were of real children, each child had his picture taken with a Polaroid camera when he arrived. Each child always chose from two photographs of children of the same sex, one black and one white. Children's choices were based on five questions, the most important of which was the first: "Which of these boys (girls) would you like as a partner to play (work) with?" The results are summarized around four points:

1.   When children did not anticipate any interaction, black children chose photographs of other black children 57 percent of the time, while white children chose black photographs only 18 percent of the time.

2.   When anticipating future interaction, black children chose black photographs *less often* (only 15 and 26 percent in Play and Work conditions, respectively). However, in anticipated interaction circumstances, white children chose black photographs *more often*, but *increased* the percentage of black choices 31 percent in both Play and Work conditions).

3.   Among black subjects, those who correctly selected the black photo in response to "Which of the photographs resembles you?" were more likely to choose a black partner. This comparison made no difference for white children.

4.   In addition, friendliness choices produced similar racial differences. Black children felt black photos were more friendly in the Photo Only (52 percent) and Anticipated Play (61 percent) conditions, but less friendly in the Anticipated Work (33 percent) condition. White children, on the other hand, felt black photos were less friendly in the first two conditions (33

percent and 35 percent, respectively), but more friendly in the Anticipated Work condition (60 percent).

These results are intriguing, but what they mean is open to considerable speculation.

The doll-choice studies provide an appropriate point of departure from the discussion of research on attitudes to a consideration of the relationship between these attitudes and behavior. The principal assumption underlying most research on racial attitudes is that there is some relationship between holding a particular attitude and the way in which one might behave toward the attitude object. Let us turn our attention now to behavior and see if the same picture of race relations emerges.

The results of the Kiesler study suggest that among black children racial self-awareness is associated with preference for black work or play partners. A similar finding was obtained in the original Clark and Clark study. More important, racial preference is demonstrated to be affected by the behavioral implications of these preferences. The relationships are not clear enough, however, to allow us to say any more than an effect exists.

Perhaps the most thorough and illuminating doll-choice study of the development of racial attitudes is that reported by Judith Porter in *Black Child, White Child* (1971). In her investigation, Porter used creative doll play as a framework within which to study doll choice. She used four-and-one-half-inch dolls of each sex dressed like nursery school children (medium-brown and white with black and brown hair, respectively) as props for a made-up TV story. The stories involved the following sequences:

1. First we're going to make up a story about Johnny (Judy) who looks just like you. "Which of the dolls will be Johnny (Judy) in our story?"

2. Johnny is the first one to school and is waiting for his friend he plays with all the time. "Which one of these is Johnny's friend?" "Why do you think this one is Johnny's friend?"

3. They start playing. "One of these kids is nice. Which one?"

4. Fourth kid comes. Johnny says, "Let's ask him to play with us." His friend says, "Nah, he's lazy and stupid." "Why?" "Time for lunch, which one does Johnny take home?" (Porter, 1971)

Responses to the above questions produced the preference data. When the story scene moved to Johnny's home, identification data were obtained by asking the children which one of the dolls looks like the colored, which looks like the Negroes and so on. Free play with the dolls and sets terminated the experimental session.

The children in this study were three to five years old and attending nursery schools and kindergartens in the Boston area. Some schools were segregated, others were integrated. The children themselves were from varied socioeconomic backgrounds.

The results of the study can be summarized as follows:

1.   Black children rejected themselves more than whites did.

2.   Knowledge of color differences was present at age three; race and color were connected by age four; and real racial knowledge was present by age five.

3.   Appearance was more important for girls than for boys.

4.   White working-class and ADC children had more negative attitudes toward blacks than middle-class whites did. Lower-class blacks had stronger black identification and preference than middle-class blacks. Lower-class blacks also had greater hostility toward whites.

5.   Racial integration produced greater tolerance among white boys, but less tolerance among white girls.

6.   Perhaps the most important finding is that "sex, play style within sex, and personality are three factors which may account for most of the playmate selection of kindergarten-age children. In both schools race seemed to play little part in determining friendship patterns" (p. 167).

This study demonstrates that a whole range of variables introduce the complexity that the subject of development of racial attitudes demands. The simplified methodologies and naive operational assumptions that have guided research in this area have perpetuated relative ignorance of the real-life racial dynamics in this country.

It is most important to note that although the racial attitudes so frequently replicated were again found in Porter's study, they bear no relationship to actual friendship behavior. With young children, whose racial attitudes are likely to be highly unstable, this finding is quite encouraging for the positive effects of interracial contact at young ages. It should also serve as warning that attitudes (operationally defined) and behaviors are *not* the same thing. In some cases they are influenced by different variables; in others, by the same variables but in different degrees.

II. Behavior

In this section we will be concerned with behaviors in two ways: (1) as consequences of a particular attitude orientation, and (2) as antecedents to developing or changing attitudes. In the former case we shall look for a correspondence between some measure of racial attitude (usually verbal statements or questionnaire responses) and some observable racial behavior (usually an interracial behavioral encounter). In the latter case we shall look for a relationship between certain inter- (intra-) racial behavior and the attitudes or changes in attitudes that result from them. For example, under conditions of racial separation or segregation, interracial behavioral encounters are bound to be of a different sort than under integrated conditions. One would expect that the development of racial attitudes would reflect these different behavioral experiences and that changes in the conditions of behavior exchange would produce changes in existing attitudes. A great deal of theory and research has been directed toward this aspect of race relations, and has had major impact on federal legislative and judicial actions in the past two decades. Let us look now at research on attitudes influencing behavior.

Racial Attitudes Influencing Racial Behaviors

The classic study on the relationship between racial attitudes and racial behaviors was conducted by LaPiere (1934). Recall our description of this study in Chapter Two. Although he and the Chinese couple with whom he was traveling were promptly and courteously served everywhere they stopped, LaPiere found that the proprietors said later that they would not accommodate a Chinese couple. This was one of the first studies that suggested attitudes and behaviors might not be as closely related as many social psychologists at the time seemed to think.

A similar study was reported by Kutner, Wilkins, and Yarrow (1952). After two white women had entered a restaurant (in a Northeastern suburb) and been seated, a black woman joined them. The black woman was never refused admission in eleven restaurants and taverns, and the service was described as exemplary. The same establishments were later requested by letter to take reservations for a racially integrated social group. After seventeen days with no replies, followup telephone calls produced five reluctant acceptances and six clear refusals.

DeFleur and Westie (1958) measured subjects' "attitudes" toward Negroes during an interview session employing different kinds of "questions, devices and situations." From these measures a self-report index of racial attitudes was constructed and subjects were sorted into prejudiced and unprejudiced categories.

The investigators used a bit of subterfuge to obtain behavioral measures of racial attitudes. During the interview period, all subjects had viewed colored photographic slides showing interracial pairs of males and females. Subjects were told that another set of slides was being prepared and asked if he (or she) would be willing to be photographed with a Negro person of the opposite sex. Presented with a "standard photographic release form," subjects who agreed indicated a range of uses to which they were willing to allow the photographs to be put. These uses ranged from other laboratory experiments to a national publicity campaign advocating racial integration.

Considering only those who signed an agreement to be photographed, Table 4.9 shows a substantial correlation between racial attitudes and

TABLE 4.9
Relationship Between Racial Attitude (Self-Report) and
Racial Behavior (Agreement to be Photographed with Blacks)

		Racial attitude	
		Prejudiced	Unprejudiced
Racial behavior	Prejudiced	18	9
	Unprejudiced	5	14

Adapted from De Fleur and Westie (1958).

behaviors. However, 14 subjects did not demonstrate attitude-behavior consistency.

The three studies which we have described are "classic" examples of the research on the correspondence between racial attitudes and racial behaviors. There have been numerous other, greatly diversified studies of this relationship (see Wicker, 1969, for a general review). Like the preceding three, most studies show either a positive or negative relationship between attitudes and behaviors of a racial nature, or a very equivocal one. But what do these studies have to say about race prejudice?

We began this chapter by defining prejudice as, in part, "... a judgment or opinion formed before the 'facts' are known." In the studies cited above, the judgment was formed *after* the facts were known. That is, the proprietors had in fact served the Chinese and black people *before* they made their negative judgments (i.e., that they would not serve them). Prejudice as a concept which is usually associated with rigid prejudgments seems inadequate to deal with the complex determinants of behavior.

We should not, however, dismiss the relevance of prejudice as a concept and the expectation of consistency between racial attitudes and behaviors on the basis of the LaPiere and the Kutner, Wilkins, and Yarrow studies. Surely some of the attitude statements made by people like George Wallace and Lester Maddox accord very well with their behavior.

The question then becomes *which* attitudes, measured how, influence *which* behavior, measured how, and in what situations. It really should not be surprising to us that a restaurateur would serve *one* black woman in the company of two white women in a Northern city rather than "create a scene." But we may also surmise that if three black women attempted to be served (suggesting they might be planning to make it a habit), the establishment's response might well have been different. In fact, observations by Robin Williams (1964) support this surmise.

Recall our earlier discussion which suggested that attitudes only have meaning as we draw inferences from some observable behavior. In the rush to quantify attitudes, however, many social scientists have come to ignore the behaviors from which they derive their attitude assessment. Many theorists (e.g., D. T. Campbell, 1963, and Kiesler, Collins and Miller, 1969) argue that the more correct view of studies like LaPiere's is not as an example of attitude-behavior discrepancy, but as an inconsistency between behaviors in two different situations.

Kiesler, Collins and Miller frame the question specifically. They ask, "*When* are attitudes and behaviors correlated?" Historically, the emphasis on direct attitude-behavior links has oversimplified what can be a very complicated, situationally bound relationship. Furthermore, the wide-spread use of pencil-paper measures of attitude has tended operationally to reify "attitude," and to lose sight of the behavioral implications of the concept.

Another way to explain the racial attitudes-behaviors relationship is in terms of the degree of normative pressure influencing each. Racial attitudes probably conform to prevailing social norms, but are at the same time capable of highly flexible interpretation. Attitudes can only exist in relation to some attitude object. The fact that we are so capable of altering our perception of the attitude object gives attitudes their remarkable lability. Recall the study of Solomon Asch (1946) which showed how varying the sponsor of a statement produced changes in subjects' attitudes about the statement.

Behaviors, on the other hand, are not nearly so flexible. Normative prescriptions on interracial behaviors are quite clear—don't marry, don't live next to, don't entertain in your home, and so on. Of course normative prescriptions vary from region to region within the country, but the pressures exerted by social normative values are considerable.

Most discussions of prejudice view the behavior component as *discrimination.* Discrimination refers to observable behavior, and because it does, it has a more limited perspective on racial relations. Prejudice = attitude = a highly flexible set of statements which reflect generalized affect, belief, and opinion toward or about an entire group. Discrimination = behavior = a fairly tight set of behavioral prescriptions which in the final instance, often affect only one or two members of a racial group. In the LaPiere and the Kutner, Wilkins, and Yarrow studies, we would conclude that the proprietors had prejudiced attitudes, but did not evidence discriminatory behavior.

We have been talking about normative prescriptions and how they affect both attitudes and behaviors. But where do these norms come from, and how do individuals and groups react to these pressures? Psychologists have tended to emphasize individual racial attitudes and behaviors. An individual view tends to look at personal racial interactions, and the result is person-type theories such as personality (Adorno *et al.,* 1950) and frustration (Dollard *et al.,* 1939). Sociologists usually look at the relationships of larger collectivities and usually produce group (Blumer, 1958) or conflict theories. Social psychologists predictably look at individuals in group situations and produce sociopsychological theories of attitude development in a delimited social context (Allport, 1954; Pettigrew, 1964). It is with social psychology that an integration of prejudice-discrimination (attitudes-behaviors) relationships would be expected.

The division of attitudes and behaviors, indicative of the specificity of the term prejudice, should suggest to us that the theory of interracial strife in America cannot achieve maturity within the classic prejudice model. If racial conflict had been restricted to the attitude domain, it might have been grounds for social scientific research, but not likely for major social reform. Hostile racial attitudes coexist with hostile racial behaviors, even though the nature of their mutual influences is not well known.*

Here I would like to summarize the germ of an idea stated above and treated more fully in the next chapter. The term *race prejudice,* which has come to represent racial hostility and a variety of other abnegations of the American Dream, is insufficient to cover the whole range of influences on interracial attitudes and behaviors. What will be needed is a term that can encompass the psychological manifestations of generalized race hatred as well as less personalized "facts" of an oppressed location in the socioeconomic and political fabric of the society. Race prejudice has drawn heavily on the assumption of a consistent relationship between attitudes and behaviors. The facts of the past decade of racial turmoil demand a more elaborate view of the problems. At this time the more elaborate view will be provided by the term *racism*—a term which greatly extends, though it does not supplant, the analysis provided by race prejudice.

A first step toward breaking behavior's bondage to attitudes is to look at reciprocal behavioral influences on attitudes. In Chapter Three, this issue was presented in the context of the question, "Can stateways (behavioral control) change folkways (attitudes)?" Here again we confront the social psychologist in the breach. If racial attitudes develop principally out of the social milieu in which a person is raised, then changing that milieu and the prescribed behaviors to which it gives rise should produce a change of attitudes. Once attitudes begin to change we might expect that their behavioral consequences also would begin to change. The unfolding of this process might contain the ultimate hope for human relationships of decency, tolerance and mutual growth and love. But . . .

---

*Cumulative effects, however, might affect an entire race. The subject of institutional racism could be seen in part as the cumulative effects of racial discrimination.

Behaviors Influencing Attitudes

Some orientations toward attitude objects are developed in the absence of direct contact with those objects. In racial matters, stereotypes are frequently attitudes of this origin. Peers or parents may warn a young child of the evils of strange men. A young child may be fearful of adult males outside the home without ever having contact with one. A similar prior fear and/or hatred of black people can and often is established in young white children. In these cases, one would expect behavior toward the attitude object to be determined by pre-existing attitudes.

We frequently have behavioral encounters with objects for which no pre-existing attitude is held. If the behavioral encounter is in some sense satisfying, we are likely to develop a positive attitude toward the object. If the encounter is unsatisfying, a negative attitude is likely to ensue. The clearest operation of these principles can be seen by watching a young baby through the course of a day having many new behavioral encounters with various objects of many characters. Satisfying encounters invariably lead to cooing and smiling, while unsatisfying ones lead to frowning and/or crying and rapid ejection (since nearly all encounters take place in and around the mouth!). Thus do baby's *attitudes* toward many objects form under the influence of its behavior encounters.

One of the most vigorous areas of research in race relations has been on the attitudinal consequences of changing racial behavioral relations. Put simply, this research has sought to determine the extent to which new behavioral arrangements would lead to more favorable interracial attitudes. One of the most significant aspects of race relations has been residentially segregated housing. Question: How much of racial antipathy can be assigned to misperceptions and misunderstandings traceable to lack of social contact?

Reviewing several studies of the effects of contact on racial attitudes, Allport (1954) reached the following conclusion:

> Prejudice (unless deeply rooted in the character structure of the individual) may be reduced by (1) equal status contact between majority and minority groups (2) in the pursuit of common goals. The effect is greatly enhanced if this contact is (3) sanctioned by institutional supports (i.e., by law, custom or local atmosphere), and (4) if it is a sort that leads to the perception of common interests and common humanity between members of the two groups. (p. 267)*

*Note the proviso "unless deeply rooted in the character structure of the individual." It is precisely this factor which requires us to go beyond prejudice to speak of racism which is deeply rooted in the character structure of individuals, institutions, and the basic culture of this society.

These are difficult criteria for *any* two groups in American society to meet, but let us look at some of the systematic research that bears on these propositions.

One of the major tests of contact theory came as a result of the school integration decision of 1954. As mentioned, E. Q. Campbell (1958) gave a questionnaire on attitudes toward Negroes to 746 white high-school students before their school had been integrated and again six months afterward. Campbell found that white attitudes were significantly affected by contact with Negroes in the classroom but in no consistent direction. Some students' attitudes became more negative, while others' became more positive. Moreover, the direction of change was closely related to how the students perceived the racial attitudes of their parents and friends.

Webster (1961) studied both white and black students in an integrated junior high school in California. Students were tested first in their segregated schools, then six months later in their integrated schools. White student attitudes became more negative after integration, while black attitudes toward whites diverged with positive changes outnumbering negative ones.

The results of these studies are typical of the finding that racial contact in a school setting has an indeterminate effect on racial attitudes. We should not be surprised by this. The criteria set forth by Allport are not likely to be met in "desegregated" (as opposed to truly integrated) schools. First, the children from segregated black schools had been receiving poorer training with fewer general educational advantages than the whites. This condition would preclude the first criterion, equal status contact. Second, as a result of community climate and peer and parent pressures, it is highly unlikely that the black and white children were in pursuit of common goals, and certain that institutional support was lacking. Perception of common interests and common humanity is a long jump from threats and shouts of "Niggers go home."

This discussion has focused on racial contact in schools primarily during the time following school desegregation. It is interesting to note that racial strife in integrated schools (primarily in the North) still exists. In fact, a recent report on violence in high schools suggests that the majority of racial incidents occur in integrated schools where black students comprise a sizeable minority. Most research of the 1940's and 50's focused on whites because therein was seen the major problem. The realities of racial conflict and integration are markedly different now in the 70's.

Closely related to school segregation has been residential and occupational segregation. The importance of this relationship is underscored by the findings of the Coleman Report that the major influence on academic achievement was the socioeconomic status of the student body. Residential and occupational segregation leads to segregated schooling with a lower-class student body—a very unhealthy state of affairs according to the Coleman data. How does racial contact in these settings affect racial attitudes?

Racial contact has generally led to increased racial acceptance in work situations, but with little carryover to other social relationships. Harding and Hogrefe (1952) found this to be the case among department store employees, and Palmore (1955) found the same results with packing house employees. Yarrow (1958) found a similar relationship with young boys and girls in a summer camp. Interracial friendships were established among cabinmates, but were largely confined to the cabin setting. In broader settings, small segregated groups were the rule.

This same kind of friendship-specificity exists for many people at many levels. As a teenager I attended an integrated high school and participated on integrated athletic teams and was a member of several integrated school organizations. In the summers I worked on an integrated recreation maintenance crew. During none of this time did interracial friendships go outside the boundaries of school, athletics, or work.

We have already discussed at some length the classic contact study of Deutsch and Collins (1951). This study showed sizeable, positive attitude change toward blacks among whites living in integrated housing units in New York and Newark. Wilner, Walkley and Cook (1955) replicated these results in a study of white housewives living "near" or "far" from black families in public housing projects. "Near" housewives expressed racial attitudes similar to those of the integrated housewives, and "far" housewives' attitudes were similar to the segregated housewives of the Deutsch and Collins study.

However, when contact is achieved through residential immigration (whites see it as "invasion"), the effects of contact are almost universally negative. There are numerous research examples to document this effect (Kramer, 1950; Hunt, 1959; Fishman, 1961). An article in the magazine section of the *New York Times* (January 24, 1971) brings the phenomenon more up-to-date:

A civic-group leader: "We don't want our neighborhood liberated as a slum. And we don't want blacks in our group; we are for the preservation of the nationalist way of life."

A Catholic war veteran: "We Slovaks are too trusting . . . the Italians told the blacks they would kill any who moved in . . . That is not our way of life, but look what we are reaping now."

A housewife: "It's sad when women have to pin their key inside their dress and put their grocery money in their shoes."

Fear and hate are the norms in racially tense urban areas. The attitudes expressed in the *Times* article might have been seen as prejudiced responses to fears of residential "invasion." However, on the East side of

Cleveland, Ohio (from whence the statements come), these ethnic Americans talk of murders, robberies, rape, and violence in the schools; they cite incidents and a 30-percent increase in neighborhood crime rate. The civic-group leader also related an incident which reflects the changing mood and character of race relations. The respondent was confronted on the street by a black boy who said, "We gonna keel you, whi' man, so get yo' _____ out NOW." With a clear sense of ethnic identity, the civic leader's response was "Let the Anglo-Saxons turn their houses over to them. We demand a right of self-determination." The melting pot is boiling over!

Contrast the racial picture presented above with the picture of middle-class black families huddled in their new homes in previously all-white neighborhoods while neighbors picket, throw stones, and shout "Niggers go home!" Whereas prejudice might be appropriate to describe unfounded white fears of middle-class "colored people," it hardly seems appropriate to describe the frightened reactions of the people of East Cleveland. Behavioral interactions are abundantly available to buttress the negative, reactive attitudes of these ethnic Americans.

The issue of racial integration has been a major one during the past 40 years of this century. If the picture of intensely bigoted, prejudiced white individuals who refused to accept blacks into *their* white society were correct, the massive economic, legal, and social roles played by the federal government might have produced sizeable, positive changes both in the plight of blacks and in the tenor of racial relations. On several scores, these results have not been realized and point again to a complexity of racial relations which the concept of prejudice is unequipped to handle.

In this section we are speaking of the influence of behavior on attitudes. The major determinants of most Americans' behavior (the very rich perhaps have the most control over their own behavior) are the social, legal, and economic systems which prescribe, proscribe, and prevent behaviors at every turn. When blacks and whites were almost totally separated, the needed changes seemed obvious; integrate blacks into the mainstream of American life; once integration begins in earnest, new behavioral relations will foster improved attitudinal ones and this country will be making a positive step toward solving the "race problem."

Pettigrew (1971) amasses a great deal of data and makes strong arguments for the potential positive attitudinal effects of racial contact. He extends his social scientific analysis and personal conviction to the conclusion that immediate, full racial integration (as opposed to the mere desegregation that occurred in response to the Supreme Court decision of 1954) is the best—and perhaps the only—way to racial harmony in America.

In the ideal case it is probably true that contact under the conditions specified by Allport would ease racial tension. However, racial contact under nonoptimal conditions can have adverse effects as we have seen. A report from the Policy Institute of the Syracuse University Research Corporation (*New York Times,* October 4, 1970) concluded that unrest in urban schools is attributable primarily to racial conflict, as racially integrated schools are more likely to experience disruptions than those that are almost all white or all black. The report also describes what it calls a mood of "black revenge" which has a strong effect on race relations. This same mood might be ascribed to the black boy's threat to the civic-group leader in Cleveland, Ohio.

We have attempted to look at how changes in behavioral relations influence the development and change of attitudes. To the extent that new behavioral relations take place among people of substantial equality and similarity already (in terms of status, goals in life, style of life, etc.), more positive, tolerant attitudes ensue. How does one engineer such changes in behavioral relations? In light of the Syracuse report, school integration achieved by bussing may be a hazardous undertaking. In light of moods of "black revenge," many racial contacts are likely to have negative repercussions. The rising militancy of "ethnic Americans" presents yet another complication to engineered behavior change. In short, governmental changes have not given sufficient weight to the complexity of the case.

Racial behavioral encounters do influence racial attitudes. When behavioral relations occur (or do not occur) under segregated conditions, the gross status inequality of most contacts produces attitudes of white superiority and further justification for the unequal status quo. When the frequency of racial encounters increases as it has in the past two decades, one finds strong changes in both directions. Some whites have been introduced to blacks under conditions which produced positive attitude change; for others, the change has been intensely negative. Of one thing we can be certain: interracial contact is not likely to be a neutral event for either racial party.

Let us close this chapter with a brief look at some of the theoretical underpinnings of the literature on prejudice. Although we have thus far been concerned primarily with research, our discussion has inevitably made excursions into the domain of theory. We will take a quick look at classical theories of prejudice, then we will look at some specifically social psychological theories relevant to prejudice, although not necessarily formulated to account for prejudice phenomena.

THEORIES OF RACE PREJUDICE

The theory of prejudice is as complex as the society which houses its phenomena. There is no general discussion of theories of prejudice which has improved on the brief description provided by Allport (1954). Allport delineates six approaches to the theory of causes of prejudice which he presents in a telescopic analogy as indicated in Figure 4.3. To reduce successfully these six approaches to the study of prejudice into one coherent theory of human thought and action would probably take divine intervention. Lacking confidence in this likelihood, I shall simply discuss each approach briefly in the context of observations we have already made.

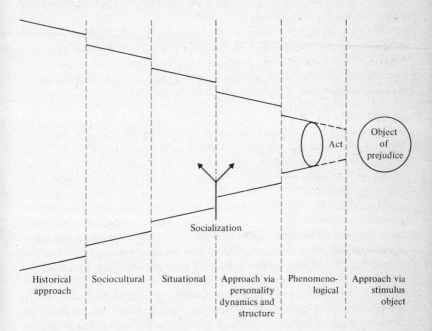

Fig. 4.3. Theoretical approach to the study of prejudice. (From G. Allport, *The Nature of Prejudice*. Reading, Mass.: Addison-Wesley, 1954.)

Historical Emphasis

My bias toward the historical approach should be evident from the nature of the first three chapters. The historical approach is usually opposed to psychological interpretations, but favors sociological, historical or economic explanations.* Recall Oliver Cox's (1948) view that race prejudice is simply a social attitude perpetuated to maintain and justify the superior, advantaged position of the upper class in relation to the underclass. This view sees race prejudice as a "mask" for exploitative intentions. I would question this interpretation by suggesting that the exploiters did sincerely believe in their superiority, and excesses of so-called race prejudice might be seen more fundamentally as an expression of racism.

*Marxist theory, notable among them, combines them all.

Prejudice has consistently implied prejudgment and, as such, almost demands either a lack of racial contact, or contact of limited variety. The substantial "contact" of imperialist expansion in the nineteenth century would suggest that racial prejudice is not the best term with which to describe early racial conflict. Historically, prejudice seems maximally relevant as an analytical tool to the period of our history between 1900 and, say, 1960. Maximal racial separation occurred during this period, and opportunities for negative prejudgment were optimal. The complexities of racial interaction and institutional bureaucracy have beclouded race relations to the point that new terms with less psychological specificity are needed.

Sociocultural Emphasis

This class of theories stresses the importance of group conflict and mobility and is characteristic of modern sociologists. Our preceding discussion of contact theory, earlier discussions of demographic variations in racial attitudes, and the sense of group position argument proposed by Blumer (1958) are characteristic of this approach. Likewise are the complexity of mass society suggested by Lohman and Reitzes (1952) and the social-problem approach of Raab and Lipset (1959).

The crises of the urban metropolis make the sociocultural approach particularly interesting now. This view suggests that the complex, impersonality of big cities places all of their inhabitants in positions of insecurity and uncertainty. Financial woes of city administrations, rising unemployment, crime, and violence contribute to these psychological tensions.

The theory continues that individuals seek to ground themselves in relevant reference groups. Strong ethnic affiliation has characterized big cities for most of this century. What emerges from strong ethnic affiliation is the sense of group position and the development of strong group conflict. The battleground has been bloody as ethnic Americans have won a succession of victories over blacks who have been handicapped by the variety of institutionalized racial inequities. But Chester Powell set the record straight when he claimed a preference for an Italian son-in-law of commonest standing to an educated Japanese. The line is drawn at the biological point.

To be sure, race prejudice contributes to the disadvantaged position held by blacks as a group competing for the scarce economic, educational, political, and social commodities of this society. However, it is more than negative prejudgments that have sustained the racial inequality of this country for so many years.

Situational Emphasis

This approach is quite simple and merely emphasizes the kinds of situational forces which influence the development of a child's racial attitudes. This approach would place great importance on the nature of the influences shaping a child's behavior and forming his attitudes. This view would see marked variations in racial attitudes and behaviors which characterize different regions of the country (North-South, urban-rural, for example) as reflections of the different situations characteristic of each region.

The major importance of the situational approach is the delineation of racial-contact situations (housing, education, recreation, and so on) and the consequent attitude development and change. The situation-specificity of many of the contact effects reflects the situational emphasis.

Psychodynamic Emphasis

We now move toward greater concern with individuals, as psychological interpretations gain ascendance. A major theoretical orientation which has been advanced to account for both white hostile prejudice and black bitter reaction is frustration and relative-deprivation theory. Frustration theory (initially advanced by the Yale group—Dollard, Doob, Miller, Mowrer and Sears, 1939) proposes simply that white Americans frequently become frustrated by repeated blocking of their attempts to achieve the goal for which they are striving, usually a comfortable economic livelihood. When thwarted by whatever means, these frustrations turn to anger which is unleashed on the nearest amenable (i.e., incapable of strong retaliation) object. The theory suggests that blacks have been the victim of displaced, frustration-produced aggression. Once hostility has been aroused it can be displaced toward any (*logically* irrelevant) victim.

Take the growing restlessness of frustrated ethnic Americans caught in the vise of economic recession plus a soaring cost of living, with expanding federal programs for blacks resulting in racial hostility. This hostility can be attributed in part to displaced aggression. Ethnic Americans are, it seems, frustrated at the prevalent assumption that they are doing okay, and that all special efforts should, therefore, be directed toward blacks. Such a source of frustration makes blacks the objects of frustration and hence the direct objects of aggression. This state of affairs produces a slight variant of the frustration-aggression hypothesis by suggesting that ethnic American hostility toward blacks is direct, and *psycho*-logically relevant. That is, massive federal spending on black-oriented projects produces the feeling that "if it weren't for the blacks, we'd be better off." Thus in a psycho-logical sense (not logically because it is the government's decision which is the last cause) blacks are seen as thwarting the goals of a better, more viable standard of living. Interestingly, the mood of frustration was discerned by President Richard Nixon in his State of the Union address on January 22, 1971. The president stated that "as the forces that shape our lives seem to have grown more distant and more impersonal, a great feeling of frustration has crept across the land."

Of course the loud voice of black demands contributes (probably correctly) to the perception of black responsibility for much of the federal

TABLE 4.10

Some Economic Indices of Racial Inequality

FAMILY INCOME DISTRIBUTION

	1947 Black	White	B/W	1960 Black	White	B/W	1968 Black	White	B/W
Under $5,000	83	51	1.63	64	32	2.00	45	20	2.25
$5,000 - 9,999	14	35	.40	29	47	.62	35	38	.92
$10,000 and over	3	11	.27	8	24	.33	21	42	.50
Median income	$2,514	$4,916	(.51)	$3,794	$6,857	(.55)	$5,590	$8,937	(.62)
Difference	$2,402			$3,063			$3,347		

MEDIAN INCOME BY EDUCATION

	1960 Black	White	B/W	1968 Black	White	B/W
Elementary:						
Less than 8 years	$1,900	$3,140	.61	$3,558	$5,131	.69
8 years	2,460	3,820	.64	4,499	6,452	.70
High School:						
1 to 3 years	2,640	4,420	.60	5,255	7,229	.73
4 years	3,020	5,060	.60	5,801	8,154	.71
College:						
1 or more years	4,390	8,608	.51	7,481	10,149	.74

Source: *The Social and Economic Status of Negroes in the United States, 1969;* Bureau of Labor Statistics Report #375.

activity. It is ironic, however, that blacks themselves look around and see a growing, rather than diminishing, gap between their collective economic plight and that of white America. This perception leads to the popular "relative-deprivation" analysis of the wave of ghetto riots during the mid-1960's. A Roberta Flack-Les McCann tune, *Compared to What?* sets the stage.

There are numerous statistics which point to the real economic gains of black Americans in the past two decades. But these gains must be measured in comparison to earlier levels of black economic achievement, levels beyond which minimal real advancement must inevitably take us far. It is against these yardsticks that many whites have measured black economic movement. But when one compares the economic level of blacks with that of whites (which many blacks do), a very different picture emerges. Promises, rising expectations—all of this is real but *compared to what?*

It is true that the income of black Americans increased from 1947 to 1968 by 122 percent (from $2514 to $5590). But compared to white family income, the relative increase is a mere 11 percent on the average (from 51 percent to 62 percent). At the higher SES levels, the income gap is closing more rapidly, but at the lower levels, it is in fact *widening*.

The data on family income in Table 4.10 show that, relative to whites, the percentage of blacks whose incomes exceed $10,000 has grown steadily since 1947. In that year there were about one-fourth (.27) as many blacks as whites earning more than $10,000. By 1960 this figure grew to one-third (.33), and by 1968 it had grown to one-half (.50). Thus at the higher income levels the gap between black and white income has been closing; still, twice as many whites are in this income bracket.

Similarly, there has been steady growth of the percentage of blacks in the middle-income range of $5000 to $10,000. The ratio of 1.00 would represent truly equal distribution, so racial equality is most closely approximated in the middle-income levels.

But now let's look at the lower-income groups. In 1947 there were 1.63 times as many blacks as white families earning under $5000. By 1960 low-income blacks had *increased* to 2.00 times the number of whites. And by 1968 black families had become 2.25 times as numerous as white families in the under $5000 category. Thus, among black people, the middle and upper-middle classes are getting more prosperous, while the lower classes are getting less prosperous. And perhaps most significantly, *this lower class for whom things are getting worse, represents 45 percent of the black population!*

It is true that black Americans have become increasingly educated— formally. In 1940 the median number of school years completed was 5.8. This figure rose to 6.9 in 1950, 8.2 in 1960, and 9.4 in 1967. Comparable figures for whites were 7.8 in 1940, 8.9 in 1950, 10.2 in 1960, 11.4 in 1967. The ratio of median school years completed for black and white has increased steadily from .67 in 1940 to .71 (1950), .75 (1960), and .78 (1967). However, there has been a constant two-year gap that has not closed during the past 27 years.

Table 4.10 tells us that in 1960 a black American with one or more years of college had an income ($4390) slightly lower than a white high-school graduate ($5060). Also, a black high-school graduate ($3020) earns less than a white elementary-school graduate ($3820). By 1968 these same inequities still exist.

Frustration and consequent anger and aggression displaced or directly focused on blacks, displaced or directly focused on white merchants in black ghettoes—these are symptomatic of psychological responses which are more general than the racial tension that they describe. The theory is compelling and correct in accounting for one aspect of the psychological problems of a mass society.

Another psychodynamic structural approach is the emphasis on personality development. This view says that prejudice is rooted in the personality structure of an individual. Thus individuals with a certain personality structure will be prejudiced. The major work of this sort was done originally by a Berkeley group headed by T. W. Adorno, resulting in the book *The Authoritarian Personality.* We have already reviewed this work and need not go into detail here. Prejudiced individuals are seen as more anxious, more close-minded, intolerant of ambiguities, in need of closure, rigid thinkers, dogmatic, and so on. There is support for this personality analysis, but the fact remains that many people exhibit these personality traits who do not show race prejudice. Similarly, people who do not fit well into the authoritarian model do show prejudice in a variety of ways. We should simply acknowledge that some types of personalities may be more likely to adopt an interracial orientation which fits a prejudice model, but that there are numerous factors which influence interracial relations beyond personality factors. As I suggested earlier, if the only problems we had were with avowed prejudiced persons, the racial problems would be considerably closer to solution.

Phenomenological Emphasis

This approach is concerned with the final cause of an individual's determination of how he will think about or act toward another. All previous generalizations (historical, sociocultural, and so on) are important to the extent that they affect a person's phenomenal representation of the present encounter between himself and the stimulus object. Generalizations are statements of probability. Consequently the correct analysis of any individual's motivation rests solely with a final phenomenal reality which instigates his behavior or influences his attitude. We cannot write a phenomenological theory of prejudice, we can only discuss individual phenomena and draw our own conclusions.

Stimulus Object Approach

Herein, we must acknowledge, lies the crux of the entire issue of race prejudice and race relations. From the white view, what are the *real* characteristics of blacks, and what implications do the whites have for appropriate attitudinal-behavioral stances toward them? From the black view the same question can be posed. At this time, answers seem to be moving people in different directions. Many blacks say whites are racist oppressors and the appropriate stances are hatred and separation, respectively. Whites seem to say they are different, perhaps, but worth getting to know and helping out. Of course this generalization needs qualification too. How many blacks and whites are actually represented by these stances is not known.

One of the principal aspects of prejudice is the assumption that what a person feels or thinks about another is in an important way wrong (usually an error toward the negative). It further assumes that this wrong judgment is maintained even though contradictory information is available. This view of prejudice avoids the crux of racial relations, specifically: (1) if there are *real* differences which serve as the basis for negative judgments, on what terms do these real differences justify the negative judgments? or (2) if the real differences place people at a disadvantage in this society, does the society change to cease punishing those who are different, or simply exclude or exploit them? These two issues are immediately raised by consideration of racism, but are largely ignored by traditional treatments of prejudice.

Let us conclude this analysis of prejudice with a brief, simple discussion. We have treated a large amount of data, and considered several theoretical orientations in this chapter. At times it seems as though we have thoroughly skirted the reality of growing from infant to adult in such a complex social environment as the United States. At other times, we have been slapped harshly in the face by the realities of these complexities. To close this chapter, let us regain our perspective on prejudice by what Fritz Heider (1958) calls the "naive analysis" of the various forces which shape what we want to call prejudiced attitudes and behaviors.

Naive Analysis of Prejudice

By "naive" we do not mean immature and ill-formed in a pejorative sense as the term is commonly used; rather, we mean it as a kind of perspective—a distance—from the rigors of scientific thought and research. This distance puts us closer to the phenomena of the world to which theory and research are ultimately addressed. To do this we must rely to a great extent on our own first hand experience, our own observations, hunches, and intuitive understanding.

A first point is that prejudice, either as an attitude or behavior, is not present in human beings at birth. Attitudes are learned orientations toward social phenomena, and require an extended period of socialization for their formation. Behaviors, in a broad sense, depend on physical maturity, the development of language, and elaboration of thought in order for a variety of behavioral alternatives to be engaged in by human beings. Thus racial attitudes and racial behaviors are both learned.

If we are to understand what prejudice is, we must understand in general how social attitudes and behaviors develop in children as they grow from infants to adults.

The racial judgments that children make are based in part on the straight transmission of judgments from adults, from older siblings, and from peers. For example, if a parent tells a child "Don't ever get close to a nigger because they carry disease," we have the direct transmission of a racial attitude. How much of a child's racial attitudes are created in this direct fashion is unknown. It certainly should be less now than in earlier periods of American history. The data on stereotyping which are presented in the previous two chapters suggest a change in the kinds of stereotypes that are drawn. Moreover, the generally more tolerant approaches to stereotyping and categorical judgments suggest that this form of attitude transmission is likely to have receded in importance (although it is still significant) in the development of racial attitudes in children.

Another form of learning racial attitudes is the direct observation of interracial events which cast the black person, or people, in a negative light. Obvious historical examples include slavery and a variety of forms of savage treatment meted out by white on black, including lynching, burning, and other forms of murder, as well as more general degradation and subjugation. Less savage, but no less instrumental in the development of racial attitudes, are the many subtle and not so subtle ways in which blacks are treated with low regard.

A third, and most subtle way in which racial attitudes are developed, derives from the automatic and largely unconscious way in which attitudes in general are learned. Learned attitudes are shaped by a hierarchy of values. This value orientation includes right versus wrong, better versus worse, moral versus immoral, good versus bad, and so on. A large portion of the upbringing of any child concentrates on the socialization of these value systems. As a child is learning these value orientations, he is continually trying out some of these valued assertions. Thus a child begins to learn that light is better than dark, tall is better than short, this street is better than that street, this house is better than that house, this man is better than that man, this color is better than that color, I am better than he. A child does not, therefore, have to be told in each instance which of two objects is better than the other, he merely needs to know that a comparative judgment can be made, and along what dimensions such comparative judgments should be made. It does not take a child long to know that big, white houses with rolling lawns are better than little teeny wooden shacks with garbage-strewn dirt yards. There soon follows the further inference that the people who live in the good, white houses are *better than* the people who live in the wooden shacks.

Even more subtly, it does not take a child long to know that a man wearing a white shirt and tie, sitting in a seat, reading a newspaper is *better than* a man who wears overalls and shines the white-shirt-and-tie-man's shoes. Along the dimensions of evaluation that are early socialized and in fact are pervasive in American society, it is very, very easy to make the value judgments corresponding to big white house over wooden shack, white collar vs. shoeshine boy or man. It also does not take long for a child to learn that there is a remarkably high correlation between white house, white collar, *white skin,* and between wooden shack, shoeshine boy, *black skin.* And the values appropriate to each are assigned very early in a child's life.

The question of prejudice, then, has been put in a reverse way. That is, the question should not center so much on what it is that produces the prejudiced persons, but rather, what it is that *keeps* some people from becoming prejudiced individuals. In the next chapter, the view that racial problems mainly concern race prejudice, as a deviation from basic idealistic norms of American democracy, has been reshaped and refocused toward the norm of racism, which more fully characterizes American society. The focus on prejudice as a *deviation* from egalitarian norms has obscured the more general and more basic level of analysis—the racism inherent in the *entire* social structure and social mind of America.

CHAPTER FIVE

Realities of Racism

Do you know what they call a black Ph.D.? NIGGER!
Malcolm X

In a small New England town I overheard the following exchange. It was two days before the funeral of Robert Kennedy, and a group of high-school kids were talking at the corner drugstore by the Green.

> Boy: "Do we get outa school for this here death?"
>
> Someone: "I don't know."
>
> Boy: "If we got off for the nigger (referring to Martin Luther King) we oughta get off for Kennedy."

We go back to the Kerner Commission Report and find that "*white racism* is essentially responsible for the explosive mixture which has been accumulating in our cities since the end of World War II." For many, this conclusion was a milestone. The Chicago Commission in 1922, the report on the Harlem riots in 1935, and the report of the Civil Rights Commission in 1946 all described the unhealthy conditions of race relations in urban areas, but for the first time, the Kerner Commission introduced *to white America* the concept of white racism.

But what is white racism? What does it mean in relation to race prejudice? Why does the Kerner Commission return to the worn theme of black pathology and the black ghettos? Why does the Commission talk about the weak family structure and social disorganization of the black community? Why does it not elaborate on what white racism IS instead of what it presumably CAUSES?

In this chapter, we will discuss these questions. We will attempt to fill in some of the gaps left by the Commission analysis. In addition, we will go beyond the overt, traditional forms of racial tensions to consider some of the more subtle causes, manifestations, and consequences of racism. Racism is a ubiquitous, cancerous phenomenon that lurks in every cranny of American society and shadows so transparently the minds of all Americans. We will not be able to understand it fully in the few pages that follow, but perhaps we will be able to illuminate some of the realities of racism.

In Chapter One, three kinds of racism were defined; individual, institutional and cultural. The remainder of this chapter elaborates these definitions by analysis and example. In Chapter Four, theories of prejudice were reviewed within the telescoping model of Allport (1954). Beginning with the most general approach—historical-cultural—the model focused in on the object of prejudice. While the Allport prejudice model moves from generality to specificity, our approach to racism will be in reverse—specificity to generality.

Whereas the final *object* of Allport's prejudice analysis is the psychology of interpersonal race relations, the final object of the following racism analysis will be the whole American culture. The difference between the prejudice and racism analyses is more than simply the order of presentation of arguments. Ultimately it is a difference in what phenomena are being explained, and what causal antecedents are attributed to them.

When you look through the wider aperture of a telescope, the objects appear smaller and farther away. When you look through the narrower aperture, objects appear larger and closer. Metaphorically the prejudice analysis, looking through the wider aperture as it does, miniaturizes the problem. The following racism analysis attempts to *de*miniaturize the problem.

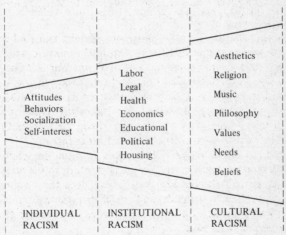

Fig. 5.1. Through a telescope *widely*—a model for the analysis of racism.

We will begin with *individual racism* because that concept contains the greatest overlap with theories of race prejudice. Confusion is expressed about the difference between race prejudice and racism. The confusion stems from the too-narrow view that is often taken of racism. Determining whether an *individual* is prejudiced or racist is a moot point in most cases. If one's understanding of racism does not go beyond the individual case, the two concepts would be interchangeable. However, expanding our view of racism reveals additional dimensions of race relations, and the overlap between race prejudice and racism diminishes.

The first expansion came from Carmichael and Hamilton (1967) who spoke of *institutional racism.* This concept is rather removed from the notions of attitudes and attitude change which characterized much of the prejudice literature. Moreover, the evidence needed for the determination of institutional racism is considerably more objective. Whereas the prejudice analysis requires value judgments, personal histories, inferences about subjective states, and the tenuous application of normative judgments, the determination of institutional racism can be very simple. One need only look for gross racial inequities in the outcomes of institutional operations to level charges of institutional racism.* Even so, for many people the racial inequities are often attributed merely to *discrimination* and hence are seen as the behavioral consequences of prejudice. Introducing the concept of institutional racism diminishes the overlap between racism and prejudice, but not completely.

The final expansion comes from the term *cultural racism.* This term encompasses both the individuals and institutions in the society. This analysis focuses on those cultural values which underlie the formation of racist institutions, and examines the values, traditions, and assumptions upon which institutions are formed and within which individuals are socialized to maturity. Since institutions reinforce and perpetuate individual racism, and since these individual values, in turn, feed back into the cultural character, the concept of cultural racism completes the chain. The culture creates or determines the nature of its institutions; the institutions socialize individuals, and individuals perpetuate the cultural character. Racism exists at each of these levels.

RACISM DEFINED

Charges of racism have flown fast and furiously in recent years, yet few people have a clear understanding of what a race is. Physical anthropologists do not agree about the number of "races" comprising the species *homo sapiens.* More enlightened ones among them have even given up trying to make careful racial distinctions. Nevertheless we must put the concept of race in some perspective if we are to make a serious attempt to analyze it here.

*Professor Thomas Pettigrew recently leveled an "institutional racism" charge at Harvard University administrators for their handling of scholarship money for black graduate students. The administrators were quite angered, probably because they knew (or felt) their *intentions* were not racist. However, the *consequences* of their policy were racist; hence Pettigrew's charge.

Recall the definition of racism proposed by van den Berghe (1967) and cited in Chapter One, which required simply a *belief* in racial inferiority. This approach makes racism very similar to race prejudice and much of the discussion of Chapter Four would be relevant here.

Furthermore, recall that van den Berghe's definition was based on the view that *race* refers to a group that is *socially* defined on the basis of *physical* criteria. A similar concept, often confused with race, is *ethnic* group which too is *socially* defined, but on the basis of *cultural* criteria. Because cultural differences often (usually) accompany physical differences, there is a strong tendency to lump physical and cultural differences under the term "race." Stated simply, preferences for (or belief in the superiority of) one's own *racial* group might be called *racism;* while preference for (or belief in the superiority of) one's own *ethnic* group might be called *ethnocentrism.* Both of these terms are frequently used.

However, racism defined as a set of beliefs or attitudes represents little advance over the concept of race prejudice. Consequently our definition of racism will go beyond belief or attitudes to include *actions.* The significant factor of ingroup preference, whether racially or ethnically based, is the POWER that the ingroup has over an outgroup.

Power is always defined in action terms. *Webster's Third New International Dictionary* defines power as

> possession of control, authority, or influence over others; . . .
> ability to act or produce an effect; . . . physical might . . .

Power is what concerns us in the definition of racism. Race prejudice is an attitude which contributes to practice of racism. Ethnocentrism is also an attitude which contributes to the practice of racism. Both race prejudice and ethnocentrism are attitudes which are building blocks for the exercise of racism. Therefore racism will be broadly defined as follows:

> Racism results from the transformation of race prejudice and/or ethnocentrism through the exercise of power against a racial group defined as inferior, by individuals and institutions with the intentional or unintentional support of the entire culture.

In American society, oppressed racial groups have separate ethnic identities. By the above definitions, black people are oppressed for reasons of both race and culture. We have had to define racism quite broadly to include both of these sources. Therefore to understand racism in America is to understand more than the simple facts of slavery, segregation, discrimination, and prejudice. To understand racism is also to understand differences in cultural heritage, the categorical suppression of the subordinate culture as well as the imposition of the dominant culture's values on members of minority cultures. When we understand this, we understand what Charles Silberman came to understand as the *Crisis in Black and White:*

... that the United States—all of it, North as well as South, West as well as East—is a racist society in a sense and to a degree that we have refused so far to admit, much less face .... (Silberman, 1964, p. 9)

INDIVIDUAL RACISM

A racist individual is one who considers that black people as a group are inferior to whites because of physical (genotypical and phenotypical) traits. He further believes that these physical traits are determinants of social behavior and moral or intellectual qualities, and ultimately presumes that this inferiority is a legitimate basis for inferior social treatment of black people in American society. A very important consideration is that all judgments of superiority are based on the corresponding traits of white people as norms of comparison.

Black people in America also represent a major ethnic group. Cultural forms and expressions of black people are also seen as inferior by white racists. Again, the determination of inferiority is based on the white cultural standards for comparison. The connection between culture and race is often made by the white racist, hence assumptions of cultural inferiority often co-occur with assumptions of racial inferiority. Both are characteristic of a racist individual.

A far more subtle form of racism concerns the analysis and interpretation of black culture. This individual correctly perceives cultural differences between blacks and whites, but evaluates the white expressions positively and the black expressions negatively. The negative evaluation of black culture is almost always based on either (a) the assumed unsuccessful attempt to copy or reproduce white culture forms, or (b) the pathological reactions to an oppressive status in American society. Congruent with these evaluations, all racially distinctive black expressions are assumed to be *lower-class* expressions.

It is important to understand that *all* reactions to oppression are not pathological. In fact it is undeniable that a certain collective strength must accompany group survival under conditions of severe oppression. However, the issue of racism raised here concerns the single-minded focus on the negative adaptations to the exclusion of the positive ones.

This view does not accord any legitimate, positive, distinctive cultural expression to middle- and upper-class black people. These blacks are assumed to be just like whites in every detail. This view produces statements like the following from van den Berghe:

Beyond the specific stigma of skin pigmentation and its numerous social and psychological consequences, Negro Americans have virtually nothing more in common than they do with any other Americans; and stigmatization itself, of course, is far from being a Negro monopoly. (1967, p. 94)

To think that a race can come from a cultural background as different as Africa's was from England's, spend 250 years oppressed by slavery and another 100 years oppressed by sheer oppression, can live among each other almost exclusively, sharing cultural background and interpreting the American experience through common pains and visions and yet conclude that because black people drive the same cars over the same highways, watch the same TV shows, and vote for the same presidents they have nothing more in common than they do with other Americans is naivete of astounding proportions! As we shall see in a later section, "They's mo to bein' black than meets the eye."

Because all major conciliatory efforts in this country have been toward drawing races together, the major stress has been on racial

STANLEY by Murray Ball

Continuing the adventures of The Great Palaeolithic Hero

Fig. 5.2. White over black? Compared to what? (Reproduced by permission, © 1970 *Punch*, London.)

similarities. But if there is no recognition of any positive contributions of black culture to the ultimate coming together of the races, then all of the giving will be black, all the taking will be white, and racism will continue to be the tie that binds.

There are many varieties of individual racists, but common to them all is a belief in the inferiority of black people (physically, morally, intellectually, culturally, and so on); and the uncompromising, unalterable use of white norms with the unquestioned assumption of their superior quality. Although an individual does not MAKE norms, he internalizes, supports, and uses them. Thus identifying people as racist involves determining the degree to which they are willing to ascribe inferiority to racial characteristics of black people on the basis of white norms.* But as the cartoon of Fig. 5.2 suggests, *it's all relative!*

A person does not have to believe that blacks are inferior in each of the ways mentioned above in order to be called a racist. For example, the most extreme form of individual racism might be someone who believed in the natural inferiority of blacks by physical criteria; that these physical differences were determinants of basic differences in intelligence, morality, and so on; that these differences produced an inferior culture; and finally, that the inferior characteristics were a legitimate basis for special, unequal treatment in American society. An individual *need not* be so thorough in his racism, however.

Thomas Jefferson believed in the innate inferiority of black people. He was a racist. Nevertheless, Jefferson's staunch advocacy of the doctrine of "natural rights" led him to propose that even though black people were inferior, the natural rights of man included them and therefore necessitated the abolition of slavery. However, in order to gain support for the creation of the Republic, Jefferson was obliged to compromise with Southern slavery interests and delete the antislavery plank from the Declaration of Independence. This deletion paved the way for the famous "American Dilemma," the contradiction between the notions of the rights of man and the facts of slavery. "We hold these truths to be self-evident, that all men are created equal, and endowed by their creator with certain inalienable rights among which are life, liberty and the pursuit of happiness."

Not only was Abraham Lincoln convinced of the innate inferiority of black people, but he felt that equality was never attainable as long as black and white lived in the same society—the superior whites would always control the inferior blacks. He too was a racist. It was this racist belief that led Lincoln to propose until the end of his life the colonization of black people—either in this country or abroad—as the only solution to the race

---

*A non-racist person would be one who was a true relativist in matters of race. Understanding that people are alike in some ways and different in others, a non-racist would not use those differences as a basis for inferior treatment of others, or the privileged treatment of his own group.

problem. It is perhaps ironic, as well as symbolic of the nature of this society, that such a man is claimed as one of the greatest white friends the American black people have ever had.*

Individual Racism–Comparative Modus Operandi: Dominative and Aversive Cases

Chapter One proposed that one of the important points of history was regional variation in patterns of race relations. In the beginning, racial attitudes did not differ in the North and the South. But as the patterns of behavioral relations diverged, the forms of racist expression and feeling similarly diverged. Slavery became institutionalized in the South, while the North traded in black bodies. As a consequence, regional differences in black-white relations have persisted throughout American history.

Most common understandings of racism have been overly influenced by the aggressive, overt, bigoted expressions which have typically characterized the Southern form. Slavery was the first and most robust expression of racism, but through the years the burnings, lynchings, Jim-Crow legislation, and violent reaction to attempts at racial integration have established the South as the *most visible home* of racism in America.

Implicit in this analysis is the view that there are more individual racists in the South than in the North, and the differences therefore are matters of the *degree* of racism rather than the kind. I would like now to propose that the differences are *not* of *degree* but of *kind.*

If a white man makes a black man ride at the back of a bus, he is a racist. If a white man chooses to stand rather than sit next to a black man on a bus, he too is racist. These are two different kinds of racism. In his book *White Racism,* Joel Kovel defines these two types of racism as *dominative* and *aversive,* respectively:

> [The dominative racist is] the type who acts out bigoted beliefs . . . he represents the open flame of race hatred. The true white bigot expresses a definitive ambition through all his activity: he openly seeks to keep the black man down, and he is willing to use force to further his ends.

> The aversive racist is the type who believes in white race superiority and is more or less aware of it but does nothing overt about it. He tries to ignore the existence of black people, tries to avoid contact with them, and, at most, tries to be polite, correct and cold in whatever dealings are necessary between the races. (Kovel, 1970, p. 54)

---

*I should mention that in spite of the obvious negative characteristics I've pointed out, of American presidents Jefferson and Lincoln are among the most sympathetic to the plight of black people in this country. I have emphasized the negative aspects to show just how unfavorable the position of black people in this country has been.

Of course by suggesting that the aversive mode characterizes the North and the dominative mode characterizes the South, I do not mean to make strict categorical distinctions. Just as some Northerners express their racism in dominative form, some Southerners express their racism in aversive form. However, there are decided differences in the language and behavior of Northerners and Southerners. The important point is that the differences do not reflect intensity of racist feelings so much as they do modes of racist expression.

Recall some of the historical figures mentioned previously. Dominative racists would include Tom Brady, or the man who slit open the stomach of the just-lynched pregnant black woman, or any member of the numerous white mobs that roamed through and plundered black communities.

The aversive racists have of course been rather subtly hidden by our history. But that astute observer Alexis de Tocqueville sniffed them out. He noted in his travels through America in 1791, "The prejudice of race appears to be stronger in the states that have abolished slavery than in those where it still exists; and nowhere is it so intolerant as in those states where servitude has never been known . . ." (*Democracy in America*, Vol. 1, p. 373).*

Woodrow Wilson's actions characterized the aversive racist. In 1912 he stated that he wished to see "justice done to the colored people in every matter; and not mere grudging justice, but justice executed with liberality and cordial good feeling."† Yet it was Woodrow Wilson who issued an executive order which racially segregated the eating and toilet facilities of federal civil-service workers. Moreover, he gave Southern federal officials the right to downgrade or discharge without due process any black employee on any ground they saw fit. His segregation order might be seen as aversive, while his discharge order is more directly dominative.

To a greater extent the dominative racist bases his arguments on physical criteria. His racism is predicated on innate inferiority of blacks, and to him that justifies almost any action he would take toward blacks. Kovel suggests that dominative racism is a more primitive form. The attitudes and behaviors sanctioned by the sociocultural ethos primarily of the North produced a pattern of race relations which required suppression of more overtly hostile actions. At moments of stress and racial tension, however, the aversive racist "regresses" to more dominative forms. This regression in the 1960's was termed "white backlash." Earlier examples were the draft riots in New York City (1863), white riots in New York

---

*In this connection it is interesting to note the recent statistics on the desegregation of public schools which show that over the last two years, Southern schools have become more racially integrated than Northern schools. In many Northern schools segregation is actually increasing.

†Quoted in Kovel, 1970, p. 31.

(1900), Springfield, Illinois (1908), East St. Louis (1917), and the so-called "Red Summer" of 1919.

The aversive racist, on the other hand, to a greater extent invokes cultural criteria for his brand of racism. The aversive racist wants to keep blacks from moving into his neighborhood not because he doesn't like blacks, but because "property values will go down." And why will property values go down? "Because they won't take care of it; they'll have loud parties; they will not maintain the 'standards' of the neighborhood." The principal standard of the neighborhood is that it is white.

One by one the dominative forms of racist expression are being eliminated or diminished in American society; first slavery, then lynchings, burnings, bombings, cattle prods, and so on. The heat and bitterness of the dominative racist characterized race relations in America for many, many years. When I traveled in Europe in 1963, everyone wanted to know about the fight between the blacks and the whites, the "racial wars" in the South. I was in Europe around the time of the church-bombings that killed four little girls in Birmingham, the slaying of Medgar Evers, and the march on Washington. The eyes of the world were riveted on the South. But the following year New York, Philadelphia, and Rochester exploded. Focus turned to teeming Northern ghettos; the world had finally caught up with the aversive racists, and de Tocqueville smiled in his grave. As the passion of the dominative racist slowly dies out, the passionless coldness of the aversive racist sets in.

Since 1965 much research has attempted to discover why black Americans are angry, why they are upset, why they have increasingly resorted to ideas of racial separation. Black Americans have been constantly trying to understand the mind of the aversive racist. Black Americans have always known and understood the dominative racist; he has been "up front." The aversive racist has lurked in the woodwork, has spoken words of conciliation, of equality, of sympathy, but for many, many years the consequences of being black in America have not improved significantly. Let us look more closely at the aversive racist and see if we can understand what he is about.

Aversive racists do not want to associate with blacks, although they do not often express this feeling. They make claims of equality and liberal or open goodwill, but stand staunchly behind the institutions they create to ensure that their goodwill is never challenged. When black people began to move into Harlem in the late 1890's, whites tried desperately to stop them by forming realty companies. They finally resorted to the ultimate control—money. Banks stopped renewing mortgages and ceased giving new ones to blacks. This practice has long been in effect and continues to maintain racial separation. It should be pointed out that it is not *banks* that adopted the policy but *individuals,* racist individuals who had an aversion to living with black people.

All racists believe in the superiority of white over black. They differ in the relative degree to which physical versus cultural criteria are important to that superiority and, correspondingly, in the kinds of actions which these beliefs sanction. As irrefutable scientific evidence has been accumulated, it has become more difficult to uphold direct physical arguments for racial differences. Racism in America has moved from a dominative to an aversive orientation.

Individuals are not born racists. The fact that racism has existed for so long in this country prompts some to suggest that it is an *inherited* characteristic of white people. For a given individual, racism is a state of mind, a set of values, and a constellation of behaviors. If racism has been perpetuated in this society for the past 350 years, it is because the same states of mind, set of values, and constellation of behaviors have been handed down (transmitted) from generation to generation in white America. These characteristics of white individuals are inherited, but not genetically. They are inherited as a natural consequence of being socialized into a culture that from the beginning has been based on the assumption of white superiority over black. Each new generation of white Americans has been socialized to that state of affairs. Let us take a brief look at that socialization process from the perspective of social psychology.

Individual Racism through Socialization

If one takes a developmental perspective, socialization may be regarded as the core of social psychology. (Clausen, 1968, p. 3)

That statement places socialization squarely within social psychology. The following statement places the socialized child squarely within the society, defining socialization as

. . . the process by which someone learns the ways of a given society or social group well enough so that he can function within it. (Elkin, 1960, p. 4)

These orientations suggest that learning to function well in society is a major result of socialization. Since we have suggested that our society can be broadly classified as racist, does this mean that to learn how to function well in this society is to learn how to be a racist? To the extent that this is and has been true, the problem of individual racism is a problem of socialization.

There are two views of the socialization process. The first, the *active* view, stresses the important role the child plays in his own socialization development. The temperament, character, and ability of the child will have an important effect on the course socialization will take. The second, or *passive* view, stresses the process whereby a child is molded to the social requirements of his environment. This approach assigns no responsibility to the child, rather it envisions a kind of cultural determinism, shaping the child totally.

If socialization is critically responsible for the development of individual racism, then the matter of which view predominates in a particular case will have important implications for the extent to which racist attitudes and behaviors are likely to characterize a child's life.

One important social psychological concept for the analysis of *active* socialization is the notion of *social comparison processes* developed by Leon Festinger in 1954. Stated very simply, the idea is that people have a need to evaluate themselves, and to do this they compare themselves to others. The basis for this comparison is primarily the similarity of the other persons with whom the comparison is made. The more similar they are to you, the more appropriate and hence informative the comparison will be.

Active flexibility is generated by the selection of criteria for determining similarity. For example, if a woman wanted to judge her beauty, she could compare herself to *any* other women (similarity of sex), to women in her particular social set (similarity of status), or to women in her old high-school graduating class (similarity of age), and so on. The salience of the situations and the reasons for making the judgments will have important implications for which similarity criteria are employed.

The crucial point of these examples is the active role a person can play in the outcomes of his self- and other-evaluations. This active role has been captured most dramatically in subsequent theoretical and empirical writings by Festinger in *A Theory of Cognitive Dissonance* (1957). This theory suggests that when an individual is confronted with two mutually inconsistent cognitions (thoughts, ideas, beliefs, attitudes), there exists pressure to reduce that inconsistency. The state of inconsistency is termed *cognitive dissonance* and the pressure to change may result in *dissonance reduction.* The reduction of cognitive dissonance is also an active process. Thus social comparison and dissonance reduction processes provide one theoretical structure for the analysis of active socialization.

The passive socialization model is quite simple. With respect to development of racist attitudes, if a child were socialized in a strongly racist environment where all relevant socializing agents (family, peers, neighborhood adults and authorities) instilled racist beliefs, we could simply note that the child was a product of his environment. Further, it would seem that the passive model would be more appropriate to segregated environments where active cross-racial interactions were minimal or of a sort consistent with the socializing dogma.

In a sense, the passive view does not require real comparison; hence the racist judgments tend to be anchorless and unstable. When whites from segregated environments and passive-racist socializing influence encounter blacks in nonstereotypic situations, often one sees the most dramatic reversals of racist beliefs and actions.

The passive model fits most appropriately in a large-scaled analysis of racism which would treat substantial sociological categories rather than individuals. This treatment, then, would attribute the racism of an individual to the socializing influences of his socioeconomic-ethnic stratification.

However, all children from apparently similar backgrounds do not develop the same attitudes and behaviors. Some come from liberal environments and express quite racist feelings. Others come from quite racist backgrounds and express genuinely egalitarian feelings. Why these discrepancies? The answer must lie somewhere in the active role taken by the child in his own socialization.

The value of white over black implies a comparative judgment. Since this value has characterized this society from its inception, the critical question might be, *what keeps a child from becoming racist?* Or, what factors produce individual differences in the degree of racist sentiment and expression? One factor, one discussed here, is the active role played by the child in his own socialization.

When social comparisons are made, social standards must be employed. When a white child compares himself to a black child, his social referent is of course his own white culture. The child is created in his culture's image, and it, in turn, is reflected in the child's eyes. When the child begins learning about himself, he makes comparisons—social comparisons. He finds that he has a big house while his black age-mates have small ones. He has bright new clothes yet his black age-mates have shabby hand-me-downs. He finds that his teacher calls his black age-mates stupid, incapable of learning, disadvantaged. He finds that his black age-mates talk loudly, play roughly, and think school is a bore. He sees that he gets A's and B's; his black age-mates get D's and F's. He keeps a mental record of all of his comparisons. He counts up the score and concludes that he is superior to his black age-mates. He concludes further that his father is superior to his black age-mates' fathers, that his mother is superior to his black age-mates' mothers: that white is superior to black. This child has become a racist.

Suppose that the main reason black people were disliked was their skin color. It could be argued that skin color is not an acceptable criterion for dislike. If that happens to be the real reason, a state of cognitive dissonance could exist. The active dissonance reduction process might follow the lines of recruiting cognitions consistent with disliking blacks but unrelated to skin color, Thus notions of genetic inferiority in intelligence, morals, and low motivation for achievement might be generalized judgments which attempt to rationalize simple race hatred predicated on skin color.*

---

*This analysis was suggested in an undergraduate paper at Harvard University by Francis Barron. His essay was provocative and although there do not exist experimental data to support this theoretical surmise, it seems worthy of experimental attention.

Of considerable importance in the socialization of racial sentiments and expressions is the family. Socialization always involves self and others. Family members are usually among the most significant others. Parents, too, take active or passive roles in the racial socialization of their children. Furthermore, their active role can be positive or negative. In one family parents might actively teach their children to hate blacks; in another, not to hate blacks.*

The socialization process, then, is quite complex. The principal factors influencing the socialization of racism are (1) the extent and character of the personal involvement of a child in his own socialization, (2) the opportunity for and nature of interracial contact during formative socialization periods, and (3) the extent and character of the parents' involvement in the child's racial socialization. If you examine your own backgrounds, you might find some clues to your own racial sentiments and expressions. You might be able to locate the socialization influences on your own racial awareness and identity.

Racism and Race Prejudice Compared

Individual racism and race prejudice have a great deal in common. Race prejudice has been analyzed as negative racial attitudes held in disregard of facts which contradict them. If a racial attitude is based on physical inferiority, there are plenty of "facts" to contradict negative attitudes. Individuals who put all blacks together into one category (presumably on the basis of physical characteristics), and adopt a negative attitude toward them all, are considered to demonstrate race prejudice. This kind of analysis applies primarily to what we have been describing as the dominative racist.

The analysis of race prejudice has always had to use overt *behavior* as a starting point. That criterion has placed undue emphasis on the dominative type because he is the type who *behaves* or acts-out his feelings most visibly. Since the dominative expression of race hatred is primal and emerges under situations of stress, it has also been possible to include less dominative individuals in a race-prejudice analysis. But the true aversive racist has not been flushed out by the prejudice analysis.

Few people would call someone who commented that a talented black individual is "a credit to his race" a prejudiced person. Yet most black people consider that comment insulting rather than complimentary, and view its speaker as a racist. The comment seems to be based on the assumption that the talented person is *unusual* among his race—unusual in the sense that he is talented. Many subtleties of racial expression which the prejudice analysis does not uncover are primarily associated with what we have called the aversive racist.

---

*It is probably quite rare that white children are taught to *love* blacks, although some do arrive at this orientation.

Race prejudice, as traditionally analyzed, coincides roughly with the dominative-racist type, or with the aversive racist who behaves "regressively." Race prejudice is an individualistic orientation in that it emphasizes attitudes and judgments, and relies on behavior for evidence of its applicability. Individual racism and race prejudice are quite similar in these regards.

To the extent that racism is considered to be synonymous with what we have called individual racism, most observers would make little distinction between the two. To hold to the prejudice analysis, though, is to preclude the analysis of many important institutional and cultural phenomena that are integral parts of racial conflict. Carmichael and Hamilton (1967) and the Kerner Commission saw the need to go beyond the individual analysis and spoke of institutional racism. Here we will go beyond the institutional analysis to touch on *cultural* racism. It is important to understand that by using different terms we are not talking about different problems, we are merely distinguishing different aspects of the same problem—the problem of the color line.

Individual Racism—Conclusion

Individual racism abounds in this society. In more emotional overstatements of the case, all white individuals are considered racists of varying degrees. This section has attempted to broaden the scope of individual racism and to place in perspective its relation to race prejudice, while avoiding the emotional racist charges that fan the flames of conflict without advancing our understanding of the problem.

Racism infects individuals in many different ways. The most important determinant of whether and/or how an individual becomes a racist is the environmental norm to which he is socialized. If there is a norm of hating blacks, then a child is likely to grow up doing so. If there is a norm of feeling blacks are inferior but a counsel of polite avoidance, a child is likely to become an aversive racist. Most subtle is the ethnocentric norm which is not avowedly racial but which, when applied to blacks, produces unchallenged feelings of white superiority. This child is neither aversive nor dominative, but bases his judgments of black people solely on norms which greatly restrict the range of black people with whom any association at all is desirable.

Individuals who contribute to the perpetuation of another person's racist practices or beliefs might also be considered part of the racism problem. When a white person rents property from a white racist he is contributing to both individual and institutional racism. When a white person listens to uninformed racist slander without rebuttal, he is contributing to individual racism.

We have examined many forms of individual racist expression. We must conclude that individual racism is more widespread than many analyses have acknowledged. We must also conclude that many people who benefit from the wealth and opportunity this country offers also contribute to the perpetuation of racism. To understand the broader pressures that are exerted on each of us, we must turn now to the racism of institutions.

INSTITUTIONAL RACISM

... it is our thesis that institutional racism is deeply embedded in American society. (Knowles and Prewitt, 1969, p. 6)

The plot thickens and the indictments become more general. American institutions are racist. We have understood this for a long time, but the significance of this fact has somehow eluded our understanding of current forms of racial conflict. Everyone knows that the "Peculiar Institution" was the earliest and most blatant form of institutional racism. Everyone also knows that the "American Dilemma" suggested by the contradiction inherent in the American Creed was not a dilemma to all, as the Federalist Paper No. 54 so rationally pointed out:

... we must deny the fact, that slaves are considered merely as property, and in no respect whatever as persons. The true state of the case is, that they partake of both these qualities: being considered by our laws, in some respects, as persons, and in other respects as property. In being compelled to labor, not for himself, but for a master; in being vendible by one master to another master; and in being subject at all times to be restrained in his liberty and chastised in his body, by the capricious will of another,—the slave may appear to be degraded from the human rank, and classed with those irrational animals which fall under the legal denomination of property. In being protected on the other hand, in his life and in his limbs, against the violence of all others, even the master of his labor and his liberty; and in being punishable himself for all violence committed against others,—the slave is no less evidently regarded by the law as a member of the society, not as a part of the irrational creation; as a moral person, not as a mere article of property. The federal Constitution, therefore, decides with great propriety on the case of our slaves, when it views them in the mixed character of persons and of property. This is in fact their true character. It is the character bestowed on them by the laws under which they live; and it will not be denied, that these are the proper criterion; because it is only under the pretext that the laws have transformed the negroes into subjects of property, that a place is disputed them in the computation of numbers; and it is admitted, that if the laws were to restore the rights which have been taken away, the negroes could no longer be refused an equal share of representation with the other inhabitants .... Let the case of the slaves be considered as it is in truth, a peculiar one. Let the compromising expedient of the Constitution be mutually adopted, which regards them as inhabitants, but as debased by servitude below the equal level of free inhabitants; which regards the *slave* as divested of two fifths of the *man.**

As American institutions proliferated from these basic racist beginnings we can discern the widespread practices of institutional racism.

Yet it has taken Watts, New York, Chicago, Detroit, Rochester, Philadelphia, Washington, D.C., and other riots to bring the point home. That racist shadow was revealed by those violent acts. The Kerner Commission opened its eyes and acknowledged:

> What white Americans have never fully understood—but what the Negro can never forget—that white society is deeply implicated in the ghetto. White institutions created it, white institutions maintain it, and white society condones it. (p. 2)

Institutions are created by people—white people. White people are racists in different ways, as we suggested in the last section. White institutions are racist in different ways also. Those white racists who correspond to the dominative types could be expected to create and perpetuate institutions whose racism corresponds to the overt character of the dominative racist. Those white racists who correspond to the aversive types could be expected to create and perpetuate institutions whose racism corresponds to the covert character of this racist type.

Recall the reaction of the whites in Harlem when blacks began moving in. Their brand of institutional racist control was to prevent the equal application of institutional policies to black people—an aversive reaction which creates what we now call *de facto* segregation. The dominative racist would simply make it against the law to make mortgages to blacks or, further, to sell property to blacks if they could get the money elsewhere. This pattern created what we now call *de jure* segregation. Institutions support both patterns of racism, and both institutional patterns are extensions of individual racism.

There exist other patterns of institutional racism that are not direct extensions of conscious racist decisions and acts. Institutional racism also exists when the norms of an institution are predicated on assumptions of racial equality that are not met in the society. The application of the institutions' policies and procedures produce racist consequences. For example, it is well known that one has the legal right of a trial by a jury of peers. It is also well known that rarely do black people or other ethnic minorities from culturally different backgrounds get such trials. The American judicial system is based on an assumption of cultural and racial homogeneity. It is only in relatively recent years that black people have even been included in the judicial process. The legal system in America has numerous inherent inequities in it. Racism is one of the most noticeable ones.

---

*From *The Federalist* (No. 54), written by Alexander Hamilton, John Jay, and James Madison. It was first published in book form in 1788. The above quotes were taken from the Modern Library edition, with an introduction by Edward Mead Earle.

Another example would be the use of standardized test scores as criteria for admission to colleges, graduate and law schools, to job openings, and so on. First of all, the tests tend to be culturally biased against blacks and other Third World minorities. Secondly, racism in economics, real estate, and elementary and secondary education make these tests often unrepresentative and poor predictors for black people. Consequently, to use test scores as a basis of exclusion (or admission, depending on your perspective) is a racist practice.

It is only in recent years that this has been understood in racism terms, and some institutions are trying to make corrections. However, there are so many "qualifications" imposed on movement up the education, labor, and business ladders that, on balance, it is unlikely that recognition of the racism in standardized test criteria makes a big dent in institutional-racist practices.

Institutional racism can be defined as those established laws, customs, and practices which systematically reflect and produce racial inequities in American society. If racist consequences accrue to institutional laws, customs, or practices, the institution is racist *whether or not the individuals maintaining those practices have racist intentions.*

Institutional racism can be either overt or covert (corresponding to *de jure* and *de facto,* respectively) and either intentional or unintentional. Both overt and covert forms of racism are intentional, usually. Unintentional forms of racism often occur when the complex interrelations among institutions in this society conspire to make the long-range effects of one institutional practice negative for black people. These consequences may be both unforeseen and undesirable by the responsible institution.

For example, recently in Massachusetts a racial-imbalance law has been enacted which demands that school systems be racially balanced or lose state financial support. It further prohibits building new schools that are to be attended by a substantial majority of one race. The purpose of the law was to promote racial integration in the public schools and thereby ensure better educational opportunities for black children. One of the consequences, however, has been that city administrators have used the law to stall on the building of new schools in black communities. Thus already-overcrowded classrooms in black communities become even more overcrowded, and educational opportunities become even fewer. Whether administrators are simply using the law or the law is using them, black children are getting increasingly inferior education as a result.

Let us now look at the major institutions in America and see what forms racism takes. Following Table 5.1 we will consider the problems of institutional racism within the major institutional categories of economics, education, and justice.*

---

*This is not meant to be an exhaustive review and analysis of all aspects of institutional racism in America. Rather it is meant to provide some flavor of the simple and subtle forms of institutional racism, as well as its depth. For a more detailed treatment, see Knowles and Prewitt (1969).

Institutional Racism—Economics

The American economic system is still considered a free enterprise system. It is "free" in that anyone who can raise sufficient capital can engage in entrepreneurial business enterprise. Through such enterprises American white men are the most wealthy in the world. Free enterprise has always been held before Americans as the ideal economics, the free system, the principal ideal in this land of opportunity—an ideal which hundreds of thousands of Europeans immigrated to America to realize.

Free enterprise without social responsibility was the first active component of racism in the history of America. The slave trade began as "enterprising" young commercial seekers left England to explore new lands, waters, and ways of making money. The first stage of slavery was the commercial trade in black bodies that was carried out during the latter half of the 16th century. You will recall that the Wall Street Market first engaged in the trade of black bodies. Largely in the name of free enterprise did many of the institutionalized forms of racism begin.

An economic corollary of free enterprise is private property. Those individuals who are successful as entrepreneurs also control the land. Perhaps the *sine qua non* of success in American society is the ownership of land or property. One need only ride through Newport, Rhode Island, and see the "summer" homes of the Vanderbilts and others to see the incredible opulence that land ownership suggests. One can drive the entire length of the Eastern seaboard and find precious few stretches of public beach. Most of the choice seaside land is well ensconced in the hands of private-property-no-trespassing-owners. Since black people have never been admitted in any numbers into the free enterprise system—at least not on the *enterprising* end—it follows that private property has never been a viable means for integration of blacks into the American economic system.

But things really hang together in this society, and if you miss out at the first levels of economic viability, you find yourself slipping further and further behind at every succeeding level. Having missed out on the enterprise system, blacks missed out on property. By not having property, blacks miss out on all of the advantages property ownership can provide. For example, when one owns his home the mortgage payments include a large percentage of interest. That interest can be deducted from taxable income. The net effect is that monthly mortgage payments in addition to creating equity in the home also diminish Federal Income Tax payments. Paying the same monthly amount for rental property has neither equity nor tax advantage. In addition, the home-owning family has the possibility of realizing profit in the sale of the house at some future time. The spiral continues, and again black people find themselves coming up short.

But even if a black family is able to buy a house, there are other ways it remains at a disadvantage. It was recently brought to public attention in Boston that the value assessment of houses in black neighborhoods was proportionately higher than in other areas. The average assessed value of property in black neighborhoods was declared to be approximately 56 percent of the market value, while in other areas of the city, the assessed value was estimated at 28 percent. In Boston, one pays property tax of $160 per one thousand dollars of assessed value.

If we have two families, one black, one white, who own homes valued at $10,000 and $20,000, respectively, the assessed value of both homes would be $5600. The taxes paid by both families would be the same, $896, even though the value of the white-owned home was twice as much. Institutional racism confronts black Americans at every turn.

We have already seen one of the ways in which black people are excluded from the private-property market, through selective activities of banks. Banks play an even more significant role that may not be intentionally racist. We all know that to get a loan from a bank one needs to be solidly middle-class—steady job, good credit references, and so on. It is exceedingly difficult for most people who are heavily entrenched in lower echelons of economic society to get bank loans. We also know that the interest rate on bank loans is lower than any other kind. Being rebuffed by banks, lower class people go to easy sources who are happy to grant loans at very high interest rates. Thus poorer people pay more for the money they borrow. But that is not all of the story. Where do high-interest loan companies get the money they loan to our poor people? From the same banks that rebuffed the poor people in the first place! Institutional racism presses black people relentlessly further and further into the periphery of this society. In the BLACKS and WHITES game published by *Psychology Today,* white players begin with $1,000,000 and black players begin with $10,000. Property rarely costs less than $70,000. These odds are not far from reality!

The most exciting aspect of American society has been the feeling of unlimited opportunity. Those opportunities fall squarely within the capitalist economic system: "you, too, can be a capitalist." American black people have been kept squarely *without* the capitalist economic system: "you can never be a capitalist."

American blacks, as a group, have been relegated to the level of laborer and servant (see Table 5.1). President Nixon recently attempted to glorify the servant occupations by stating that there was dignity in changing bedpans—his mother apparently did it. That President Nixon's mother changed bedpans is not a convincing argument to the thousands of black people who have been denied access to every major avenue of economic advancement, and who now, oppressed (not blessed, as some whites seem to feel) with welfare payments, are being asked to ease the oppression by accepting "dignified" menial employment.

It is not enough that blacks are herded into low-paying, low-status jobs, but in many cases they are obliged to fight to get those. For example, in many cities garbage collection is a very low status job and blacks have a corner on that labor market. However, if whites in positions of political power decide that this labor market is desirable to their constituents, one

TABLE 5.1

What Jobs do Black People Have?

	1910		1930		1950		1960	
	White	Black	White	Black	White	Black	White	Black
White collar	23.8	3.0	33.0	4.6	39.9	10.2	44.1	13.4
Professional and Tech.	4.8	1.4	6.5	2.1	8.6	3.4	11.9	4.7
Props., mgrs., and offcls.	7.4	.8	8.3	1.0	9.8	2.0	9.1	1.4
Clerical and sales	11.6	.8	18.2	1.5	21.5	4.8	23.1	7.3
Manual and service	48.2	46.6	47.6	59.3	47.7	69.3	45.5	70.3
Skilled	13.0	2.5	14.2	3.2	14.4	5.5	14.3	6.1
Semiskilled and operative	16.1	5.4	17.2	9.4	20.3	18.3	18.3	19.6
Laborers	14.3	17.4	11.7	21.6	5.0	15.7	4.0	12.6
Service	4.8	21.3	4.5	25.1	8.0	29.8	8.9	31.9

Percent distribution adapted from Ginzberg and Hiestand (1966), Table XIV; p. 220.

finds blacks virtually unrepresented among garbage collectors. That is apparently the case in Boston, as I have not seen during the past year and one-half a single black garbage collector.*

The significance of such an observation is this: Nearly every major institution which provides the economic livelihood of people in this country is controlled by whites. That control is so thorough that in very few instances can a black man or family make a decent wage without first being hired, promoted, or otherwise accepted by a white man.

We have seen in the previous section how pervasive are racist attitudes in this country. Since economic advancement is now and always has been predicated on certain opportunities which have constantly been denied black people, institutional racism is easily perpetuated and advanced with the aid of racist attitudes and restricted opportunities.

It is not surprising that the consequence of occupying the lowest-paying and lowest-status jobs is a lower income. Recall Table 4.9 which showed just how low the income of black people is in comparison to that of whites. The median black family's income is approximately 60 percent as large as the median white family's. It was pointed out, however, that as the racial gap is closing somewhat for middle and upper-middle income groups, it is in fact widening for lower income groups. That is, the number of blacks (relative to whites) with income lower than $5000 has increased since 1947.

There are three ways of looking at these gross racial inequities. The problem lies either with (a) the "inferior skills, mentality, and culture of black people," (b) the consistent racist practices of American economic institutions, or (c) some combination of black incapacity and racist exploitation. Many people (we have generally called them racists) believe racial inequities are explained by the first alternative.

For many in America, inferior black economic positions are attributed to inferior education, not to exclusionary, discriminatory, racist practices. Yet recall again in Table 4.9 that a black man with a college education can expect a yearly salary ($7481) comparable to that of a white man with but one to three years of high school ($7229). The comparable salary for a white man with a college education is $10,149. These figures suggest that in this society a white skin is worth $2668 annually—a conservative estimate.

Having been denied, deprived, and discriminated against at every level of economic activity, black people are finally dealt the ultimate racist blow—they are exploited as consumers.

We have already shown that black people have inferior jobs and lower incomes. Moreover, the exclusion of blacks from free enterprise is nowhere

---

*Institutional racism creates strange paradoxes. It is indeed strange to consider all-black garbage collectors an indication of racism at the same time you consider all-white garbage collectors an indication of racism.

more evident than in Northern black ghettoes where most of the merchants are white.

Just as black people pay more for the money they borrow, they also pay more for the clothes, furniture, appliances, and food they buy. The biggest source of exploitation is the continuous come-on blaring over radio stations that cater to black listeners. "Get a beautiful 3-piece bedroom suite, only $5 down and $1 a week!" Following up such ads, one finds a warehouse of inferior-quality furniture, selling at prices not much below regular department store prices in downtown areas, and a raft of installment and interest charges.

At $1 per week how many weeks does it take to pay for a $179 item of furniture? Over three years. All the time the weekly payments are being made, interest charges are being added at rates between 18 and 36 percent per annum on the total cost. Thus the total amount and period of indebtedness is large and long indeed.

The Federal Trade Commission recently showed that 92 percent of the sales in furniture and appliance stores catering to low-income households were credit sales involving installment purchases. Stores dealing in general retail of the same merchandise have only 27-percent installment sales.

Furthermore, FTC chairman Paul Rand Dixon testified that an item selling wholesale at $100 would retail at an average price of $165 in a general merchandise store but $250 in a low-income specialty store. This difference amounts to a 52-percent average price premium for being a poor, black, urban dweller.*

As if the oppression of installment practices were not enough, the use of garnishment—diverting the wages of an employee to a creditor by court action requiring *no hearing*—is another form of harassment to ensure that the poor ghetto resident remains locked in the clutches of the exploiter. An FTC study in Washington, D.C., observed that the courts were used to collect from one out of every eleven customers in low-income consumer transactions. The comparable figure in department stores in the same area was one out of every 14,500 customers.

The economic picture is a very grim one. Institutional racism is not always directly responsible for exploitative conditions, but in one form or another always contributes to the unequal racial distribution of jobs, income, and general access to the economic opportunities that are available. Let us move now to the issue of education.

---

*These statistics come from the *Report of the National Advisory Commission on Civil Disorders,* 1968, p. 275-277. Of course these statistics are not exclusively race determined but are principally influenced by class. Since racism, as we have seen, operates to keep blacks as an underclass group, they are presented as manifestations of institutional racism.

Institutional Racism—Education

The educational system in the United States has in the twentieth century been the most important institution in this society. For most children the skills and values which this society rewards are instilled during their formative years in educational institutions.

Education has always been bound closely to racism in this country. During slavery, many Southern states had laws which forbade teaching slaves to read. It was felt that reading knowledge might create a rebellious spirit.* It is perhaps this insular belief that produced the current aphorism, "Ignorance is bliss." When slaves were taught to read, it was usually to read the Bible. Under these circumstances reading was countered by religious instruction based on the values of black servitude and humble obedience to white authority.†

In the North, belief in the inferiority of blacks led abolitionists to argue for segregated schooling on the basis that blacks could not compete with whites. Later, when public schools were formally segregated and monies were distributed unevenly over black and white schools, the arguments were changed toward integration. By then the racial cleavages had become firmly entrenched.

These brief notes are presented to illustrate the simple point that *educational institutions, like all other institutions in this society, reflect racist beginnings.*

There are three principal ways in which educational institutions are racist: (1) by giving inferior education to black children; (2) by willfully not educating black children in order to perpetuate existing racial inequalities; and (3) by miseducating white children about their own racist heritage, and black children about their own racial history.

Black children have always received an inferior education in the United States. There are many different reasons for this, but all can be linked directly to racism. We encountered *Plessy* v. *Ferguson* in an earlier context, but one of the most significant consequences of "separate but equal" was the establishment of separate, *unequal* educational facilities for black and white children.

In 1947 Mordecai W. Johnson, then president of Howard University, summarized statistics which suggest the degree of general racial inequality in education. He reported that of $137,000,000 annually spent on higher education in Southern states, *92 percent* ($126,541,795) was spent on institutions restricted to white only. Sixty-eight percent, or $86,000,000, of this amount was allocated to so-called public, state-supported schools.

---

*According to Herbert Aptheker (1969), slaves were rebelling from the beginning of their period of bondage. It seems reading was not necessary to that rebellious spirit.

†President Nixon's assurance of the dignity of bedpan meniality strikes me as a modern manifestation of this same tactic.

Only $10,500,000 reached black students in any way, and of that only $5,000,000 was allocated to state-supported schools.

These differences in higher education are reflected in elementary and secondary education as well. As the 1954 Supreme Court decision has been successfully circumvented until recently, these gross inequalities have persisted. As the Federal government has become more adamant about school desegregation, Southern segregationists have elevated evasion to a higher form—the "private" educational institution.

White children have been withdrawn from public schools to be placed in newly created private schools (all white, naturally) which enjoy tax exemption and, in some particularly blatant impecunious situations, public tax-dollar support. The federal government has recently voiced the intention of cracking down on these evasionary tactics, and recent statistics on school integration suggest their efforts have achieved some success.

In the North as well, unequal educational opportunities prevail, although the form of injustice differs from that of the South. As the black population of cities increases, the black enrollment in public schools increases even faster. For example, from 1950 to 1965 the proportion of black residents in Milwaukee, Oakland, and Washington, D.C., increased by 7.3, 17.6, and 20.0 percent, respectively. Corresponding increases in the proportion of black children in public schools were 16.3, 31.0 and 39.3.* Black increases in population can be attributed in large part to white migration to the suburbs. Black increases in public schools can be attributed to whites withdrawing their children from public schools and sending them, at great expense, to private or parochial schools.

Thus racially segregated schooling exists in the North and South alike. The report by Dr. James S. Coleman on educational opportunity (see Chapter Three) presents all of the statistics relevant to the unequal education black and white children receive in this country. What these statistics do not capture, however, is the prevalent feeling among many teachers in the North (a large majority of whom are white) that black children are dumb and incapable of learning.† These attitudes are most often found in middle-aged teachers who usually have tenured positions and return year after year to *not*-educate class after class of black children.

The classic study by social psychologists Robert Rosenthal and Lenore F. Jacobson (1968) shows just how insidious these teacher attitudes can

---

*Figures from *Report of the National Advisory Commission on Civil Disorders,* Table 11.1, p. 431.

†I have received many personal communications from teachers around the country substantiating the prevalence of these negative attitudes. In addition, these reports have been corroborated by my own experiences in Northern educational institutions. One interesting variant on the inferior intelligence of blacks, is the inferiority of courses about blacks. The popular impression at most predominately white schools is that Afro courses are "gut" courses.

be. These investigators told the teachers of a South San Francisco school that certain children (randomly picked) were "potential academic spurters." On the basis of tests administered at the beginning of the year and on several occasions over the next two years, "children from whom teachers expected greater intellectual gains showed such gains" (p. 22). The average gain of these children was over 27 IQ points. Not only did the children perform better on IQ tests, but their teachers saw them

> . . . as having a better chance of being successful in later life and as being happier, more curious and more interesting than other children. . . In short, [they] became more alive and autonomous intellectually, or were at least so perceived by their teachers. *(ibid.)*

Thus a child could expect to do better in school, to learn more, and to be liked and evaluated more highly simply because the teacher expected positive things from him. There are great advantages to having a teacher who thinks highly of you.

On the other hand, when improvement was not expected, children who made real IQ gains were rated unfavorably by their teachers—*the more so the greater their improvement!* In education, as in economics, the deck is stacked, but to add racist insult to racist injury the controlling power deals from the bottom.

Beyond noting that the Rosenthal Effect exists (i.e., teacher's expectations influence student's performance) it is not easily detectable *how* the influence is transmitted. It seems obvious that some rather subtle form of nonverbal communication is going on; that is, somehow the teacher communicates confidence and support and thereby facilitates academic growth.

But teachers are unfavorable toward those children whose improvement was not expected. Why? We do not know for sure, but teachers, like many of us, prefer a stable and predictable environment. If their expectations are continually confirmed, then traditional or prior judgments will not have to be checked and they will be free to think about other things. When their expectations are not confirmed, they are obliged to recheck their judgment process or otherwise explain the disconfirmation. This is not convenient.

The Rosenthal Effect also suggests that students are highly sensitive to nonverbal cues emitted by the teachers. In schools outside the South most black children are taught by white teachers, many of whom are thorough racists (i.e., believe in natural inferiority of blacks). Needless to say, the black students pick up these cues and react to them. (I can still recall some of my elementary and high-school teachers whose racism was most apparent.) The reaction is often dislike or hatred, or in milder forms simple apathy or ennui. Teachers complain that black students are discipline problems and, as is typical of white society, look away from themselves to blacks for the causes.

The Rosenthal Effect, coupled with prevalent negative feelings about the abilities of black children, serves to ensure that these children get an inferior education. The negative attitudes of teachers are also shared by administrators. When administrators put into practice their racial biases, the Rosenthal Effect becomes institutionalized. Here we face clear examples of institutional racism.

Administrators, like high-school deans, counselors, and so forth, are responsible for the curriculum of all students. If people in these positions have negative biases toward black students, manifestation of these biases leads directly to institution-wide racial inequities.

It has been true in most Northern high schools that unless a black student has outstanding grades *and* parental pressure is exerted, he will be put in a technical- or business/clerical-skills curriculum. Over the years, black students have rarely been placed in the college-preparatory curriculum. This has been true even of most black students who go on to college. These students usually must spend one or two years making up deficiencies in their curriculum training. Thus excluded from the relevant college preparatory courses, these black students not only consume valuable time "catching up," but are *never* able to enter the competition for scholarship aid. This problem has been even worse for black female students who, no matter how bright, are frequently channeled into typing, shorthand, and home economics.

Perhaps the worst aspect of the entire education process has been mis-education of all children. The excessive denigration of African history and culture has been matched by a comparable denigration of Afro-American history and culture. Just as excessive, but no less inaccurate, has been the glorification of Western Anglo-American history and culture.

American children are "taught" about sweetly singing, happy-go-lucky, childlike slaves devoted to mint-julep drinking, paternalistic plantation owners. The slave trade and the horrible "Middle Passage" have been ignored.

Children have been taught about the courageous settlers who fought against the harsh wilderness and savage attacks of hostile Indians. We have learned that Columbus "discovered" America instead of "finding" it—along with the Indians who were already here. That the settlers "bought" the island of Manhattan from the Indians is seen as a shrewd business deal made with ignorant savages who loved trinkets and firewater. White-Western-Anglo-American culture has been wrapped in a white shroud and placed on the top shelf. Black-nonWestern-Afro-American culture has been wrapped in dirty, soiled rags and tossed on the floor. American Indian culture has been stripped bare and locked up in that dungeon called a reservation.

Institutional Racism—Justice

I pledge allegiance to the Flag of the United States of America. And to the Republic for which it stands. One Nation, under God, indivisible with Liberty and *Justice for All.*

The administration of justice begins with law-enforcement officers. It does not begin on a very just note. In major American cities the average white population of 65 percent produces the average white police population of 95 percent. Put the other way, although nonwhite city residents account for about 35 percent of the population, they contribute only 5 percent of the policemen. It is in reaction to this kind of inequality and the blatant, brutal exploitation that too frequently follows, that the Black Panther Party was organized in Oakland, and the Deacons for Defense and Justice were organized in Louisiana.

TABLE 5.2

*Percent of White Population and White Policemen
of Some Major American Cities*

City	Percent white population	Percent white policemen
Atlanta, Ga.	62	90
Baltimore, Md.	59	93
Boston, Mass.	89	98
Buffalo, N. Y.	82	97
Dayton, Ohio	74	96
Detroit, Mich.	61	95
Memphis, Tenn.	62	95
New Orleans, La.	59	96
Oakland, Cal.	69	96
St. Louis, Mo.	63	89
Washington, D. C.	37	79

Adapted from the *Report of the National Advisory Commission on Civil Disorders,* p. 321.

Given these staggeringly lopsided statistics, it is not surprising that residents of black urban communities view policemen as occupation forces. Incidents like one which I will now describe reinforce this feeling:

One evening last winter I was preparing to go out, when a squadron of police cars pulled up in front of my house, sirens wailing and lights flashing. They blocked off the street while 15 policemen piled out of the cars and shortly brought forth one handcuffed, 17-year-old black youth from the alley to the paddy wagon. The size of the squad suggested that an armed robbery had been committed, or at least that a major drug raid was in progress. The offense was stripping a car that was parked on the street. Every one of the policemen was white. After the boy had been safely locked up, the policemen sat lightheartedly chatting for a few minutes before driving away.

A far more devastating example comes from the Boston police records.* Claris Blake was a 12-year-old black girl who lived in Dorchester, a black section of Boston. One late afternoon about 4:30 she went to the corner store to buy her mother a pie. When Claris had not returned by 5:30, her mother became anxious, and after looking all over the neighborhood she finally called the police at about 8:30 p.m. It was April 27, 1971.

The police response was nonchalant, apathetic, and unhelpful. They advised Mrs. Blake that she was probably visiting friends and would probably be back later. Mrs. Blake pleaded that her daughter never stayed away from home without permission. The police were not sympathetic.

The complete story is long, and sad. It is enough to make anyone give up on a belief in justice—it reinforces the felt need for blacks to control their own institutions. The police *never* made a search for the girl. They did not file an official missing-person bulletin until *May 6!* The newspaper published a brief article on April 29 *with a picture of the wrong girl!* A tap was to be put on the Blake phone in case a ransom call was received. Claris did call her home at 7:10 a.m. on May 7. She sounded dazed and asked her mother if she loved her. The phone clicked. Mrs. Blake called the operator and asked for a trace. There was no tap and she was informed that a trace was not possible.

The F.B.I. refused to enter the case because it did not involve interstate flight. *How did they know?* The telephone company said the phone could not be tapped because the police said the girl was not kidnapped. On May 15, 1971, Claris' body was found with a bullet in her head. It was not immediately known how long she had been dead.

> Telephone official: Look, let's face it, the wheel turned damned slowly in this case. It's not just the police. It's the double standard of our whole society. If a 12-year-old girl disappears on her way to buy a pie and she's *white,* the presumption is she's met foul play. If a little girl disappears on her way to buy a pie and she's *black,* everyone assumes she's just run away.†

> Mrs. Blake: Let me tell you something. I'm sick and tired now. . . . The child is gone and dead and there's nothin' that can bring her back alive. . . . I was begging. But I'm poor and I'm black. It didn't do no good, and now she's dead.

When whites control 95 percent of the police force and are openly hostile to poor urban minorities (mainly black and Puerto Rican), the words of the Declaration of Independence and the Nation's Pledge are

---

*This account and quotations are from an article in the *Boston Globe Sunday Magazine,* July 11, 1971.

†A postscript on this story. About a month later there were reports that a young, teen-age white girl from a suburban Boston community had been kidnapped. There were stories and photos, and searches beginning the night she disappeared. She was found two days later—*she had run away from home!*

recast in survival terms.* Violence breeds violence.

Many of the problems of injustice for blacks accrue because of their lower-class economic status. For many blacks, stealing is a way of "making a living." For example, I overheard a conversation in an Atlanta, Georgia, bar in which a couple of men were citing the various ways in which crime pays. A shoplifting conviction apparently drew $200 in fines and/or 30 days in jail. The economics of the situation were such that shoplifting $500 worth of goods each day would more than pay the $200 every two weeks or month when the man got caught. Shoplifting was a good paying *vocation.*

The fact of justice in the United States is that there are many legal ways in which injustices are perpetuated. The most frequent legal injustices occur to people who are poor. A large segment of the black population is poor, therefore classism and racism overlap a great deal. Yet within class strata there are still clear examples of racist practices.

One of the principal ways in which the judicial system practices discrimination is through the bail system. The judge can set bail at any amount he chooses, although there are some *suggested* guidelines that link the amount of bail with the severity of the alleged crime and the defendant's financial circumstances. A recent investigation of the Boston Courts by Bing and Rosenfeld (1970) revealed some startling statistics.

These investigators studied urban Boston courts (Boston Municipal Court, Roxbury, and Dorchester) where 64 percent of the defendants are poor (53 percent of this figure are unemployed); and suburban courts of Chelsea, Malden and Waltham.

In the urban courts, 55 percent of the defendants are committed for failure to post bail. The comparable figure in the suburban courts is 41 percent. The racial discrepancy is even greater. Black defendants fail to raise bail money 62 percent of the time, compared to white defendants' 43 percent. This discrepancy is not due simply to the lower income of blacks, for in the Roxbury and Dorchester courts (serving predominantly black defendants) bail is set at or above $10,000 in 20 percent and 38 percent, respectively, of all bail cases. The comparable figure in the other four

---

*In a *New York Times Magazine* article (May 16, 1971) several allegations of brutality in law enforcement and, more importantly, open hostility toward blacks were attributed to James Rizzo, Police Commissioner of Philadelphia. One of the cited incidents alleged that a black radio disc jockey reported a black gang fight and while waiting in his car for the police to arrive, was startled by the muzzle of a gun pointed at his head. Rizzo, answering the call, greeted the disc jockey with "Make one false move, you black son-of-a-bitch, and it'll take 36 doctors to put you back together again." In connection with his campaign for mayor of Philadelphia, one Rizzo aide enlists voter support by asserting that "If it weren't for Rizzo, the Zulus would be running the city." Now, Mr. Rizzo runs the city. Admittedly Rizzo is an extreme case, but the model of white domination and strong antiblack feeling is all too familiar in American cities.

courts is *3 percent.*

It might be expected that these figures reflect the more serious nature of crimes committed by black defendants. However, over one-half of those subjected to bail of $10,000 or more in Dorchester are charged with nonsupport or illegitimacy. In addition, those who are committed before trial are found guilty more often than those who are not.

At the end of the Knowles and Prewitt (1969) book, Harold Baron has written a chapter called "The Web of Urban Racism." As we have seen, that web is a large, all-encompassing net which is quite efficient at capturing the poor, the black, and the brown urban dwellers.

In a general sense, the most important aspect of inequality in the administration of justice concerns the enormous power contained within the legal profession. The law is so flexible that any skillful lawyer or interested judge can manipulate it to achieve a desirable end. We have already seen how bail money can be used as a kind of preventative detention. Other forms of stalling or simple bureaucratic complexity can serve the same function. It is important, in this connection, to note the recent ruling in New York State that any defendant who has not been tried within six months of his original charge must be set free.

Beginning with the killing of Bobby Hutton and a policeman in Oakland, California, a series of legal entanglements between Black Panther Party members and police and judicial authorities have had enormous effect on the Party's national organization. The national leadership was decimated by various charges resulting in incarceration for several years (as with Huey Newton), or flight into exile (as with Eldridge Cleaver), or detention for charges pending and during trial (as with Bobby Seale). Each of these leaders was legally removed from effective leadership on a day-to-day basis. In the cases of Newton, Seale, Ericka Huggins in New Haven, and the New York 13 (held on bomb-plot conspiracy charges), each was finally released from jail without being found guilty. Yet in each case the defendants spent from one to three years in jail. The overall effect seems to be that a one- to three-year jail term can be given legally to someone at the whim of a police force and prosecuting attorney. In addition to the years spent in jail, many thousands of dollars have been spent litigating case after case.

I have said nothing of the guilt or innocence of the defendants; I have only pointed out that extended detention and large legal fees have accrued to members of the Black Panther Party around the country. This form of legal detention is mild compared to that lethal search-warrant shoot-out tactic that claimed the life of Fred Hampton in Chicago. The point is that the laws are made by whites, enforced by whites, can be used and circumvented by whites. Rather than being protected by the law, black people are too frequently exploited in the name of the law.

People who manipulate and control the legal machinery of this country have tremendous power over those people who are either relatively ignorant of its workings or powerless to do anything about it.

Public Defender Offices and legal-aid agencies have helped to reduce the disproportionate legal power now enjoyed by the rich, the white, and the educated; still we are a long way from the idea of *justice for all.* *

*One of the most compelling indicators of racial inequality is the racial composition of penal (the current euphemism is "correctional") institutions. In Massachusetts, where black people comprise approximately three percent of the state's population, black inmates in state penal institutions number about forty percent. For many, these lopsided statistics are simply reflections of the myriad ill effects of disadvantage and poverty that describe ghetto conditions in America. However, in the black community these figures are seen as objective confirmation of the systematic exploitation and oppression of black men.

Penal institutions exist as a repository for people who commit crimes against society—that is the traditional rationale. However, the institutional inequities by race suggest to many that in a realistic sense being black is a crime against American society. In the economic ledger one can compute a poverty or racial "tax" on goods, summarized in Caplovitz's study, *The Poor Pay More* (1967). In the ledger of justice, where the stakes are considerably higher than dollars and cents, *the black pay more!*

The end of the Civil War supposedly represented the end of slavery in the South. However, a neo-slavery institution was created in the South to take up the labor slack brought about by the Civil War—the Prison Farms. One of the most famous of these is Parchman Farm, or more accurately Parchman Plantation.

> The state penitentiary system at Parchman is simply a cotton plantation using convicts as labor. The warden is not a penologist, but an experienced plantation manager. His annual report to the legislature is not of salvaged lives; it is a profit and loss statement, with accent on the profit. . . (*New York Post,* January 9, 1957).

With prisons, as with other institutions in America, the racist practices were more blatant in the South than in the North. But as we suggested at the beginning of this chapter, the regional differences were not of degree but of kind. The growing restlessness and rebellious mood in Northern penitentiaries were hinted at by the events at San Quentin, and dramatically demonstrated by the events at Attica. Black minds and bodies are abused by the spectre of racism even until death.

The "facts" of George Jackson's death at San Quentin and of the massacre at Attica are not well known. Secrecy and blatantly contradictory testimony probably assure that they will never be fully revealed. What should be clear, however, is that these events mark the beginning—not the end—of a very volatile condition in American penal institutions. We have already seen how American institutions close off options for black people at every turn. By the time a black man ends up in a penal institution, he has become desperate. Not a desperate criminal, as he is so often portrayed, but a desperate human being struggling for survival.

Although black people are represented disproportionately in penal institutions, the immediate cause is not simply institutional racism in the administration of justice, but institutional racism in every facet of American society. Incarceration for blacks is too often the culmination of frustrating and degrading and anger-provoking experiences.

It would take another book to unfold the many ramifications of racism in and around penal institutions. I mention it here briefly to alert the reader to the critical importance of this most severe consequence and manifestation of institutional racism in America.

Institutional Racism—Conclusion

Institutional racism is pervasive in this society. Indeed, it is the very foundation upon which this society was built. This section has taken a brief overview of the beginnings and current practices of institutional racism. The major institutions—economic, educational, and legal—were reviewed in some detail. The major conclusion is that racism exists in practically all institutions by design or by effect, by intention or by ignorance. It is quite clear that many of the problems attributed to institutional racism are better understood in class terms, but to make the isomorphism between class and race in America is to obscure the institutional effects of individual racist practices and attitudes.

For example, black children do not get inferior education just because they have a lower-class background, a lower-class school environment, inadequate school facilities, and so on. They also get an inferior education because they are often taught by white teachers who think they are incapable of learning and who therefore do not teach them. Also, the unequal bail-setting procedures show greater variations by race than by class. The unequal treatment received by blacks at every class level also belies the assumed isomorphism of race and class.

It was suggested earlier that racist consequences could be either intentional or unintentional. Intentional institutional racism can be attributed to the institutionalization of individual racist desires. This form might be seen as the institutional counterpart of the dominative racist mode. The unintentional racist consequences can arise from one of two things: (1) Functioning of institutions to favor middle- and upper-class people is the variant most often cited in recent major works on the problems of cities (cf. Banfield's *The Unheavenly City*). Those young people and older ones as well who see the major problem of America as the need for a more equitable distribution of resources and wealth also see the problems of class disadvantage as paramount. Since black people as a group are disproportionately represented in the lower class, racial inequities are attributed primarily to class membership. (2) A more subtle but perhaps more pervasive problem of unintentional institutional racism concerns the cultural assumptions upon which institutions are based. These assumptions form the bases of institutions which reward individuals insofar as they possess cultural forms and modes of expression congruent with the institution's value system. It is at this level of practice that most Americans have been insensitive to the problems of racial conflict. It is from this point that we must move beyond individual racism, beyond institutional racism, and get to the real heart of the problem—that of cultural racism.

CULTURAL RACISM

"They's mo' to bein' black than meets the
     Eye!
Bein' black, is like the way ya walk an'
     Talk!
Bein' black, is like sayin', "Wha's happenin',
     Bebeee!"
An' bein' understood!
Bein' black has a way'a makin' ya call some-
Body a mu-tha-fuc-kah, an' really meanin' it!
An' namin' eva'body broh-thah, even if you don't!
Bein' black, is eatin' chit'lins an' wah-tah-
Melon, an' to hell with anybody, if they don't
Like it!
Bein' black has a way'a makin' ya wear bright
Colors an' knowin' what a fine hat or a good
Pair'a shoes look like an' then—an' then—
It has a way'a makin' ya finger pop! Invent a
New dance! Sing the blues! Drink good Scotch!
Smoke a big seegar while pushin' a black Cadil-
lac with white wall tires! It's conkin' yo'
Head! Wearin' a black rag to keep the wave!
Carryin' a razor! Smokin' boo an' listenin' to
Gut-Bucket jazz!
Yes! They's mo' to bein' black than meets the eye!
Bein' black is gittin' down loud an' wrong! Uh-huh!
It's makin' love without no hangups! Uh-huh! Or,
Gittin' sanctified an' holy an' grabbin' a han'ful'a
The sistah nex' to ya when she starts speakin' in
Tongues!
Bein' black is havin' yo' palm read! Hittin' the
Numbers! Workin' long an' hard an' gittin' the
Short end'a the stick an' no glory! It's
Knowin' they ain't no dif'rence 'tween
White trash an' white quality! Uh-huh!
Bein' black is huggin' a fat mama an havin'
her smell like ham-fat, hot biscuits
An' black-eyed peas!
Yes! They's mo' to bein' black than meets
     The eye!
Bein' black has a way'a makin' ya mad mos'
Of the time, hurt all the time an' havin'
So many hangups, the problem'a soo-side
Don't even enter yo' min'! It's buyin'
What you don't want, beggin' what you don't
Need! An' stealin' what is yo's by rights!
Yes! They's mo' to bein' black black than meets the
     Eye!

It's all the stuff that nobody wants but
    Cain't live without!
It's the body that keeps us standin'! The
    Soul that keeps us goin'! An' the spirit
    That'll take us thooo!
Yes! They's mo' to bein' black than meets the eye!"*

Like individual and institutional racism, cultural racism has a long history. In fact, I would argue that cultural racism is fundamental to all forms of racism in the United States. The assumptions guiding the following discussion of cultural racism are that (1) black and white Americans come from two quite different cultural backgrounds; (2) the origin of racial contact (English-white and African-black) precipitated conflict at a basic cultural level; (3) with the development of the slave trade and subsequent settling of America, cultural conflict escalated into cultural racism; (4) cultural racism was the premise upon which institutional racism flourished; and (5) institutional racism has had a major role in the perpetuation of racism by transmitting cultural values and thereby socializing individual racists.

The *Funk and Wagnalls Standard Dictionary of the English Language* (International Edition, 1967) defines culture as

> The sum total of the attainments and activities of any specific period, race, or people, including their implements, handicrafts, agriculture, economics, music, art, religious beliefs, traditions, language and story.

Cultural racism in the United States has two forms: (1) the belief in the inferiority of the implements, handicrafts, agriculture, economics, music, art, religious beliefs, traditions, language, and story of African peoples; and (2) a neoracism in current American thought which suggests that black Americans *have no* distinctive implements, handicrafts, agriculture, economics, music, art, religious beliefs, traditions, language, or story apart from those of mainstream white America and those deriving from the pathology of years of oppression in American society.

---

*This monologue is reprinted from Charles Gordone's Broadway play, *No Place to be Somebody*. I have chosen this excerpt because the basis for much of this section depends on an understanding of black culture. One does not, however, learn about black culture through the popular media nor through most books available in educational institutions. One learns best by direct experience. Since this is not immediately available to many of you, the next-best way is by reading black literature, and listening to and viewing black music, poetry, theatre, and art. Although the fullness of black culture still awaits the discovery and creation of the total black experience, not only in America but throughout the world, this section attempts to ease the Black Man's Burden (Killens, 1965) by illuminating some facts of white cultural racism.

In its broadest sense, cultural racism is very closely related to ethnocentrism. However, a significant factor which transcends simple ethnocentrism is power. This power to significantly affect the lives of people who are ethnically and/or culturally different is the factor which transforms white ethnocentrism into white, cultural racism.

Origins of Culture Contact: Statement of a Theme*

In the beginning was Africa (Black) and England (White), separate and different; equality was not an issue. Our description of the differences is a description of two different cultures. The opposition of skin color is but one of the significant manifestations of the degree of culture difference. Table 5.3 outlines some comparisons of African and English culture around the year 1550. These characterizations are generalized abstractions, and although close inspection might reveal somewhat greater similarity than that which is portrayed here, the extent and nature of the cultural differences are basically accurate.

Englishmen of the 16th century were very ethnocentric and hence were predisposed to dislike or judge negatively any group of people who were different from themselves. Ethnocentrism is not, of course, a peculiarly British phenomenon, as most culture groups tend to think their way is the best way. But within the context of English-African contact, British ethnocentrism was particularly salient: the culture of Africans was not merely different, but at the opposite end of the continuum on practically every major cultural criterion. Most significantly, British ethnocentrism included the glorification of the color white and the vilification of the color black. With the omniscience of historical perspective we might ask if there were any other way the contact of white Englishmen with black Africans could have turned out.

Skin color. According to Jordan (1969), upon first meeting, the English found the two most salient aspects of Africans to be skin color and sexuality. These reactions are vividly portrayed in the travel logs of British seafarers and English writers. For example

> And entering in [a river], we see
>   a number of blacke soules,
> Whose likelinesse seem'd men to be,
>   but all as blacke as coles. (quoted in Jordan, 1969, pp. 4-5)

seems to suggest that being a man and being black were not compatible states of existence. Further, upon noting that when a white Englishman

---

*For a good account of racial and cultural contacts see Winthrop Jordan's *White Over Black* (1969), and E. Franklin Frazier's *Race and Culture Contacts in the Modern World* (1957). For an account of the impact of Africanisms on the development of Afro-American culture, see Herskovits' *The Myth of the Negro Past* (1958).

TABLE 5.3

Some Cultural Comparisons ca. *1550—Africa and England*

Cultural component	AFRICA	ENGLAND
Religion	Relativistic Pragmatic Magical Secular Family oriented	Absolutist Faith Moralistic Sacred Privileged

Social organization	Matrilineal
	Polygamous
	Status based on
	   type of work
	"Man is what he does"
	Stratified-fluid
	Family discipline
		Patriarchal
		Monogamous
		Status based on
		   lack of work
		"Man is what he owns"
		Stratified-rigid
		Institutional dis-
		   cipline

Economics, property	Agrarian, artisan commerce Hunting, fishing Collective property	Capitalist commerce Artisan Private property

Education	Informal (family, peers)
	Oral tradition
	Requires interpersonal
	   contact
		Formal (tutor, schools)
		Written tradition
		Facilitates inter-
		   personal separation

Time	Present, past fused
	Traditional (primitive)
	Little change over time
		Past, future, no present
		Progress—positively
		   evaluated change
		   over time

Music	Rhythmic—body Songs secular	Tonal, melodic—mind Songs sacred

World view	Intuitive, superstitious
	Tolerant, open
		Rational (cogito—
		   Descartes)
		Intolerant, manipu-
		   lative (Machiavelli)

married a black Ethiopian woman she bore him black children, one observer concluded that the blackness of Africans

> proceedeth of some natural *infection* of the first inhabitants of that country, and so all the whole progenie of them descended, are still *polluted* with the same blot of infection. (*Ibid.*, p. 15; italics mine)

And yet another reaction suggested that "*though* they were black, they were civill" (italics mine). The white Englishmen had universally negative reactions to the blackness of the Africans. But this is not really surprising if we consider the *Oxford English Dictionary* definition of the color black *prior to the 16th century:*

> Deeply stained with dirt; soiled, dirty, foul. . . . Having dark or deadly purposes, malignant; pertaining to or involving death, deadly; baneful, disastrous, sinsister. . . . Foul, iniquitous, atrocious, horrible, wicked. . . . Indicating disgrace, censure, liability to punishment, etc.

If that is how the color black was commonly used in white England prior to contact with black Africa, imagine the power of a Rosenthal Effect on the Englishmen's impressions and reactions. More importantly, imagine the power of that effect on the history that followed from these culture contacts. That is, if the color black had such strong negative connotations, then evaluations of and reactions to black people were bound to be very negative also. Feeling quite negative to start, the English were also exposed to a culture that was *very* different from their own. It does not seem idle speculation to suppose that a basic aversion to black "colored" the Englishmen's judgments of all elements of African civilization and culture.

It is important to note that it was not simply the negative reaction to blackness that was involved here, but a super-positive regard for the purity of whiteness.

> Everye white will have its blacke,
> And everye sweete its sowre. (quoted in Jordan, p. 15)

And for William Shakespeare, the natural order of things included

> Tis beauty truly blent, whose red and white
> Nature's own sweet and cunning hand laid on. (*Ibid.,* p. 8)

White is good and beautiful, while black is bad and ugly. We have been inundated with so many theories, hunches, and assumptions about racial attitudes and behaviors that the very simple fact of *color* rarely is entertained as a *cause* of racial antagonism. Opposition and conflict of basic cultural, physical dimensions preceded the complexities of individual, institutional, aversive, and dominative racism by many centuries.

An interesting observation on the relation between color-name and culture is suggested by a classic clinical report of a multiple personality. In 1954, Thigpen and Cleckley wrote a clinical report of a multiple personality involving three distinct identities. The case was popularized when a motion picture *The Three Faces of Eve* based on the study was made. Of interest to us are two of the personalities named by the authors as Eve White and Eve Black. The choice of white and black is intriguing in light of the personalities to which they were ascribed. The following partial list of characteristics is offered for your consideration:

Eve White	*Eve Black*
Demure, retiring, in some respects almost saintly.	Obviously a party girl. Shrewd, childishly vain, and egocentric.
Face suggests a quiet sweetness; the expression in repose is predominantly one of contained sadness.	Face is pixie-like; eyes dance with mischief as if Puck peered through the pupils.
Voice always softly modulated, always influenced by a specifically feminine restraint.	Voice a little coarsened, "discultured," with echoes or implications of mirth and teasing. Speech richly vernacular and liberally seasoned with spontaneous gusts of rowdy wit.
An industrious and able worker; also a competent housekeeper and a skillful cook. Not colorful or glamorous. Limited in spontaneity.	All attitudes and passions whim-like and momentary. Quick and vivid flares of many light feelings, all ephemeral.
Though not stiffly prudish and never self-righteous, she is seldom lively or playful or inclined to tease or tell a joke. Seldom animated.	Immediately likable and attractive. A touch of sexiness seasons every word and gesture. Ready for any little irresponsible adventure.
Her presence resonates unexpressed devotion to her child. Every act, every gesture, the demonstrated sacrifice of personal aims to work hard for her little girl, is consistent with this love.	Dress is becoming and a little provocative. Posture and gait suggest lightheartedness, play, a challenge to some sort of frolic.
Cornered by bitter circumstances, threatened with tragedy, her endeavors to sustain herself, to defend her child, are impressive.	Is immediately amusing and likable. Meets the little details of experience with a relish that is catching. Strangely "secure from the the contagion of the world's slow stain," and from inner aspect of grief and tragedy.*

*This summary is adapted from Thigpen and Cleckley (1954).

Is there a suggestion of racial comparison underlying this split personality? The color-name and personality characteristics are not, I would argue, haphazardly associated. In the mind of the therapists, as in the mind of America, black is associated with a "troublesome presence."

Sexuality. Sexuality was the other remarkable white English response to black Africa. Francis Bacon envisioned the Spirit of Fornication as "a little foul ugly Aethiop." Black men were alleged to sport "large Propagators." This sexuality was not merely a fanciful conception of these white adventurers, but based on experience as the

> hot constitution'd Ladies [with] temper hot and lascivious, [made] no scruple to prostitute themselves to the Europeans for a very slender profit, *so great was their inclination to white men.* (Ibid., p. 35; italics mine)

But the white man cannot be held responsible for his sexual activities for

> she comes to the place of the white man, lays beside him, and arouses his passion with her *animal arts. (Ibid.,* p. 35; italics mine)

Thus the white man attributes the price of prostitutes in Africa to the strong desire of black women for white men. Morever, since it seems the white men do not want to be responsible for their sexual interests, they place all fault with the black temptress who, with her animal arts, arouses him in ways that ordinary men could not resist.* This relationship between white males and black females has not waned over the centuries as the laws of progeny during slavery consistently favored the white male's sexual profligacy with black women.†

This very brief review of early stages of culture contact has summarized some of the basic differences between black Africa and white England. We reviewed in Chapter Four the "contact hypothesis" of resolving interracial conflict. It is important for us to note that it was interracial, intercultural contact that *created America's racial problem in the first place!*

---

*We still find the same relationships between black female prostitutes and white clients today, only men come to the women now. Any late afternoon or early evening one can stroll to the corner of Massachusetts and Columbus Avenues in Boston and watch a stream of white males making arrangements with the black prostitutes. The men appear to be middle class suburbanites.

†To do this, laws were passed during slavery which made a child the race of his mother in any biracial unions. Consequently a white man could produce as many offspring as he wanted with black women without "contaminating" the white race. This particular view might also be seen as one reason why prosecution of black-male/white-female relations was done with such violent thoroughness. To ensure his own sexual outlets with black women, the white man had to deprive his white female of any and all cross-racial sexual contact.

Returning again to DuBois, the problem of the color line is not just a twentieth-century problem, but one which goes back several centuries. There are numerous theories and proposed solutions for racial conflict in twentieth-century America. It seems to me that any theory of race relations in the twentieth century must be informed by an historical analysis of the cultural heritage of *all* American peoples. The dynamics of racial contact and *mutual* influence must be better understood if modern theories are to bear any relationship to the realities of racism.

Toward cultural racism. The discussion thus far has concentrated on ethnocentrism, but the main issue of this section is cultural racism. Therefore we must determine the relationship between ethnocentrism and cultural racism. The ethnocentrism upon which the white reactions to black Africans was predicated still exists. Foreigners are often looked on with suspicion, as their customs and modes of dress frequently seem bizarre.* Ethnocentrism might be seen as an attitude, a common prejudice in favor of one's own group. Like prejudice, ethnocentrism is characterized as a judgment. The attitudes of the English toward the Africans were judgments about their physical appearance, customs, values, beliefs, and so on. In short, the ethnocentric reaction of white Englishmen was a cultural reaction. Jordan (1969) suggests that

> [the consequence of] the Englishman's ethnocentrism tended to distort his perception of African culture in two opposite directions. While it led him to emphasize differences and to condemn deviations from the English norm, it led him also to seek out similarities (where perhaps none existed) and to applaud every instance of *conformity to the appropriate standard.* (p. 25; italics mine)

African culture was seen as inferior to the extent that it deviated from English norms; it was given modest recognition for achievements that "measured up" to those same norms. The important point of this is that *all judgments of African society were made with respect to white, English norms.*

But ethnocentrism is a judgment and, like prejudice as we have defined it, is basically an attitude. Ethnocentrism becomes cultural racism when attitudes escalate into behaviors. When ethnocentric judgments become prescriptions for action, and those same ethnocentric judgments serve to justify those actions, cultural racism is the appropriate label. Ethnocentrism is transformed to cultural racism by the accumulation of POWER. The ability to control, through the exercise of power, the lives and destinies of black people becomes cultural racism when those destinies

---

*In some cases, minor cultural differences are labeled "quaint." What determines the nature of the response to cultural differences is probably related to racial similarity.

are chained to white ethnocentric standards. Glenn (1965) frames the picture of white power as follows:

> Whites are almost 90 percent of the population, are more than 95 percent of the college graduates, and have perhaps 95 percent of the wealth, and since they occupy almost all key positions in the social order and control the armed forces and law enforcement agencies, they could, by acting in unison, prevent any economic, educational, or other gains by Negroes. (p. 105)

Not only do whites control all of the major institutions and nearly all of the education and wealth, but Glenn gives them major credit for every advancement that black people have made in this country:

> The harshness of the fact that Negroes are largely at the mercy of whites is tempered [for whom?] by the fact that they have had many white benefactors. White abolitionists worked to free them, a white president gave them legal freedom, and the efforts of thousands of white soldiers made that freedom a reality. White people are responsible for the Thirteenth, Fourteenth and Fifteenth Amendments to the Constitution. They were more numerous than Negroes among the founders and early leaders of the National Association for the Advancement of Colored People. ... An all-white Supreme Court rendered a series of decisions favorable to the rights of Negroes, and in 1964, a predominantly white Congress passed, and a white president signed into law, a sweeping civil rights bill. ... (*Ibid.*, p. 105-106)

With this statement Glenn creates the image of black people as so many toy dolls, cared for and manipulated at the whim of white people. While this statement grossly exaggerates the singular contribution of allegedly sympathetic whites, the general character of white people "calling the shots" is correct.

It is important, however, to understand that WHITE POWER, whether in the hands of "benefactors" or detractors, has sought in every instance to evaluate and control the destinies of black people in America with respect to those same ethnocentric white standards that so heavily influenced the reactions of white Englishmen in 1550. Cultural racism will never be understood or eliminated until these facts are understood, until white America evaluates the cultural assumptions upon which their exercise of white power is based.

Cultural Racism: Development of the Theme

White England's ethnocentrism was transformed to cultural racism by the expansion of British commerce to include the slave trade and, most significantly, the institution of slavery in America to meet the labor needs of the British settlers. The more commonly discussed and analyzed forms of racism (particularly those associated with atrocities of slavery and the supportive roles taken by Northern commercialists) are derivative of the fundamental cultural and racial inferiority ascribed to Black African peoples.

Over the years cultural racism has been clouded by the mutual cultural exchanges of blacks and whites in America, as well as by the unquestioned belief in the superiority of western European culture as represented by the United States of America. The negative distortions of African culture and the positive distortions of European culture have falsified the heritage of *all* Americans. Falsifications have glorified the notions of "White Man's Burden" and "Manifest Destiny" in the eyes of America's youth for generation after generation. They are instructed that the white man's burden was eased "as more Africans became educated and learned about life in the rest of the world, [and] they came to believe that they would have better lives *if they could govern themselves*... [To assist them] The British government has worked hard to train the people in its colonies for self-government" (Allen, 1964, pp. 53-54; italics mine). This is written in modern history texts in spite of the fact that African peoples had sophisticated political forms of self-government for centuries before England or the United States of America ever existed.

Excessive enthnocentrism produces many half-truths and in some cases gross distortions which, if people in power act on them, can have severe negative consequences for the victims of these distortions. One of the most important ways in which theories and research in social psychology aid us in our analysis of racism is by pointing out some of the mechanisms by which people acquire distorted views of themselves and others. One of the most serious distortions made is the erroneous analysis of collective identity based on a misunderstanding of cultural heritage. Let us take two examples using attribution theory for purposes of analysis.

Misattributing intention or character. Recall the earlier quote concerning the "hot constitution'd ladies" who "were so inclined toward the white man" that they prostituted themselves for a "very slender profit." Edward Jones and Keith Davis (1965) have attempted to analyze the process by which people come to understand the personality dispositions underlying and causing the actions of others. Attribution is the process of establishing cause-effect linkages. As with our prejudice analysis the starting point is behavior, the question is what causes the behaviors we observe. The white Englishmen attributed the act of prostitution for slender profit to the underlying disposition of a strong inclination or desire for white men. Presumably the significant piece of evidence was the slender profit. Critical to the attribution was the assumption that profit was the important criterion for being a prostitute, as well as that a profit margin of a certain magnitude was commensurate with the business-transactional dimensions of the relationship.

It is entirely possible that the women enjoyed sex regardless of the business relationships, and also that the profit margin required for a "successful" business transaction was considerably smaller in Africa than in England. Thus the attribution of strong inclination for white men may have been gratuitous because of erroneous cultural assumptions which were important to the final assignment of intention.

Similiar attributional errors are made today. Abrahams (1964) writes about the so-called masculine self-doubt of black men in terms of an ambivalent love-hate relationship toward women. Abrahams suggests that this ambivalence "is undoubtedly responsible for many of the apparent effeminate traits of this otherwise masculine group" (p. 33). Among the effeminate traits Abrahams includes "the importance of falsetto voices in quartet singing." In white Western culture, the falsetto or high-pitched voice of male singers is associated with the *castrati* in early Italian opera. These singers were castrated men who sang the high parts because women were not allowed to perform publicly.* Of course castration did have the clear consequence of creating very effeminate-acting males.

However, from observing the act (singing in falsetto) to attributing the causal disposition (effeminate character) an important cultural link is omitted. The result is a misattribution because, as Keil (1966) points out,

> Falsetto singing comes directly from Africa, where it is considered to be the very essence of masculine expression. The smallest and highest-pitched drum in a West African percussion ensemble or "family" is designated the male drum because its tone is piercing and the role it plays is colorful. (p. 27)

If there is any doubt about the role of falsetto singing in contemporary black culture, one need only listen to the unmistakable sexual reactions of *women* to the falsetto singing of male performers (B. B. King is an outstanding example, but the lead singers of most black groups use falsetto to good advantage).

Once again we see an analysis, an attribution of intention or disposition which is ill-informed because of an ethnocentric reference point, the assumptions of which are not applicable to the attribution situation. These two examples are not of great importance because they do (or did) not have important consequences for the survival of black people. However, I point them out to suggest that the distortions thus produced are a very likely consequence of employing ethnocentic standards in making judgments about others from different cultural backgrounds. When these ethnocentric standards are used as a basis for national policy prescriptions, and are buttressed by white power, the problems become increasingly acute. The issues of cultural racism are inextricably bound up with these cultural and power differentials.

---

*And so a sexist-based practice of early Italian theater is the modern basis for attributing ambivalent masculine character to black males. Considerations of culture lead to myriad subtle ironies.

Social comparison with white standards. Earlier we discussed the importance of social comparison theory (Festinger, 1954; Pettigrew, 1967) with
reference to prejudice. Briefly, the theory states that we have a need to
evaluate our abilities and opinions. To do this, we compare ourselves to
others. If we compare favorably, our self-evaluation is positive; if we
compare unfavorably, our self-evaluation is negative. There are two
dimensions to social comparison, one stressing the *accuracy* of our
evaluations and the other emphasizing the *favorableness* of our evaluations. In addition, our judgments can be based on physical or objective
criteria or on social or more subjective criteria. It can be generally stated
that the former (objective) criteria facilitate the accuracy of our evaluative
judgments, the latter (social) facilitate the favorableness of those
evaluations.

The idea of *cultural relativity* assumes the relative social-subjective
nature of cultural differences. Thus cultural relativists view cultural forms
as simply the expressions of unique ecological, biological, and anthropo-
logical conditions of a group of people. It does not attempt to compare,
evaluatively, any two cultures but simply to describe them. The cultural
absolutists, on the other hand, establish what they consider to be the *best*
cultural forms for *any* group of people and proceed to evaluatively
measure all cultures by those yardsticks. This view tends to merge the
social or subjective with the physical and objective aspects of culture. As a
result, the favorableness *and* accuracy of their evaluations are based on
comparison with the *same* standards.

I suggest that the absolutist quality of white western (American)
ethnocentrism has precisely that quality of cultural absolutism. Now
cultural absolutism is not unique to Western culture. But no other culture
has had the power to impose its cultural values and assumptions so widely.
As a consequence, social comparison with darker and different cultures of
the world produces not only favorableness of self-evaluations, but the
feeling of *accuracy,* i.e., not I like (think, feel) our way better, but we
KNOW our way is BEST. This feeling or belief is so ingrained in American
culture that a large majority of our people believe it, and our institutions
function in accordance with this presupposition. It is so ingrained, in fact,
that many if not most people do not even feel there is an issue to be
considered concerning the supremacy of white American ideals and way of
life.

One manifestation of this cultural supremacy is the continued
analyses of black pathology which recur. Social scientists, politicians, and
others continually define black cultural differences as aberrations and as
part of the "problem" that black people face. Cultural supremacy is by no
means restricted to black people; Jews change their names and fix their
noses, Orientals deslant their eyes, eastern Europeans change their names.
For too long, favorable self-judgments in this country have been made
with respect to white, Anglo-Saxon, Protestant norms. These norms have

been so rigidly entrenched that all groups have had to establish their worth with respect to them.*

Let us return to cultural racism. The issue of social comparison is that black people in this country now, as in 1550, deviate most from the rigid norms which carefully contain the aspirations of all groups in the United States. Beginning with skin color and continuing with sexuality, the attitudes and basic life styles of black people in this country are sufficiently different that, as a group, they are excluded from the rewards of this society. I would also argue that this is also true of other culturally different minorities, such as American Indians, Chicanos, and Puerto Ricans. Cultural racism is the appropriate label for the act of requiring that these cultural minorities measure up to white standards in order to participate in the economic and social mainstream of this country.

I would like to close this section with two examples of what I consider cultural bias, or racism, in social scientific research. The first is the well-known and controversial research on intelligence; and the second is research on a personality variable called *delayed gratification.*

Intelligence.

> It should be obvious that IQ tests do not directly measure innate gene-determined intellectual capacity but do measure current intellectual performance *as defined by a particular culture or at least by its psychologists.* (Gottesman, 1968 p. 25. Italics mine)

In his *Harvard Educational Review* article on intelligence, Arthur A. Jensen (1968) argued that although it was not possible to define intelligence, it could be measured. Although he stated, "There is no point in arguing the question to which there is no answer, the question of what intelligence *really* is," (p. 5-6) Jensen proceeded in effect to "define" intelligence as *what intelligence tests measure.*

Let us briefly consider the argument that Jensen advanced to suggest that blacks were genetically inferior in IQ to whites. His argument runs as follows:

1. IQ is under genetic control—studies with twins show that IQ correlations between identical twins are greater than fraternal twins, which are greater than individual siblings. Further, siblings are more similiar in IQ than randomly selected children.

2. There are racial differences in IQ—holding other factors constant (insofar as this is *really* possible), racial differences remain.

*Cultural relativism is a two-pronged idea. On one hand, objectivity demands it. On the other, it is unreasonable to think there are no values or adaptations that are universally good—necessary to adaptive human survival. We cannot resolve the extent to which the absolute or relative view should or can be applied to cultures, but the hegemony enjoyed by the absolute view suggests the relative view merits favor.

Jensen's argument, then, is that IQ is under genetic control, there exist racial differences in IQ, therefore racial differences are due to genetic factors. Professor Jerome Kagan (1969) rejects this argument. Height is obviously under genetic control. However, Kagan observes, to conclude that differences in height between urban- and rural-dwelling South American Indians were due to genetic factors would be erroneous—disease and malnutrition are more accurate explanations for the differences.

Furthermore, a study of 38 pairs of identical twins reared in different environments showed average IQ differences of 14 points, and in at least one-quarter of the cases different environments produced IQ differences of more than 16 points. This difference is larger than the average difference between black and white populations and led investigator I. I. Gottesman (1968) to conclude: "The differences observed so far between whites and Negroes can hardly be accepted as sufficient evidence that with respect to intelligence, the Negro American is less endowed" (p. 27).

I have waited until this point to discuss Jensen's research because the most significant aspect of this work is the unchallenged ethnocentric definition of intelligence. In what, if any, sense should a college professor who graduated Phi Beta Kappa be considered more *intelligent* than, say, the eminently successful high-school drop out, Frank Sinatra? In the strict biological sense, intelligence means simply the ability to adapt to environmental circumstances so as to perpetuate the species. By this criterion, the cockroach *is* very intelligent while the dinosaur *was* not.

Intelligence defined as what intelligence tests measure does have great importance in this society. School achievement is considered very important in this society; it is what people want to predict and control; it is that with which intelligence test scores are correlated. School achievement and general intelligence are considered the foundations of this country. When Russia orbited Sputnik I in 1958, the United States became frightened that it was falling behind in the training of young would-be scientists. Massive amounts of money were poured into education and earmarked for science and math. Male teachers were exempted from military service if they taught math or science. Intelligence test scores are correlated with school achievement and this achievement is obviously very important in this society.

An insidious element of intelligence tests is the implicit assumption that people who score high on them are in some sense better than people who score low. Over the years, formal education has served to elevate people who obtained it above the masses who did not. It somehow seemed that educated people were *better* than uneducated people. Perhaps more than any other single trait, intelligence is the yardstick by which superiority is measured—white over black, male over female, rich over poor. It is important to understand that having an IQ-test score of 150 does not make a person *better* than a person with a test score of 100. There are a lot of dimensions to human potential and no one person or index of personal qualities embodies all of those dimensions.

Jensen attempted to prove that black intelligence was genetically inferior by showing that, even when all possible controls for variables known to be related to intelligence test performance were controlled, blacks still scored lower than whites. In the end he suggested that there are two different kinds of learning ability: Level I, or associative ability (blacks are good at this); and Level II, or conceptual ability (whites are good at this). Level II, he contends, is a higher-order ability, as a person must be proficient at Level I in order to perform well at Level II, but not vice versa. Since generalized intelligence or "g" is associated with Level-II abilities, Jensen's argument becomes more subtly not that blacks are of inferior intelligence per se, but they are simply at a genetically less-advanced stage of intellectual development.

The point I want to make is very simple. The notion of intelligence as the ability to manipulate abstract symbols and concepts (this is what IQ tests measure) is a culturally biased one. Accepting this standard absolutely is to fall into the trap of cultural ethnocentrism. What criteria support this concept of intelligence as an absolute? And to what kind of society does such acceptance lead? To bottle in the form of culturally biased IQ tests the numerous value judgments which a term like "intelligence" carries is to engage in the highest form of cultural racism.

Obviously I cannot, nor do I wish to, argue absolutely against the good of abstract, conceptual thought, for it is the foundation of scientific thought and discovery. We can attribute many desirable advances to the fact that some people, mostly Europeans, had these abilities. However, there are other ways of thinking which are most frequently represented in people of different cultural (and usually different racial) characteristics. That is, the "culture-free" test has not been created which would allow an unbiased measuring of generalized intelligence. Perhaps such a test is not possible. The current anti-intellectual wave among many college students is not so much a rejection of those modes of thinking embodied by the concepts of intelligence tests as it is a reaction against the hegemony which those modes have enjoyed over the education process and all that it influences.

"Knowledge" is not totally contained by the abstract conceptual processes of Level-II intellect but can accrue to Level-I type of associative thought, as well as to even less-structured modes of "knowing"—e.g., intuition, mysticism, emotionalism, and so on. The point of importance is that consequences of conceptual thought are scientific discovery and the "advancement" of Western civilization. In our society, *Western* civilization and civilization are considered synonymous; therefore intellectual functioning relevant to the growth of that civilization is *ipso facto* the best, highest, or whatever term you choose.

We are speaking of cultural racism. Since the advancement of an individual in this culture depends in large part on his school achievement (although the statistics cited earlier suggest that this advancement is greatly affected by race), the functioning of school systems is predicated on cultural assumptions which define the most important aspect of performance in terms of a measure which has black inferiority programmed into it. This unidimensional view of intelligence excludes possible differences in cognitive and behavior adaptations of black children. Contents or experience play a very important part in the way one processes information, whether in abstraction or by association. Consider the following research example.

Michael Cole (1971) was interested in a cross-cultural investigation of memory. He selected a twenty-item list of common objects (for example, a rake and a fork) and presented them to college students in the United States and Africa. He found that the number of presentations needed to memorize the entire list was considerably less for the Americans than for the Africans. In fact the Africans were never able to memorize more than ten items on the list. Cole proceeded to test various explanations for this difference in terms of the way in which the objects were encoded, categorized in memory, and recalled. He tried experiments which attempted to categorize the objects for the Africans in the way that the American students did, since it seemed that their way was superior. It made no difference in the Africans' recall. One might conclude from this that the Africans simply had inferior memory.

Cole was not content to stop there, because obviously for a culture to survive the thousands of years that African civilization has, memory must be more highly developed than that. Cole proceeded to use the distinctive features of African culture, in particular the oral tradition, as the basic structure for presenting the objects. He told a very simple story about the marriage of the daughter of a chief. On the day of her wedding the daughter learned that the man she was marrying was an evil witchdoctor, and she feared he would take her away to his kingdom and she would never be able to escape. As she left her father's house she left a trail so they could find her. She dropped along the way a rake, then a fork, and so on. In this context, the students learned every item on the list and recalled them in exactly the order in which they were dropped!

It is not important that as a group, black children score 15 points lower than white children on IQ tests. It is important to understand the contributions of a different cultural heritage to the way black children think, and the role that different experiences have in influencing modes of cognitive and behavioral adaptation. Furthermore, it is important to understand ways in which relationships between and among people are represented in cognitive functioning.

Recently a new dimension to the genetic determinants of IQ controversy was added by Harvard psychologist Richard Hernstein. In an article in *Atlantic Monthly* (September, 1971), Herrnstein focused on the provocative notion that *class* differences have a genetic determinant based in IQ scores. Herrnstein develops his point around the following syllogistic form:

1.   If differences in mental abilities are inherited and

2.   if success requires these abilities, and

3.   if earnings and prestige depend on success, then

4.   social standing (which reflects earnings and prestige) will be based to some extent on inherited differences among people. (Herrnstein, 1971, pp. 58, 63)

It should be clearly noted that Herrnstein said very little about racial differences, but all of the implications are there. Citing the work of Jensen, and claiming basic class differences (we have already seen the gross over-representation of blacks in the lower class), one can infer the author's assumed genetic contribution to black lower-class status.

Returning to the syllogism, we note that the three minor premises are *if*-statements. However, unlike formal logic wherein if-statements are *givens,* the if-statements offered by Herrnstein reflect questionable empirical generalizations. Scientists and social scientists of great prestige are divided in their endorsement of the validity of these minor premise assertions.

Furthermore, the principal assumption that American society is properly conceived as a meritocracy—one advances by the merit of his or her deeds—is open to considerable question.

The real kick of this article is contained in the following quote:

What is most troubling about this prospect [willy-nilly sorting into inherited castes] is that the growth of a virtually hereditary meritocracy will arise out of the successful realization of contemporary political and social goals. (p. 63)

This point suggests that the ideal of equality in American society has the inevitable consequence, by Herrnstein's analysis, of creating an inherited caste system.

One of the previously suggested consequences of human society is role conflict. The tendency to see (or not see) human beings as roles, categories, or abstractions with little more life than x's, π's or α's can be attributed in part to abstract conceptual thought. Military logistics and strategic-planning social scientific demographic statistics are among the most visible examples.

Labels facilitate cognitive manipulation via Level II processes. When human beings are reduced to labels for easy cognitive manipulation, we must ask how such impersonal abstractions contribute to the difficulties of interpersonal relations we experience. Perhaps it is the manipulation of human life in abstract symbolic terms that is responsible for the inhumanity that plagues us today.

Delayed gratification. "Progress is our most important product." This motto of the General Electric Company might well be the motto of the

United States. From a small frontier colony to a mighty industrial giant in just 350 years is indeed progress. One of the strongest catalysts of progress in the United States is what Max Weber called the "Protestant Ethic."

The Protestant ethic is a belief in hard work, thrift, and frugality, in anticipation of just rewards that will come in the future. This ethic requires that one subordinate his whims and fancies of the present to the hard work which future success dictates. The accumulation of capital requires acceptance of mentality, and it seems, the economic strength of this country is based upon the successful and pervasive socialization of generation after generation of youth who practice this ethic.

Perhaps the psychological study most relevant to our understanding of the Protestant ethic is the work of Walter Mischel on delayed reinforcement or gratification. We would assume that if children are socialized to a Protestant ethic norm, they should possess personality characteristics which such a norm would dictate. The first investigation of this issue of delayed reinforcement was conducted by Mischel in 1958 in Trinidad.

At the time, Mischel was interested simply in testing an observation that there were fundamental differences between East Indian and Negro Trinidadians. These differences were described by the following characterizations:

> Negroes: impulsive, indulge themselves, settle for next to nothing if they can get it right away, do not work or wait for bigger things in the future but, instead, prefer smaller gains immediately.

> East Indians: deprive themselves and are willing and able to postpone immediate gain and pleasure for the sake of obtaining greater rewards and returns in the future. (Mischel, 1958, p. 57)

It would seem from these characterizations that the East Indians are more attuned to the cultural demands of a Protestant ethic and hence would likely be more successful in such a culture as the American than would the Negroes or Africans who displayed characteristics exactly opposite those that are likely to be rewarded.

Mischel (1958) had school children perform several paper-and-pencil tasks for him, then offered them rewards for their cooperation. Children were offered a one-cent unattractive candy immediately, or ten-cent attractively wrapped candy a week later. He found that only 37 percent of the Africans but 67 percent of the East Indians chose the larger, but delayed, reward. Mischel reasoned that acceptance of the delayed reward would likely be associated with trust of male socializing agents and would hence be related to the presence of the father in the home. The overall proportion of Africans choosing delayed, larger rewards increased to 52 percent when only those with fathers present in the home were included.

Mischel extended his work to cover the relationship between preference for delayed reinforcement and social responsibility (1961a) and need for achievement. In these studies he found that preference for larger, delayed reinforcement was positively associated with Social-Responsibility-Scale scores, and with measured need for achievement. He further found an association between preference for immediate smaller rewards and acquiescence in an ambiguous situation. Finally, Mischel (1961c) replicated the relationship with father-absence, but found that while it applied to younger children aged 8-9, it broke down for 11-14 year olds.

Now let us return to cultural racism. Individual and institutional racism aside, the ability to get ahead in this society is predicated on being socialized to a Protestant ethic and firmly believing in the value of delaying immediate gratification for the larger benefits that may come later. These studies by Mischel, as well as common observation, suggest that black people in this country *as a group* show less preference for delayed reinforcement than do whites. This fact alone accounts for some portion of the disadvantage experienced by blacks in America.

An immediate strategy might be suggested to the effect of instilling in black people greater tolerance for delayed gratification. This is precisely the counsel given by Booker T. Washington at the turn of the century. But if this characteristic is in fact a cultural one, not a reactive but a positive, indigenous characteristic of peoples of African descent, then such strategy for improving the position of black people in this society requires socialization of blacks as a group *away* from the values and expressions of their African and Afro-American heritage and *toward* a basically European system of values and expressions.

The argument here does not concern the relative merits of cultural values, but the power to make one set of values overwhelmingly prescriptive. Many groups are crying now for a right of self-determination. Self-determination in essence means the ability to choose one's future course from a range of options. Black people have not had such a range of options; these come only with power.

Again we must recognize that the issue is not a completely racial one, as the industrial state rules the world today. Any group who would prosper in this world arena must develop the mentality which a successful industrialism requires. Small countries without the resources required by an industrial economy do not have that decision to make and, in a cultural sense, are relatively uninfluenced by the world economy. However, considering black people in America there are no choices. To be successful, to be able to care adequately for oneself and one's family, it is necessary to be culturally attuned to those values and socialization procedures which our industrial economy demands.

It is important to note the change in acceptance of delayed reinforcement as a cultural norm in America. It seems that young Americans today have considerably less stake in the Protestant ethic. The Pill, as well as changing sex mores, has rendered obsolete the young woman's counsel to "save herself for her husband." A recent TV interview with elderly people revealed an almost unanimous feeling that if they could do it over again, they would not postpone so many things, but would do them while they were young and could enjoy them. The booming credit market has created the widespread practice of spend-now pay-later. The ethos of American culture seems to be changing from a future to a *now* orientation.

These characterizations are of course what seem to be trends, not a full description of cultural reality. It still takes rigid adherence to the delayed-reinforcement mentality for people on the bottom rungs of our economic ladder to move up a few notches. Black people are heavily represented here, therefore the luxury of living in the present is one they, as a group, cannot afford.

This discussion has strayed a bit from the point of cultural racism. To integrate with the economic mainstream of American life, black people are obliged to change certain characteristics. To the extent that these characteristics are products of an indigenous cultural heritage, black people are obliged to give up a substantial portion of their own heritage and adopt a different one. This means accepting new norms which may be fundamentally antagonistic to the indigenous cultural modes of expression which derive from an African past. There is nothing inherently wrong about cultural evolution. However, when it is forced by a powerful group on a less-powerful one, it constitutes a restriction of choice; hence it is no longer subject to the values of natural order.

I began this section by suggesting some cultural differences that existed between Africa and England around the year 1550. I began there because I feel the core of today's racial problems is indeed linked to those same fundamental differences. To counteract gross bigotry, social scientists have spent a great deal of energy attempting to prove the extent of similiarity between races. Those attempts have always be guided by acceptance of the superiority of Western cultural norms. Black people, it is argued, are just like whites (not vice versa), therefore deserving of similar treatment. The norm has been "you must be melted before you can have a chicken in your pot."

Johnetta Cole argues in *Black Scholar* (1970) that black culture consists of three components:

American Mainstream—material culture, values, behavior patterns

Minority Sense—continued need to detect hostility for self-protection

Blackness—the unique inputs of being black with all of the cultural heritage (African and American) that entails

Only the first and third of these components are positive. The second is basically reactive and occurs because of hostility to difference. When the American mainstream and the blackness components of black subculture are in conflict, black people are obliged to make choices. To the extent that success in this society is predicated on American mainstream values, then black choices are foreclosed. It is a matter of cultural racism that black people must give up a too-extensive portion of their own cultural heritage to enjoy the basic rights and privileges advertised by this society.

Cultural Racism: Conclusion

In Chapter One, we noted sociologist Lee Rainwater's charge to "tell it like it is." That is certainly an honored and noble goal of social science. However, there are many pitfalls which sabotage our noblest efforts in this regard. One such pitfall is that people and statistics lie. A second is that even when they do not, we as social scientists are limited by our humanity. We are, each of us who pretends to analyze race relations, caught up in the living of it. The responsibility of the social scientist should be more humble than Rainwater demands. Perhaps we should, rather, take as a more realistic goal the baseball umpire's simple charge to "call them as we see them."

In this chapter, I have attempted to analyze racism as I see it. My analysis is not idiosyncratic; I am sure there is great agreement among my colleagues and others on many points. I am equally sure, however, that disagreements will occur. Frequently my general point of view biases my interpretation of data and events. I only suggest that, like it or not, one's personal point of view always biases to some degree his interpretation of things. Consequently, to summarize this chapter is to point out the general goals which directed the writing of it.

1. My first goal was to demonstrate the inadequacy of the concept of race prejudice as the framework for studying the racial problems which beset this country.

2. The second aim was to show by analysis and example why racism is a more accurate concept.

3. Finally, it was my purpose to show the depths of the problems of racism in the foundations of this society.

The most important aspect of racism is its interlocking network of antecedent-consequent components, so diffuse that I believe nearly every major symptom of the malaise in the society can be traced to problems of race. It is debated whether the elimination of racism or sexism is more crucial to the salvation of this society; but that the two are closely related is often overlooked.

The student movement began over issues related to civil rights activism. The so-called generation gap widens over numerous living examples of American hypocrisy, the foundations of which were written into the Declaration of Independence and even the Constitution. Now white America is beginning to learn what black America has known for 350 years. Perhaps that is a start.

Chapter Six

Epilogue — The Problem of the Culture Line

In the preceding pages I have attempted to conduct the reader over the long, sometimes tortuous course of the subject of race relations. It has been personally very difficult because I have endeavored to reach several diverse audiences, yet at the same time to maintain a common focus and theme.

The primary audience, projected at the outset by the publishers and editor, is college sophomores taking an introductory course in social psychology. Among other things, I felt a responsibility to this audience to review a significant portion of the relevant literature of prejudice and racism without becoming excessively involved in the tedium of academic discourse.

Second, I felt an obligation to present a professional perspective that might be illuminating to my colleagues. In many cases this has involved reinterpretation of, or an alternative perspective on a given body of literature or particular theoretical or empirical approach to problems.

My third motivation was to write about prejudice and racism in such a way that anyone interested in the subject could read this book and gain something from it. Accordingly, I have attempted to tie my discussions as closely as possible to everyday events that occur within this society.

And finally, realizing there is relatively little I can say to my black audience about prejudice and racism that they do not already know from first-hand experience, I have considered the major portion of this book to be directed toward a white audience. Many of the points of view I have expressed are not unique to me as a professor, but are common to us who have lived the black experience in America. I have attempted in part to reflect white America to my white audience from a black perspective.

In this epilogue, I will (1) summarize what I have presented in the preceding five chapters; and (2) suggest what I consider to be the significance of the preceding discussion toward the reduction of racial animosity or hostility.

PREJUDICE AND RACISM: A BRIEF REVIEW

In the first chapter I sought to place the issues of prejudice and racism in historical perspective. Covering the period from the origins of racial contact in the middle of the sixteenth century to the beginning of the twentieth century, I suggested three major historical aspects of the problems of prejudice and racism.

First, *racist attitudes* followed by *racist behaviors* constituted the beginnings of racial problems in America. Potentially racist attitudes preceded initial contact between black Africa and white England, but became thoroughly racist and escalated to racist behaviors with the development of the slave trade and subsequent enslavement of black peoples in the United States. Important here was the observation that individuality and freedom, which we now cherish so much in this society, formed the cornerstone of the development of racism in America. Individuality without social responsibility is mere license for individual exploitation.

The second important point in the early history of prejudice and racism concerned the *regional variations in black oppression.* Emanating from common racist attitudes but different *forms* of racist behaviors, the evolution of the racial problems in America followed different regional courses. Entrenched in the system of slavery with all its psychological, sociological, and religious implications, the South developed very strict codes for racial relations. The repercussions led not only to intense, dogmatic feelings of racial superiority, but also to a whole system of distorted images and beliefs which have sustained them.

Development of racial relations in the North followed a slightly different pattern which, though no less racist in origin, gave the impression of being a more open and tolerant attitude toward race relations. The complexities of an industrial economy and the general economic sophistication which characterized the North seemed to provide opportunity for blacks. In some cases the opportunity was real, but only in comparison to Southern poverty and blatant racism. Thus, from the days of slavery onward, the popular impression of racism and bigotry in the South and racial tolerance and equality in the North tended to obscure the whole society's involvement in the practice of racism.

The third important point in this early history concerned what Myrdal called the American dilemma, but which I refer to as *the great American lie.* The contradiction between the ideals of American democracy and the realities of racist oppression have been with this country from its beginning. The importance of this contradiction is that for many it was not seen as a contradiction at all. That is, it was felt that blacks were innately inferior and hence should be deprived of *full human status* (see the quote in Chapter Five from Federalist Paper 54). This racist view of a lowly phylogenetic status was seen as *evidence* that subjugation was the natural lot of black people. Equality, liberty, and freedom only applied to those from a "higher" European civilization and were correspondingly granted to them alone. These racist arguments were included in the Constitution and sanctioned by silence in the Declaration of Independence. The great American lie has been eating at the heart of this country for 200 years.

In Chapter Two, I attempted to chart the modern course of the racial problem from the time of DuBois' 1903 statement of it through the first four decades of this century. A social scientific analysis of racial problems dealt particularly with the concept of attitudes and correspondent methodological and statistical approaches necessary to their measurement. These early developments in social psychology tended primarily to orient the analysis of race relations toward the concept of racial attitude. A major interest developed around the study of stereotyping and various other attitudinal indications of racial bias. This focus on attitudes had a tendency to guide theorists away from racial behaviors except as they attempted to predict them from their measurements of racial attitude. Not all researchers and theorists, however, joined the attitude bandwagon.

Analysis of attitudes could not account for the complexities of situational variance, and we saw in the late 1930's and the 1940's a move toward specifying more general theories of racial bias which tended to emphasize personality traits. Research on the authoritarian personality and on frustration and aggression, or the scapegoat theory of prejudice, was given greater attention in the 1940's.

Perhaps the most important event in the country-at-large during the first four decades of this century was the Great Depression and the federal bureaucratic response to it. The legacy of those policies has been federal paternalism, which perpetuated black people in marginal economic situations while not dealing directly with the more basic problems of discrimination at every level of economic activity in this country. Many of the current problems of welfare and unemployment for black people are not unrelated to the government's response to the Great Depression.

There were three important points in Chapter Three. First in the 1950's the social scientist became a significant input to the character of race relations. From the time when the Supreme Court cited "modern authority" (1954 school desegregation decision), social scientific analysis and testimony has been utilized in drafting and presenting legislation, and its influence has been felt in legal decisions. It is important to understand that theory and research of social science is in part a reflection of itself. That is, the phenomena to which theory and research are addressed are also influenced by the theories and research from which public policy is in part derived. I briefly reviewed the Moynihan Report, the Coleman Report, and the Kerner Report as examples of how social science has been used in influencing government policies.

Our second emphasis was the analysis of role conflict in mass society. As the roles which each of us must play proliferate, it becomes increasingly difficult to relate to another person in role-independent ways. Therefore one finds a growing sense of impersonal standard, uniform determinants of interpersonal relations which tend to overshadow the simple relationships of black and white individuals.

The problem of race relations becomes more complex when, in addition to attempting to analyze strictly racial conflict, we attempt to analyze numerous role conflicts which sometimes are correlated with racial conflicts and other times are not. While we might be able to analyze role conflict in some structural sense, we must recognize that roles do not have attitudes and roles do not engage in behavior. The role-conflict analysis of race relations emphasizes the importance of understanding both the individual, his attitudes, behaviors, *and* the social milieu within which his roles are socialized and from which he develops attitudes and behaviors.

Our third point in Chapter Three was recognition of the depth of racial conflict and hostility in the North. The wave of riots in the 1960's and the development of militant, political, and para-military philosophies were symptoms of a growing malaise in the Northern black communities which began to erupt in the past decade. I suggested in Chapter One that our analysis must contain two separate dimensions, representing the Northern and Southern cases. Although people were presumably aware of racial problems in the North, these problems were not given sufficient attention until the outbreaks of the 1960's. By the conclusion of Chapter Three, the historical background for our analysis of prejudice and racism had been completed.

In Chapter Four, the lengthy analysis of prejudice had several objectives. Initially, an attempt was made to review the research and theoretical literature on race prejudice. The chapter began with a brief introduction to definitions and theoretical concepts relevant to the analysis of prejudice. Prejudice was defined as:

> the prior negative judgment of the members of a race, or religion or the occupants of any other significant social role, held in disregard of facts that contradict it . . . . [and as] an affective, categorical mode of mental functioning involving rigid prejudgment and misjudgment of human groups.

Next I introduced a paradigm for the analysis which would allow us to understand that prejudice basically involves the relationships between and among people and human groups. We further observed that at some point prejudice involves one's conception of himself. Thus to the extent that prejudice is seen as a negative attitude toward an outgroup, it embodies the suggestion of a positive attitude toward an ingroup. Just as the negative stereotyping of outgroups is a problem of prejudice, so is the positive stereotyping of ingroups.

A general point was made that prejudice as an attitude is too narrow a concept to deal with all the complexities of race relations. The ultimate goal of the prejudice analysis was to establish why an individual develops an enduring emotional and rigid negative attitude toward other individuals or human groups. This *is* a problem, and when a significant percentage of an enormous aggregate group (such as white America) develops these attitudes, race prejudice can become a critical issue as it has in the United States. However, of equal importance is the analysis of where attitudes come from. Here it was suggested that the conditions which produce early negative racial attitudes in children are just as important, if not more important, than the specific attitudes themselves.

We should remember that the analysis of race prejudice has been appropriate for many years in identifying a particular problem in American society. However, it has not been sufficient or adequate to deal with the whole range of social problems that are involved with the problems of race. I suggested that a general conception is necessary and could be provided by the broad-based term *racism.*

In Chapter Five, the analysis of racism was broken down into three parts: individual, institutional, and cultural. Racism was broadly defined as follows:

> Racism results from the transformation of race prejudice and/or ethnocentrism through the exercise of power against a racial group defined as inferior, by individuals and institutions with the intentional or unintentional support of the entire culture.

My approach to the analysis of racism was contrasted to Allport's approach to the analysis of prejudice. Whereas the ultimate object of the prejudice analysis was the individual, the ultimate object of my racism analysis is the entire culture. I began with individual racism because that element characterized the major overlap between race prejudice and racism. However, individual racism is found not only in the traditional view of the bigot (here represented as the dominative racist), but also in the more quiet, covert form of racism (here called the aversive racist). It was suggested that the prejudice analysis was somewhat insensitive to the more subtle form of aversive racism.

It was pointed out, however, that individual racism is not inherited but is transmitted and nurtured by the socializing influences of institutions. We consequently broadened our view of racism to include institutional racism in both intentional and unintentional forms. Institutional racism was significant (a) because of the consistently negative consequences of institutional practices for blacks (and low-income whites as well), and (b) because institutions consistently socialize generation after generation of American youth to be individual racists.

Institutions in America were founded on the principles of white supremacy. Moreover, they were founded on cultural assumptions which, I suggested, were in conflict with the cultural assumptions of sixteenth-century Africa. Those conflicts combined with the power to influence and control the destinies of black Americans and produced what I called cultural racism. Cultural racism was seen simply as the attitude characterized by ethnocentrism (buttressed by race prejudice) coupled with the power to make normative one's ethnocentric values. They were seen as inherent in American culture and formative in the establishment of American institutions.

The dynamics of the development and perpetuation of racism were such that cultural racism provided the background for the development of institutions and led to institutional racism. Subsequently, individuals were socialized to racist norms by racist institutions, and thus evolved individual racism. The final effect is seen when these individuals perpetuate and support the culture, and the entire process forms a chain of relationships and associations of such complexity that after 350 years the beliefs in and practices of racism have produced an interlocking network of racist disadvantage.

I would like now to move toward what I see as the significance of the discussion in this volume. Beginning with some very important research on intergroup conflict, I will offer my personal views on the ultimate elimination of inequality and hostility in this country.

TOWARD A CULTURAL REVOLUTION

Muzafer Sherif conducted several interesting experiments on intergroup conflict which he reports in his book *In Common Predicament* (1966). In 1953, white boys from very similar backgrounds went to a three-week summer camp in Robber's Cave, Oklahoma. The purpose of setting up the camp was to investigate friendship formation and, later, development of intergroup conflict and some techniques for conflict reduction. When the boys arrived at camp they all stayed in one bunkhouse and were free to engage in camp-wide activities, choosing friends from among the entire compliment of boys. It was expected and found that friendship choices were based on sheer personal attraction.

After the formation of initial friendship choices, Sherif divided the boys into two groups, putting them in separate bunkhouses. The groups were divided in such a way that for each boy two-thirds of his friends were in the *other* bunkhouse. What followed was a series of contests between the two bunkhouse teams, the "Rattlers" and the "Eagles."

The games produced intense rivalry and developed a very high level of conflict. Boys who had initially been friends now found themselves intensely disliking each other and calling each other names. Although the majority of each boy's initial friends were on the other team, the development of conflict tended to produce an increase in solidarity within the new groups, such that friendship choice switched dramatically to almost entirely *within* the competitive groups. Moreover, the perception of achievements of own-group members and outgroup members was remarkably distorted. Systematically, the performance of the members of one's own group was judged to be superior to objectively comparable performances by members of the outgroup. Sherif summarizes the basic facts of the development of group conflict as follows:

> When members of two groups come into contact with one another and a series of activities that embody goals which each urgently desires, but which can be attained by one group only at the expense of the other, competitive activity toward the goal changes, over time, to hostility between the groups and their members. (p. 81)

The critically important element of this hypothesis or observation is that two people or groups are competing for goals that are very desirable, but which can be attained only by one person or group and at the expense of the other person or group. This observation can be summarized in the following statement: *The active competition for desirable, scarce resources produces group conflict.*

The history of race relations is frequently analyzed in terms of group conflict. However, if we use the Robber's Cave experiment as a model of intergroup conflict, the historical accuracy of the conflict analysis becomes less compelling.

First of all, the competition for desired goals with one group winning at the expense of the other assumes that each group has a *real* opportunity for success. That is, both the Rattlers and the Eagles felt they had every opportunity to win and that it was a matter of competition and effort as to who would ultimately triumph. In the history of race relations the power differential has been so great that in a real sense blacks and whites have not been "competing" for mutually desired goals. Whites have simply been competing among themselves for the highest attainment in this society, while each white enjoys an advantaged position with respect to blacks as a group. Thus the history of racism is not the history of racial conflict.

In the same connection however, there are recent advances in racial relations which have led to a greater legal attempt to ensure equality; the courts attempt to enforce the statutes of equality, and the economic machinery is relaxing so that blacks in increasing numbers are able to move up the economic ladder in this country. We are perhaps now in the last decade truly beginning to move toward a situation of *real* intergroup conflict. It is ironic in my view that after all these centuries of racial tension, animosity, and hostility, it seems that we are only now, at this time, moving to a serious level of competitive conflict. Thus contemporary aspects of racism do embody racial conflict.

However, the free-enterprise, capitalist system is predicated on competition. Competition is seen as an important goad to progress. Consequently the present structure of this society provokes competition and ultimately conflict over the resources, which necessarily must be limited. Thus moving to a level of conflict and competition, blacks as a group are *beginning* to realize the promise of America.

It is my view that as long as black people constituted a consistent underclass above which any white person or white group could rise, whites in competition *with each other* never have faced the challenge of winning *or* losing, but have simply competed for a degree of success. With blacks entering into the competition it now promises to become real competition for resources, where whites can *in principle* lose. The intense conflict within unions suggests the level to which this conflict has risen.

In the early part of this century, when industrial growth of the late nineteenth-century had produced real opportunities for all white Americans (and for a few blacks), the scarcity of goals was not the reality. In 1972, however, money is scarce, jobs are scarce, and the belief that one man's win means another man's loss is not far from reality. In game theory, these rules describe what is known as a "zero sum" game. Under this popular mental set, everyone and every group is vying mightily to ensure that his outcome is on the plus side of zero.

But let us return for a moment to Robber's Cave. Having established conditions for intense intergroup conflict, Sherif did not find it easy to reduce the level of conflict. He found that *contact* between groups on an equal status in activities that, in themselves, were pleasant for members of both groups *did not* decrease conflict when the activities did not involve interdependence between the groups. Such things as going to movies, shooting off fireworks, and eating together simply presented new opportunities for conflict (e.g., the team that lost the shoving contest for first in the dining hall called out "Ladies first!" at the winner.)

Sherif did find, however, that when

> conflicting groups come into contact under conditions embodying goals *that are compelling for the groups involved, but cannot be achieved by a single group through its own efforts and resources,* the groups will tend to cooperate toward this *superordinate goal.* (p. 88; italics are Sherif's)

Sherif's experiment suggests that the best and perhaps only way to reduce intergroup conflict is by subsuming the hostilities aroused by competition for scarce resources under the broader need for cooperation to achieve a superordinate goal. In the American culture the superordinate goal has been and continues to be economic achievement. The capitalist economic system thrives on competition. Competition, as we have seen, produces conflict. Therefore it seems in a society where competition is a traditional cultural value, and heterogeneity of ethnic and racial character is a matter of fact, intergroup conflict is inevitable. This simple analysis suggests that in the United States an ameliorative superordinate goal requires a fundamental change in cultural values.

Because of the American cultural norm of individuality without social responsibility, individual freedom has been greatly abused. The rights of the individual have been placed above the common good. Consequently, privacy has come to be the norm and now represents America's basic exclusionary character. Private property keeps people from desirable beach land; private clubs keep people from social events; private enterprise keeps people from realizing the promise of economic opportunity; private colleges keep quality education from the people. In this society "mine" always seems to conquer "ours." Individual sovereignty seems to have created national anarchy. As Anthony Lewis has noted so well: "In a world of nation-states, we are fools not to eat, drink and be merry because there is not and cannot be any 'we' who can prevent 'us' from dying tomorrow. *And I and mine expect to die last*" (*New York Times*, February 5, 1972).

The persistence of racism in American culture is but the most consistent manifestation of a serious defect in the American character. Ability to produce intergroup harmony is dependent upon achieving superordinate goals. In the context of the competition and conflict inherent in the American way, superordinate goals are difficult to conceive. In a country where a few get most, many get a little, and a lot get almost nothing, something is wrong. When a powerful Senator and a wealthy actor can get hundreds of thousands of dollars from the federal government *not* to plant cotton, while welfare payments are curtailed if a family head works and makes some very small amount of money, something is wrong. If the total amount of farm subsidies is three billion dollars, while impoverished black families living in tenements in urban ghettos are decried for the burden they place on the welfare budget, something is wrong. When large-scale farmers are able "legally" to create businesses which rechannel payments to large farm owners in order to circumvent laws which would limit their subsidy payments, while social workers snoop around trying to catch welfare violations so they can cut off meagre $80 checks to ghetto residents, again, *something is wrong*.

The principal superordinate goal is the perpetuation of and support of human life. Its attainment demands the cooperation of every relevant group in this society, indeed in the world. To this end each and every one of us can play an active part. In the name of individual freedom, the powerful people of this country have undertaken options which truncate the life possibilities of large numbers of powerless people. Historically the life options of black people have been consistently truncated. It is this truncation of black life options that is the crux of racism in America.

If intergroup harmony of any consequence is ever to be achieved, we must adopt a superordinate goal which stresses the value of human life. We must continually scrutinize our actions and goals and attempt never to constrict or constrain, to threaten or to eliminate the life of another

"This land is your land, this land is my land, for le-gal loop-holes in the cot-ton cei-ling..."

Fig. 6.1. King Cotton remains a symbol of racist disadvantage. (Reproduced by permission of the Register and Tribune Syndicate, Inc. © 1971.)

human being. In my opinion such a goal is incompatible with the competition and conflict inherent in current values of American society. In my opinion, if the value of *human life* were truly to dominate American society, we would have successfully achieved a cultural revolution.

Eldridge Cleaver framed the issues quite clearly when he noted that one was "either part of the problem, or part of the solution." Ask yourself; "Do I practice or support racism? Do I practice or support sexism? Do I practice or support classism? Do I practice or support religious oppression? Do I practice or support militarism?" If the answer to any of these questions is yes, you are part of the problem. Many of you will surely say no to the "practice" questions, but do not be too quick to reject your complicity in "support" of various practices of inequality and suppression in this country. In one way or another we all contribute to and are victimized by inequality and oppression.

Neither I nor anyone else can impose a value system on you. I can only ask each of you to examine your actions constantly; to judge them in relation to the values of human life and social responsibility, and hope that you would retain only those actions which help make this world a more humanly decent place to live for *every* human being.

References

Abrahams, R., *Deep Down in the Jungle*. Chicago: Aldine, 1964. (First revised edition, 1970).

Adorno, T. W., E. Frenkel-Brunswik, D. J. Levinson, and R. N. Sanford, *The Authoritarian Personality*. New York: Harper, 1950.

Allen, W. D., *Africa*. Sacramento: California State Department of Education, 1964.

Allport, F. H., The influence of the group upon association and thought, *J. exp. Psychol., 2,* 1920, 159-182.

Allport, G. W., The composition of political attitudes, *Amer. J. Sociol., 35,* 1929, 220-238.

Allport, G. W., *The Nature of Prejudice*. Reading, Mass.: Addison-Wesley, 1954.

Aptheker, H., *A History of Negro Slave Revolts*. New York: International Publishers, 1969.

Asch, S. E., Forming impressions of personality, *J. soc. Psychol., 41,* 1946, 258-290.

Asher, S. R., and V. L. Allen, Racial preference and social comparison processes, *J. soc. Issues, 25,* 1969, 157-167.

Banfield, E. C., *The Unheavenly City*. Boston: Little, Brown, 1968.

Bayton, J. A., The racial stereotypes of Negro college students, *J. abnorm. soc. Psychol., 36,* 1941, 97-102.

Bayton, J. A., L. B. McAlister, and J. Hamer, Race-class stereotypes, *J. Negro Ed., 41,* 1956, 75-78.

Bennett, L., *Before the Mayflower: A History of Black America.* Chicago: Johnson Publishing Company, 1969.

Berscheid, E., and E. Walster, *Interpersonal Attraction.* Reading, Mass.: Addison-Wesley, 1969.

Bettelheim, B., and M. Janowitz, *Dynamics of Prejudice.* New York: Harper and Brothers, 1950.

Bing, S., and S. S. Rosenfeld, *The Quality of Justice in the Lower Criminal Courts of Metropolitan Boston.* September, 1970.

Blumer, H., Race prejudice as a sense of group position, *Pacific sociol. Rev., 1,* 1958, 3-7.

Bogardus, E. S., Measuring social distances, *J. app. Sociol., 9,* 1925, 299-308.

Bogardus, E. S., *Immigration and Race Relations.* Boston: D. C. Heath, 1928.

Brady, T. P., *Black Monday: Segregation or Integration . . . America Has its Choice.* Winona, Mississippi: Association of Citizens' Councils, 1955.

Brimmer, A., The Negro in the national economy, in J. P. Davis (ed.), *The American Negro Reference Book.* Englewood Cliffs, N.J.: Prentice-Hall, 1966, Chapter 5.

Brown, C., *Manchild in the Promised Land.* New York: Macmillan, 1965.

Byrne, D., and C. McGraw, Interpersonal attraction toward Negroes, *Hum. Rel., 17,* 1964, 201-213.

Byrne, D., and T. J. Wong, Racial prejudice, interpersonal attraction, and assumed dissimilarity of attitudes, *J. abnorm. soc. Psychol., 65,* 1962, 246-253.

Campbell, A., and H. Schuman, *Racial Attitudes in Fifteen American Cities.* Ann Arbor, Michigan: Institute for Social Research, 1969.

Campbell, D. T., Social attitudes and other acquired behavioral dispositions, in S. Koch (ed.), *Psychology: A Study of a Science.* New York: McGraw-Hill, 1963, 94-172.

Campbell, E. Q., Some social psychological correlates of direction in attitude change, *Social Forces, 36,* 1958, 335-340.

Carmichael, S., and C. V. Hamilton, *Black Power: The Politics of Liberation in America.* New York: Vintage Books, 1967.

Caplovitz, D. *The Poor Pay More.* New York: Free Press, 1967.

Chicago Commission on Race Relations, *The Negro in Chicago: A Study of Race Relations and a Race Riot.* Chicago: University of Chicago Press, 1922.

Clark, K. B., *Prejudice and Your Child.* Boston: Beacon Press, 1963.

Clark, K. B., *Dark Ghetto.* New York: Harper and Row, 1965.

Clark, K. B., and M. Clark, Racial identification and preference in Negro children, in T. M. Newcomb and E. L. Hartley (eds.), *Readings in Social Psychology,* first edition. New York: Holt, 1947.

Clausen, J. A., Socialization as a concept and as a field of study, in J. A. Clausen, (ed.), *Socialization and Society*. Boston: Little, Brown, 1968.

Cleaver, E., *Soul on Ice*. New York: McGraw-Hill, 1968.

Cohen, N. (ed.), *The Los Angeles Riots: A Socio-psychological Study*. New York: Praeger Publishers, 1970.

Cole, J. B., Culture: Negro, black and nigger, *Black Scholar, 1,* 1970, 40-44.

Cole, M., and J. Gay, Culture and memory, *Amer. Anthropol.,* 1971.

Coleman, J., et al., *Equality of Educational Opportunity*. Washington, D.C.: Government Printing Office, 1966.

Cox, O. C., *Caste, Class, and Race*. Garden City, N.Y.: Doubleday, 1948.

Cronon, E. D., *Black Moses: The Story of Marcus Garvey and the Universal Negro Improvement Association*. Madison, Wisconsin: University of Wisconsin Press, 1955.

Daniels, R., *The Politics of Prejudice*. New York: Atheneum, 1968.

de Tocqueville, A., *Democracy in America*. New York: Vintage Books, 1945.

DeFleur, M. L., and F. R. Westie, Verbal attitudes and overt acts: an experiment on the salience of attitude, *Amer. sociolog. Rev., 23,* 1958, 667-673.

Deutsch, M., and M. E. Collins, *Interracial Housing*. Minneapolis: University of Minnesota Press, 1951.

Dewey, J., *Human Nature and Conduct: An Introduction to Social Psychology*. New York: Henry Holt, 1922.

Dollard, J. *Caste and Class in a Southern Town*. New Haven: Yale University Press, 1937.

Dollard, J., L. Doob, N. E. Miller, D. H. Mowrer, and R. R. Sears, *Frustration and Aggression*. New Haven: Yale University Press, 1939.

Drake, St. C., and H. R. Cayton, *Black Metropolis: A Study of Negro Life in a Northern City,* two volumes. New York: Harcourt, Brace and World, 1945.

Elkin, F., *The Child and Society: The Process of Socialization*. New York: Random House, 1960.

Festinger, L., *A Theory of Cognitive Dissonance*. Evanston, Ill.: Harper and Row, 1957.

Festinger, L., A theory of social comparison process, *Hum. Rel., 7,* 1954, 117-140.

Festinger, L., and H. H. Kelley, *Changing Attitudes Through Social*

Contact. Ann Arbor: University of Michigan, Institute for Social Research, 1951.

Fishman, J. A., Some social and psychological determinants of intergroup relations in changing neighborhoods: an introduction to the Bridgeview study, *Social Forces, 40,* 1961, 42-51.

Frazier, E. F., *The Negro Family in the United States.* Chicago: University of Chicago Press, 1939.

Frazier, E. F., *The Negro in the United States.* New York: Macmillan, 1944.

Frazier, E., *Race and Culture Contacts in the Modern World.* Boston: Beacon Press, 1957.

Garvey, A. J., *Garvey and Garveyism.* London: Collier-McMillan, Ltd., 1970.

Gilbert, G. M., Stereotype persistence and change among college students, *J. abnorm. soc. Psychol., 46,* 1951, 245-254.

Ginzberg, E., and D. L. Hiestand, Employment patterns of Negro men and women, in J. Davis (ed.), *The American Negro Reference Book.* Englewood Cliffs, N.J.: Prentice-Hall, 1966, Chapter 4.

Glenn, N., The role of white resistance and facilitation in the Negro struggle for equality, *Phylon, 26,* 1965, 105-116.

Goldman, P., *Report from Black America.* New York: Simon and Schuster, 1970.

Goodman, M. E. *Race awareness in Young Children.* Cambridge, Mass: Addison-Wesley, 1952.

Gordone, Chas., *No Place to Be Somebody: A Black-black comedy in three acts.* New York: Bobbs-Merrill, 1969.

Gottesman, I. I., Biogenetics of race and class. In M. Deutsch, I. Katz, and A. R. Jensen (eds.), *Social Class, Race, and Psychological Development.* New York: Holt, Rinehart, & Winston, 1968.

Greenwald, H. J., and D. B. Oppenheim, Reported magnitude of self-misidentification among Negro children — artifact? *J. pers. soc. Psychol., 8,* 1968, 49-52.

Hamilton, A., J. Jay, and J. Madison, *The Federalist Papers.* First published in 1788. Modern edition published in New York: Modern Library, 1937, with an introduction by E. M. Earle.

Handy, W. C., *Father of the Blues.* New York: Macmillan, 1941.

Harding, J., H. Proshansky, B. Kutner, and I. Chein, Prejudice and ethnic relations, in G. Lindzey and E. Aronson (eds.), *Handbook of Social Psychology, Vol. 5.* Reading, Mass.: Addison-Wesley, 1969, 1-76.

Harding, J. and R. Hogrefe, Attitudes of white department store employees toward Negro co-workers, *J. soc. Issues, 8,* 1952, 18-28.

Hartley, E. L., *Problems in Prejudice.* New York: Kings Crown, 1946.

Heider, F. *The Psychology of Interpersonal Relations.* New York: Wiley, 1958.

Herrnstein, R., I.Q., *Atlantic Monthly, 228,* 3, 1971, 43-64.

Herskovits, M., *The Myth of the Negro Past.* Boston: Beacon Press, 1958.

Hofstadter, R., *Social Darwinism in American Thought,* Revised edition. New York: Braziller, 1955.

Hraba, J., and G. Grant, Black is beautiful: a reexamination of racial preference and identification, *J. pers. soc. Psychol., 16,* 1970, 398-402.

Hunt, C. L., Private integrated housing in a medium size Northern city, *Soc. Prob., 7,* 1959, 195-209.

Jensen, A. R., How much can we boost IQ and scholastic achievement? *Harvard educ. Rev., 38,* 1968, 1-123.

Johnson, J. W., *Black Manhattan.* New York: Atheneum, 1930.

Johnson, M. W., Hearings before Subcommittee of the Committee on Appropriations, House of Representatives, 80th Congress, February, 1947, p. 245.

Johnson, N. J., and P. R. Sanday, Subcultural variations in an urban poor population, *Amer. Anthropol., 73,* 1971, 128-143.

Jones, E. E., and K. E. Davis, From acts to dispositions, in L. Berkowitz (ed.), *Advances in Experimental Social Psychology, Volume I.* New York: Academic Press, 1965.

Jordan, W. D., *White over Black: American Attitudes Toward the Negro, 1550-1812.* Baltimore: Penguin Books, 1969.

Kagan, J. S., Inadequate evidence and illogical conclusions, *Harvard educa. Rev., 39,* 1969, 126-129.

Kardiner, A., and L. Ovesey, *The Mark of Oppression.* New York: Norton, 1951.

Karlins, M., T. L. Coffman, and G. Walters, On the fading of social stereotypes: Studies in three generations of college students, *J. pers. soc. Psychol., 13,* 1969, 1-16.

Katz, D., and K. Braly, Racial stereotypes of one hundred college students, *J. abnorm. soc. Psychol., 28,* 1933, 280-290.

Katz, D., and K. Braly, Racial prejudice and racial stereotypes, *J. abnorm. soc. Psychol., 30,* 1935, 175-193.

Keil, C., *Urban Blues.* Chicago: University of Chicago Press, 1966.

Kellicott, W. E., *The Social Direction of Human Evolution.* New York: D. Appleton and Co., 1911.

Kiesler, C. A., C. E. Collins, and N. Miller, *Attitude Change: A Critical Analysis of Theoretical Approaches.* New York: Wiley, 1969.

Kiesler, S. B., Racial choice among children in realistic situations. Unpublished manuscript, University of Kansas, 1971.

Killens, J. O., *Black Man's Burden*. New York: Trident Press, 1965.

Klineberg, O., *Negro Intelligence and Selective Migration*. New York: Columbia University Press, 1935.

Knowles, L. L., and K. Prewitt, *Institutional Racism*. Englewood Cliffs, N. J.: Prentice-Hall, 1969.

Kovel, J., *White Racism: A Psychological History*. New York: Pantheon, 1970.

Kramer, B. M., Residential contact as a determinant of attitudes toward Negroes. Unpublished, Harvard College Library, 1950.

Kutner, B., C. Wilkins, and P. R. Yarrow, Verbal attitudes and overt behavior, *J. abnorm. soc. Psychol., 47,* 1952, 549-652.

Landreth, C., and B. C. Johnson, Young children's responses to a picture and insert test designed to reveal reaction to persons of different skin color, *Child Devel., 24,* 1953, 63-80.

LaPiere, R. T., Attitudes vs. actions, *Social Forces, 13,* 1934, 230-237.

Lasker, B., *Race Attitudes in Children*. New York: Henry Holt, 1929.

Lerner, M., in J. Macauley and L. Berkowitz, *Altruism and Helping Behavior*. New York: Academic Press, 1970, 205-229.

Lippitt, R., and M. Radke, New trends in the investigation of prejudice, *The Annals of the American Academy of Political and Social Science, 244,* 1946, 167-176.

Lippman, W., *Public Opinion*. New York: Harcourt, Brace and World, 1922.

Lipset, S. M., New perspectives on the counter-culture, *Saturday Review,* March 20, 1971, 25-28.

Lohman, J. D., and D. C. Reitzes, Notes on race relations in mass society, *Amer. j. Sociol. 58,* 1952, 240-246.

Marlowe, D., R. Frager, and R. L. Nuttal, Commitment to action-taking as a consequence of cognitive dissonance, *J. pers. soc. Psychol., 2,* 1965, 864-867.

Marx, G. T., *Protest and Prejudice: A Study of Belief in the Black Community*. New York: Harper & Row, 1969.

Marx, G. T. Editor's introduction to Racism and Race relations, in M. Wertheimer (ed.), *Confrontation: Psychology and the Problems of Today*. Glenview, Ill.: Scott Foresman, 1971.

Mckay, C., *Harlem: Negro Metropolis*. New York: Dutton, 1940.

Mischel, W., Preference for delayed reinforcement: an experimental study of a cultural observation, *J. abnorm. soc. Psychol., 56,* 1958, 57-61.

Mischel, W., Preference for delayed reinforcement and social responsibility, *J. abnorm. soc. Psychol., 62,* 1961a, 1-7.

Mischel, W., Delay of gratification, need for achievement, and acquiescence in another culture, *J. abnorm. soc. Psychol., 62,* 1961b, 543-552.

Mischel, W., Father-absence and delay of gratification, *J. abnorm. soc. Psychol., 63,* 1961c, 116-124.

Moynihan, D. P., *The Negro Family: The case for national action.* Washington, D.C.: U.S. Government Printing Office, 1965.

Myrdal, G., *An American Dilemma: The Negro Problem and Modern Democracy.* New York: Harper, 1944.

National Advisory Commission on Civil Disorders, *Report of the National Adivsory Commission on Civil Disorders.* New York: Bantam, 1968.

Palmore, E. B., The introduction of Negroes into white departments, *Human Organizations, 14,* 1, 1955, 27-28.

Pettigrew, T. F., Personality and sociocultural factors in intergroup attitudes: A cross-national comparison, *J. conf. Resol., 2,* 1958, 29-42.

Pettigrew, T. F., *A Profile of the Negro American.* Princeton: D. Van Nostrand, 1964.

Pettigrew, T. F., Social evaluation theory: convergences and applications, in D. Levine (ed.), *Nebraska Symposium on Motivation,* 1967. Lincoln, Neb.: University of Nebraska Press, 1967.

Pettigrew, T. F., The metropolitan educational park, *The Science Teacher, 36,* 1969.

Pettigrew, T. F., *Racially Separate or Together.* New York: McGraw-Hill, 1971.

Pitts, J. R., The hippies as contra-meritocracy, *Dissent, 16,* 4, 1969, 326-337.

Porter, J. D., *Black Child, White Child: The Development of Racial Attitudes.* Cambridge, Mass.: Harvard University Press, 1971.

President's Committee on Civil Rights, *To Secure These Rights.* Washington, D.C.: U.S. Government Printing Office, 1947.

Raab, E., and S. M. Lipset, *Prejudice and Society.* New York: Anti-Defamation League of B'nai B'rith, 1959.

Radke, M., J. Sutherland, and P. Rosenberg, Racial attitudes of children, *Sociometry, 13,* 1950, 154-171.

Radke, M. H. G. Trager, and J. Davis, Social perceptions and attitudes of children. *Genet. Psychol. Mono., 40,* 1949, 327-447.

Rainwater, L., Crucible of identity, in T. Parsons and K. B. Clark (eds.), *The Negro American.* Boston: Houghton Mifflin, 1966, 160-204.

Rainwater, L., and W. L. Yancey, *The Moynihan Report and the Politics of Controversy.* Cambridge: MIT Press, 1967.

Rokeach, M., *The Open and Closed Mind.* New York: Basic Books, Inc., 1960.

Rokeach, M. Belief vs. race as determinants of social distance: comment on Triandis' paper, *J. abnorm. soc. Psychol., 62,* 1961, 187-188.

Rokeach, M., and S. Parker, Values as social indicators of poverty and race relations in America, *The Annals of the American Academy of Political and Social Science, 388,* 1970, 97-111.

Rokeach, M., and L. Mezei, Race and shared belief as factors in social choice, *Science, 151,* 1966, 167-172.

Rokeach, M., P. W., Smith, and R. I. Evans, Two kinds of prejudice or one? in M. Rokeach (ed.), *The Open and Closed Mind.* New York: Basic Books, 1960.

Rose, A., *Studies in the Reduction of Prejudice.* Chicago: American Council on Race Relations, 1947.

Rosenthal, R., and L. F. Jacobson, Teacher expectations for the disadvantaged, *Scientific American, 218,* 1968.

Rudwick, E. M., *Race Riot at East St. Louis, July 2, 1917.* New York: World Publishing Company, Meridian Books, 1966.

Ryan, W., Savage discovery: the Moynihan report, in L. Rainwater and W. L. Yancey (eds.), *The Moynihan Report and the Politics of Controversy.* Cambridge: MIT Press, 1967.

Selznick, G. J., and S. Steinberg, *The Tenacity of Prejudice: Anti-Semitism in Contemporary America.* New York: Harper and Row, 1969.

Sherif, M., *In Common Predicament.* Boston: Houghton-Mifflin, 1966.

Silberman, C. E., *Crisis in Black and White.* New York: Random House, 1964.

Simpson, G. E., and J. M. Yinger, *Racial and Cultural Minorities: An Analysis of Prejudice and Discrimination,* third edition. New York: Harper and Row, 1965.

Social Science Institute, *Racial Attitudes, Social Science Source Document No. 3.* Nashville, Tennessee: Social Science Institute of Fisk University, 1946.

Stein, D. D., J. A. Hardyck, and M. B. Smith, Race and belief: an open and shut case, *J. pers. soc. Psychol. 1,* 1965, 281-289.

Taeuber, K. E., and A. F. Taeuber, *Negroes in Cities.* Chicago: Aldine, 1965.

Thigpen, C. H., and H. M. Cleckley, A case of multiple personality, *J. abnorm. soc. Psychol., 49,* 1954, 135-151.

Thurstone, L. L., Attitudes can be measured, *Amer. j. Sociol., 33,* 1927, 529-554.

Tower, I. V., *Soul on Rice: The Black Soldier in Vietnam.* New York: Racquet Press, 1969.

Trager, H. G., and M. R. Yarrow, *They Live What They Learn.* New York: Harpers, 1952.

Triandis, H. C., A note on Rokeach's theory of prejudice, *J. abnorm. soc. Psychol., 62,* 1961, 184-186.

Triandis, H. C., and E. E. Davis, Race and belief as determinants of behavioral intentions, *J. pers. soc. Psychol., 2,* 1965, 715-725.

United States Commission on Civil Disorders, *Racial isolation in the public schools: Report of the U. S. Commission on Civil Rights,* two volumes, Washington, D.C.: U.S. Government Printing Office, 1967.

van den Berghe, P., *Race and Racism: A Comparative Perspective.* New York: Wiley, 1967.

Webster, S. W., The influence of interracial contact on social acceptance in a newly integrated school, *J. ed. Psychol., 52,* 1961, 292-296.

Whitmore, P. S., Jr., A study of school desegregation: attitude change and scale validation, *Dissertation Abstracts, 17,* 1957, 891-892.

Wicker, A. W., Attitudes versus actions: the relationship of verbal and overt behavioral responses to attitude objects, *J. soc. Issues, 25,* 1969, 41-78.

Williams, R. M., Jr., *The Reduction of Intergroup Tensions.* New York: Social Science Research Council, Bulletin 57, 1947.

Williams, R. M., Jr., *Strangers Next Door: Ethnic Relations in American Communities.* Englewood Cliffs, N.J.: Prentice-Hall, 1964.

Wilner, D. M., R. P. Walkley, and S. W. Cook, *Human Relations in Interracial Housing: A Study of the Contact Hypothesis.* Minneapolis: University of Minnesota Press, 1955.

Wilson, W., Rank order of discrimination and its relevance to civil rights priorities, *J. pers. soc. Psychol., 15,* 1970, 118-124.

Wright, R., *Native Son.* New York: Harper, 1940.

Yarrow, M. R., Interpersonal dynamics in a desegregation process, *J. soc. Issues, 14,* 1958, 63.

Name Index

Abrahams, R., 157
Adorno, T. W., 26, 32, 33, 98, 110
Ali, M., 85
Allen, V. L., 92, 93
Allen, W. D., 156
Allport, F. H., 21
Allport, G. W., 2, 3, 26, 37, 42, 99,
    100, 103, 104, 105, 114, 172
Aptheker, H., 12, 137
Asch, S. E., 70, 98
Asher, S. R., 92, 93

Baldwin, J. M., 18
Banfield, E. C., 146
Baron, A., 144
Barron, F., 126
Bayton, J. A., 25, 68, 69, 70
Bennett, L., 17
Berscheid, E., 83
Bethune, M. M., 24
Bettelheim, B., 34
Bing, S., 143
Blake, C., 142
Blumer, H., 3, 65, 99, 106
Bogardus, E. S., 21, 22, 23, 26, 29,
    33, 89
Brady, T. P., 39, 42, 76, 122
Braly, K., 24, 25, 26, 29, 68, 70,
    71, 72, 89

Brown, C., 52
Bunche, R., 24
Byrne, D., 83, 84

Calvin, J., 9
Campbell, A., 85, 86
Campbell, D. T., 98
Campbell, E. Q., 43, 101
Caplovitz, D., 145
Carmichael, S., 5, 7, 45, 46, 116,
    128
Cayton, H. R., 29
Chicago Commission on Race Rela-
    tions, 19, 114
Clark, K. B., 39, 40, 41, 43, 52, 90,
    91, 92, 94
Clark, M., 39, 40, 41, 43, 52, 90,
    92, 94
Clausen, J. A., 124
Cleaver, E., 76, 144, 178
Cleckley, H., 151-152
Coffman, T. L., 68, 71, 72, 89
Cohen, N., 45
Cole, J. B., 166
Cole, M., 162
Coleman, J. S., 52, 53, 54, 55, 56,
    57, 101, 102, 138, 171
Collins, C. E., 98
Collins, M. E., 34, 35, 36, 39, 102

Subject Index

American Dilemma, 11, 29, 120,
   129, 169-170
Antislavery activity, 12-13
Attitudes, 21, 67
  and behavior, 26-27, 62-63,
   94-104
  definition of, 25-26
  demography of, 73-80, 89
   white on black, 73-77
   black on white, 77-80
  race versus beliefs, 80-85, 89-90
  racial, and doll-choice techniques,
   92-93
  and interracial contact, 34,
   100-104
  and social action, 21
  and social distance, 21-22
  and social norms, 98
  and social scientific investigation,
   21, 29, 170
  black and white compared,
   85-89, 90
  social psychological investigations
   of, 21, 62
  socialization of, 111-113
Authoritarian personality, 33-34,
   110, 170

Behavior, 62-63, 95-104
  and doll-choice techniques, 93
  relation between attitudes and,
   62-63, 95-104, 107
  and social norms, 98
  social psychological investigation
   of, 62, 170
Black cultural revolution, 45
Black family, 47-52
  matrifocality of, 50
Black migration, 28
Black militancy, 27, 37, 45
Black Muslims, 45
Black Panther Party, 45, 47, 141
  and police and judicial authorities,
   144
Black Power, 45-47
  and white liberals, 46
Black pride, 45
Black revenge, 104
Busing, 55
Brown v. Board of Education, 38,
   42-43

Chicago Commission on Race Relations, 19
Civil Rights movement, 28, 42, 44
  white roles in, 46

definition of, 2-3, 60-62, 171
and interracial contact, 43, 106
and prejudgment, 60-61, 66, 72,
    106
psychological position on, 3
and racism, 115
scapegoat theory of, 31-32, 170
and self-concept, 172
social norm criteria of, 65
sociological position on, 3
Prejudiced personality, 32-33, 66,
    80-81, 110
and belief dissimilarity, 84-85, 90
and rationality, 66

Race, 116-117
and cultural differences, 117-118
Race prejudice, 4, 37
and aggression, 31, 107, 110, 170
and behavior, 127
definitions of, 25, 31
and economic exploitation, 33,
    104
and frustration, 31, 107, 110, 170
and individual racism, 5, 7, 115
and interpersonal attraction
    theory, 83
personality theories of, 32-33, 66,
    80-81, 98, 110, 170
and racism, 99, 127
theories of, 104-113
    naive analysis, 111-113
    phenomenological emphasis, 110
    psychodynamic emphasis,
        107-110
    situational emphasis, 106-107
    sociocultural emphasis, 106
    stimulus-object approach, 111
Race riots, 16-17, 19, 24, 28,
    45-46, 122-123
and Northern States, 16, 19, 171
Racial conflict, 1, 15, 18, 23, 64,
    99, 106
in the North, 171
and social scientific investigation,
    23
Racial identification, 39-40, 90-95
class factors in, 95
and color of dolls, 90, 91-92
development of, 91, 95

and racial awareness, 40
regional differences in, 40, 41, 91
and skin color, 40, 91-92
in white children, 92
Racial preference, 40, 90-95
and anticipated future interaction,
    93-94
behavioral implications of, 94
class factors in, 95
and color of dolls, 90
development of, 91
and integration, 95
and skin color, 91
regional differences in, 91
Racism, 4-7, 19, 114-167, 172-173
aversive, 121-124, 172
    and the use of white norms, 122
    in the North, 122
and behavior, 117
cultural, 6-7, 115-116, 128,
    147-167, 172-173
    cultural absolutism, cultural rela-
        tivity, and, 158
    and ethnocentrism, 149, 172
    social comparison processes and,
        158-159
    two forms of, 148
    and the use of white standards,
        158-159
definitions of, 4, 117, 172
dominative, 121-124, 127, 172
    and race prejudice, 128
    in the South, 122
and ethnocentrism, 117
individual, 5, 27, 115-116,
    118-129, 172-173
    and belief in black inferiority,
        118-121
    and black culture, 118-119
    relation between race prejudice
        and, 115-116, 128
    socialization of, 124-126
    and the use of white norms, 120
institutional, 5-6, 27, 115-116,
    128-146, 172-173
    de facto, de jure segregation and,
        131
    definition of, 131
    in economics, 131-136